THE

ISLAMIC MOSES

THE

ISLAMIC MOSES

How the Prophet Inspired Jews and Muslims
to Flourish Together and Change the World

MUSTAFA AKYOL

ST. MARTIN'S
ESSENTIALS
NEW YORK

First published in the United States by St. Martin's Essentials,
an imprint of St. Martin's Publishing Group

THE ISLAMIC MOSES. Copyright © 2024 by Mustafa Akyol.
All rights reserved. Printed in the United States of America. For information,
address St. Martin's Publishing Group, 120 Broadway, New York, NY 10271.

www.stmartins.com

The Library of Congress Cataloging-in-Publication Data
is available upon request.

ISBN 978-1-250-25609-6 (hardcover)
ISBN 978-1-250-25608-9 (ebook)

Our books may be purchased in bulk for promotional, educational, or
business use. Please contact your local bookseller or the Macmillan
Corporate and Premium Sales Department at 1-800-221-7945, extension
5442, or by email at MacmillanSpecialMarkets@macmillan.com.

First Edition: 2024

10 9 8 7 6 5 4 3 2 1

To all members of my beloved family
in the United States, Turkey, and Bosnia,
hoping that they will grow, live, and age happily,
in a better world of peace, justice, and liberty

Mahomet . . . was not a loyal son of Judaism, but he appreciated its highest aims, and was induced by it to give to the world a new faith, known as Islam, founded on a lofty basis. This religion has exercised a wonderful influence on the course of Jewish history and on the evolution of Judaism. . . . Judaism may justly consider his teachings a victory of its own truths and a fulfillment of the prophecy that "one day every knee will bend to the only God, and every tongue will worship Him."

—Heinrich Graetz, *The History of the Jews,* 1891

CONTENTS

INTRODUCTION: WHY MOSES?   1

1. THE MOSES OF MECCA   11

2. WHAT REALLY HAPPENED IN MEDINA (PART I)   36

3. WHAT REALLY HAPPENED IN MEDINA (PART II)   61

4. UNDER THE KINGDOMS OF ISHMAEL   76

5. HALAL JUDAISM, KOSHER ISLAM   108

6. HOW ISLAMIC RATIONALISM ENRICHED JUDAISM   125

7. THE JEWISH HASKALAH AND THE ISLAMIC ENLIGHTENMENT   151

8. THE GOOD ORIENTALISTS   180

9. THE OTTOMAN HAVEN   197

EPILOGUE: IN THE DARKEST HOUR   225

ACKNOWLEDGMENTS   237

NOTES   241

INDEX   295

WHY MOSES?

Islam . . . is from the very flesh and bone of Judaism.
It is, to say, a recast, an enlargement.

—Shelomo Dov Goitein, Jewish historian, 1955[1]

Islam, in many ways, is a universalized Judaism.
It is Judaism for gentiles.

—Shaykh Hamza Yusuf, Islamic scholar, 2022[2]

Y EARS AGO, ON AN AUTUMN DAY IN ISTANBUL, I RECEIVED AN email from a friend who lived in the American Midwest and frequented a mainline Protestant church. After kind greetings, he asked me for some advice. "To understand Islam better, I want to read a copy of the Qur'an," he wrote. "Can you please recommend a good English translation?"

I was happy to see my friend's interest in my faith's scripture, and advised him to get his hands on *The Qur'an: A New Translation* by Muhammad Abdel-Haleem. "It is carefully worded and has some helpful footnotes," I explained, adding that I would be happy to hear his thoughts when he could go over the text.

Several weeks later, my friend wrote back. He had indeed bought a copy of that translation and read much of it. He was touched by the teachings of piety and ethics he came across in the Qur'an, while puzzled by some other themes. He was also, as he put frankly, a bit troubled by some combative verses—but only to recall, in fairness, that his own scripture, particularly the Old Testament, had similarly harsh passages.

"But do you know what the biggest surprise was?" my friend wrote at the end of his long email. "That I was expecting to read about the life of Muhammad. But, instead, I read about the life of Moses more than anything else."

Was he exaggerating?

No, he was quite right. Because the Qur'an indeed narrates very little about its own messenger, the Prophet Muhammad (peace be upon him, as we Muslims say), at least in an explicit way. In more than six thousand verses that make up a hundred and fourteen "suras," or chapters as we will call them, the name Muhammad appears only four times. When you read the whole Qur'an, you learn almost nothing about his birth, his upbringing, his early life. Meanwhile, many events in his prophetic mission are frequently alluded to, but still hardly narrated as a story that you can follow.

In contrast, Moses dominates the Qur'an. His name is mentioned 137 times—by far more than any other human being. His story is narrated in some seventy passages dispersed throughout thirty-four separate chapters. When you read them all, you learn so many themes about Moses—from his birth in peril, to his leadership of the Israelites, to his defiance of the Pharaoh, to his amazing miracles. Therefore, when you read the whole Qur'an, you indeed learn about Moses more than anybody else.

Why is this the case? Why does the Qur'an narrate very little about its own actual Arab prophet? And why does it narrate so much about a bygone Jewish prophet?

The first question is easy enough to solve: the Qur'an does not speak *about* its own prophet because it speaks *to* him. Because the Qur'an presents itself as the word of God, transmitted by Angel Gabriel to Muhammad, whose primary function is to receive the divine revelation and to proclaim it to his people, the

Arabs of early seventh-century Arabia. He is the "messenger," truly, and not the message.

So, that is why the Qur'an is largely silent about Muhammad. But what about the second question above, the one that intrigued my Christian friend: Why it is that the Qur'an speaks about Moses more than about anyone else?

THE PARADIGMATIC PROPHET

This second question isn't also too hard to figure out. Moses is the most prominent figure in the whole Qur'an because he is the main historic precedent for Muhammad—the key inspiration from which he draws, the key example he follows.

The parallelism between the two men is in fact hard to miss. First, both were orphans who were adopted. Then, both lived normal lives until a life-changing moment where they unreadily came face-to-face with the divine. For Moses, it was the burning bush on Mount Horeb. For Muhammad, it was the angelic voice on Mount Hira. Then, the revelations that followed those first encounters formed the two scriptures these two prophets gave to their followers: for Moses, it was the Torah. For Muhammad, it was the Qur'an.

Yet neither Moses nor Muhammad merely transmitted sacred books. Both also delivered their followers from persecution to freedom. Moses and his fellow Israelites were persecuted by the Pharaoh of Egypt. Similarly, Muhammad and his fellow Arab monotheists—say, Ishmaelites—were persecuted by the polytheist leaders of Mecca. No wonder, as we shall see, the Qur'an draws parallels between these two oppressors—the Egyptians and the Meccans—when it narrates Moses to Muhammad. And no wonder the oppression ends in both stories thanks to a perilous escape: for Moses, the *exodus* from Egypt; for Muhammad, the *hijra* ("migration") from Mecca.

And yet, in both stories, the journeys do not end with mere

freedom. Both Moses and Muhammad also led bloody battles with deadly enemies, conquered new lands, and used coercive power to impose religious laws. In fact, they each established what political scientists may call a theocracy.[3]

A Western scholar of Islam who noted this parallelism between the journeys of these two prophets was the late Patricia Crone. Moses, she had observed, is the "paradigmatic prophet" of the Qur'an. Because,

> wittingly or unwittingly, Muhammad was a new Moses. Like him, he united scattered tribes in the name of God and led them on to conquest. . . . Moses was an inspiration to many people, but his admirers were not usually able to imitate him in any literal way since they lived under such utterly different conditions. This was where Muhammad differed. He could and did re-enact Moses' career.[4]

In comparison, Jesus Christ, or Isa al-Masih, who is also highly praised in the Qur'an along with his mother, Mary, does *not* seem to be a role model for the Prophet Muhammad. For while the Qur'an tells us a lot about the supernatural birth of Jesus and his own miracles—while framing them in its own "low Christology"—it says nothing about his political journey. Not a single Qur'anic verse mentions Jesus' ordeal with the Romans, which ended not with conquest and victory but rather in a painful earthly defeat. In fact, in just one verse, the Qur'an mentions the archetype of that earthly defeat—the Crucifixion—but only to assert that it was actually not a defeat.[5]

THE THREE MONOTHEISMS

For those who are familiar with the secular history of the world's major religions, all this may rightly fall into place. History tells us that monotheism—belief in one God, as opposed to polytheism, or belief in many gods—developed first among the small nation of Israelites, but then had two major expansions that reshaped the whole world.

The first major expansion was Christianity. Not too surprisingly, it was born among the Israelites themselves, when one of them, Jesus of Nazareth, began to spread "good news." He was speaking to his fellow Jews, yet his message, and persona, was so powerful that it soon began winning hearts and minds among the gentiles. In a few centuries, it also won over the Roman Empire, and ultimately became the world's largest religion.

It should not be missed, however, that Christianity universalized Jewish monotheism only by departing from it in two significant ways.

The first departure was the notion of the Divine Christ, and the subsequent doctrine of the Holy Trinity, which were unthinkable in the staunchly monotheistic Judaism, as they still are today.[6]

The second departure was the claim to supersede the Halakha, or religious law. This detailed code of private and public life, based on the Laws of Moses and later Jewish texts, was very central to Judaism, as it still is today. One can hardly imagine being a pious Jew, in the Orthodox sense, without observing the Sabbath or keeping the dietary laws. But such rules were exactly what Christianity left behind. "A person is justified not by the works of the law," proclaimed Saint Paul, the most definitive apostle of Jesus, "but through faith in Jesus Christ."[7]

Then, almost six centuries after the birth of Christianity, came the second major expansion of monotheism, which was of course Islam. Its scripture, the Qur'an, clearly defined itself as a revelation from the God of Abraham, "confirming what came before it," namely "the Torah and the Gospel."[8] It also proclaimed its version of the Ten Commandments, leaving aside only the Sabbath.[9]

It should not be missed, however, that Islam did *not* take the two departures that Christianity had taken from Judaism. First, theologically, it boldly denied the notion of a Divine Christ, and restored the strict unitarian monotheism of the Torah. As the medieval Muslim scholar Ali al-Tabari (d. 870) put it proudly, Muhammad

> did not contradict Moses in the article of the unity of God, nor did he utter on this subject ambiguities and equivocations as the Christians did, but he openly and clearly proclaimed it, and rendered faith pure and his saying precise.[10]

Second, Islam showed no interest in Saint Paul's dismissing of the law. "Instead of developing a Pauline antinomianism [anti-legalism]," as two Western scholars noted decades ago, Muslims "went on to replace the letter of the law of Moses with the letter of the law of Muhammad."[11]

In fact, the "law of Muhammad," which Muslims call Sharia, was not even a replacement of its Jewish precedent, the Halakha, but a recasting of it. The two terms, in fact, have the same meaning: "path" or "way." Also just like the Halakha, Sharia covers all aspects of human life, with similar religious practices such as male circumcision, strict avoidance of pork, dress codes, and daily prayers. It also includes a penal code with corporal punishments, which has become largely obsolete in Judaism but is still in effect in Islam—due mainly to the different political trajectories of the two faiths as well as some interesting theological nuances, which we shall see in this book. Despite these historical divergences, though, the similarity of the two legal systems is unmistakable. No wonder the great medieval Jewish scholar Moses Maimonides, to whom we will refer often in this book, did not shy away from using the very term "Sharia" for Jewish law in his writings in Judeo-Arabic.[12]

In other words, among the two major expansions of monotheism, that is, Christianity and Islam, it was the latter that proved more loyal to the precursor of both, which is Judaism.

Today, this may sound counterintuitive to many people in the West because they are used to hearing about the "Judeo-Christian tradition," while Islam is often considered, at best, a distant cousin. But the Judeo-Christian tradition is a modern concept popularized only in the twentieth century—when Western civilization finally began to question its dark history of antisemitism, while parts of the Muslim world sadly began to absorb it. However, there is an equally valid Judeo-Islamic tradition that encompasses not only the striking religious parallels between Judaism and Islam, which I just mentioned, but also the deeply intertwined history of Jews and Muslims, which we will see.

THE ROAD MAP

That is all why this book suggests the matrix between the three great Abrahamic faiths should not be imagined as two separate branches: the Judeo-Christian tradition on one side, Islam on the other side. The more accurate image is a *triangle*—with Judaism, Christianity, and Islam on its three points, each with complex connections to the other two.

In the chapters ahead, we will have a theological and historical walk through the much-neglected side of that Abrahamic triangle: the Judeo-Islamic tradition. And this is how we will proceed.

First, in chapter 1, "The Moses of Mecca," we will look into the very birth of Islam in early seventh-century Arabia—with Judaism being its "midwife," as some modern Jewish historians see it.[13] We will see why the Qur'an, especially in its Meccan chapters, narrates so much about Moses and his nemesis, the Pharaoh, with many parallels to the story of Moses in the Hebrew Bible, but also with some fascinating nuances.

In chapters 2 and 3, "What Really Happened in Medina (Parts I and II)," we will reexamine the first actual encounter between Jews and Muslims. It is a story that begins with a remarkably cordial and pluralist "constitution," but ends up with grim stories of war, expulsion, and destruction. We will see, though, that beneath this seemingly religious conflict there could be more than meets the eye: the clash of the two great empires of the time, the Byzantines and the Sassanids, which may have strained the relations in peripheral Arabia. We will also question the accuracy of the "Medina massacre" story, while also seeing the historical context of the polemics against Jews in some Medinan chapters of the Qur'an.

In chapter 4, "Under the Kingdoms of Ishmael," we will observe how the Judeo-Islamic tradition really began to take hold in history. As surprising as it may sound today, the early Islamic conquests, which built a huge empire from Spain to the borders of India in just a century, were often welcomed by Jews, if not assisted by them. The reason was not a "Jewish-Arabic cabal," as some Christians believed then, but rather the simple fact that Jews found more freedom under Islam than elsewhere. It presents a remarkable irony—a sad one—as today's reality is the exact opposite.

In chapter 5, "Halal Judaism, Kosher Islam," we will explore the "creative symbiosis" that took place between medieval Islam and Judaism, as some Jewish historians called it.[14] The two religions, with remarkably similar beliefs and practices, learned a lot from each other, in intricate ways that may surprise many of their believers today. We will also see what the two religions teach about each other's fate in the afterlife, or "the world to come."

In chapter 6, "How Islamic Rationalism Enriched Judaism," we will explore how theological and philosophical trends that appeared in the golden age of Islam influenced the Jewish tradition in intricate ways that are unknown to most people today. That includes the rational theology of the Mu'tazilites, who soon had their Jewish counterparts. That also includes the impact of *falasifa,* or Muslim philosophers, on the Jewish philosophical tradition.

Chapter 7, "The Jewish Haskalah and the Islamic Enlighten-ment," takes us to the modern world and examines how Jews, at the dawn of Western liberalism, reinterpreted their tradition with a new sense of individual liberty and religious freedom. We will focus on Moses Mendelssohn, the greatest Jewish thinker of the eighteenth century, whose ideas about the origins and values of Judaism are remarkably similar to the ideas of Islamic re-formers of the more recent time. We will also see how European suspicions about Judaism in that early modern era are quite rem-iniscent of Western suspicions about Islam today.

Chapter 8, "The Good Orientalists," challenges a cliché that has become all too popular in Muslim societies: "Orientalism," or the study of Islam in the modern West, is built only on cynical motives that serve colonial interests. The truth is more compli-cated, as we shall see, evidenced especially by the much-forgotten Jewish Orientalists of nineteenth-century Germany. Their mo-tivations toward Islam had nothing to do with colonialism or racial supremacism. Quite to the contrary, they had genuine sympathy for Islam, and even identified with it, while trying to find remedies in it against European antisemitism.

Chapter 9, "The Ottoman Haven," reminds of the safety the Ottoman Turks, my ancestors, offered to Jews in their darkest hours, such as their expulsion from Spain in 1492, and the blood libels of the nineteenth century. In return, Jews were remarkably loyal to the Ottoman Empire until its very end in World War I—in stark contrast to latter-day myths about Jewish conspiracies that supposedly ended this last seat of the Islamic caliphate.

Finally, in the epilogue, "In the Darkest Hour," we will pon-der whether the better history between Jews and Muslims is gone for good, as many would think today, especially in the darkness of the brutal conflict between the Israelis and the Palestinians, or whether there is a chance for peace and reconciliation.

Much of this book, in other words, is not about the modern conflict in the Middle East, which has built much tension and distrust between Muslims and Jews over the past three quarters of a century. Instead, it is about the much older, deeper, and often brighter story of Islam and Judaism—the Judeo-Islamic tradition—the remembrance of which, hopefully, can also help find a peaceful solution to that modern political tragedy. It can also help Muslims and Jews everywhere to look at each other with better understanding and deeper respect.

So, with that hope, let's begin excavating the Judeo-Islamic tradition.

And let's begin, naturally, where it all began: the story of the Islamic Moses.

1

THE MOSES OF MECCA

Did you not know that we have found Muhammad, a prophet like Moses described in the oldest books.

—Abu Talib, speaking to fellow Meccans, circa 616 CE[1]

Before this, the Book of Moses was revealed as a guide and mercy. And this Book is a confirmation, in the Arabic tongue.

—The Qur'an, 46:12

UNTIL THE LATE AGE OF FORTY, MUHAMMAD IBN ABDULLAH, A merchant from the Arabian city of Mecca, was a righteous, virtuous, yet still seemingly unexceptional man. He did not expect to receive divine revelations, challenge his own tribe, suffer persecution, flee his hometown, command armies, conquer cities, and ultimately change the world forever.

In other words, Muhammad, the Prophet of Islam, was not like Jesus of Nazareth, the Christ of Christianity, who had a supernatural birth, a wise childhood, a preconceived mission, and a foreknown finale. Rather, he was like Moses who, until his encounter with a burning bush on Mount Horeb, also didn't know what God expected of him.

Notably, Muhammad's first encounter with the divine also took place on a mountain: Jabal al-Nour, or "Mountain of Light," a small hill that rises a few miles outside Mecca. On this peak, there is a cave, known as Hira, where Muhammad used to withdraw periodically to contemplate. Yet in AD 610, in the month of Ramadan, his reflections were disrupted when he suddenly realized that he wasn't alone in the cave. He heard a voice telling him, "*Iqra,*" or "Recite." "Recite," the voice said repeatedly, "in the name of your Lord who created the human from a clot."[2] These were the very first words of the scripture that would be known to the world as the "Recitation," or the Qur'an.

Muhammad's first response to this initial revelation was what the Qur'an also ascribes to Moses: fear.[3] He ran back home, "with his heart beating severely," only to ask his wife, Khadija, "Cover me! Cover me!" When the latter learned what happened, she took Muhammad to her cousin Waraqa, "a Christian who used to write with Hebrew letters."[4] When this mysterious Judeo-Christian sage heard the story, he comforted Muhammad. The voice that terrified him was no demon, Waraqa said, but:

> Holy! Holy! By Him in whose hand is the soul of Waraqah, there hath come unto Muhammad the greatest namus, even he that would come unto Moses. Verily Muhammad is the Prophet of this people.[5]

The Arabic word *namus,* probably from the Greek word *nomos,* meant either "the Angel of Revelation" or "Divine Law or Scripture."[6] In both senses, it referred to a Mosaic precedent.

So, at the very first assurance of his prophecy, Muhammad was also informed about his role model: he was the new Moses whom God sent to the Arabs, the Children of Ishmael.[7] Unlike their cousins, the Children of Israel, these were "a people whose forefathers were not warned."[8] In other words, they had not yet received revelations from God. But now, a "warner" had finally come to them, with two revolutionary calls: Arabs had to give up worshipping the idols of their fathers and instead worship only the one true god, the God of Abraham. They also had to give up their immoral ways, like the exploitation of orphans, the poor, and slaves.

It was no easy task to challenge the Quraysh, Muhammad's own tribe that controlled Mecca, which was all too proud of its gods, hundreds of which were venerated at the cube-shaped sanctuary that stood in the heart of the city—the Kaaba. Hence Waraqa not only assured Muhammad but also cautioned him: "Thou wilt be called a liar, and they will use thee despitefully, and cast thee out, and fight against thee."[9]

Which is exactly what happened in the next thirteen years, when Muhammad preached an uncompromising monotheism in the face of a growingly hostile polytheism. He was ridiculed, abused, pelted, and almost assassinated. His fellow mu'minun, or believers, also faced persecution. The slaves among them were tortured by their owners. Two of them, Sumayyah bint Khabbat and her husband, Yasir ibn Amir, were executed, to be hailed in history as Islam's first martyrs. To save their lives, some believers fled to the Christian kingdom of Abyssinia, where they hoped for, and indeed found, a safe haven. Ultimately, most believers in Mecca, including the Prophet himself, fled the city in 622, in a historic hijra, or migration. Their new home was the northern city of Yathrib, which later would be known simply as "the city," or Medina.

Muslim sources write that the believers who migrated to Medina were a little over two hundred people. The other party, refugees in Abyssinia, reportedly numbered a little over a hundred people.[10] These small numbers, in a city whose population must have been many thousands, show how tiny the early Muslim community was.[11] It also gives an idea about how insecure they must have felt.

We see this insecurity also in the Qur'an, in the very words that Muhammad was commanded to convey to his followers in one of his darkest hours: "I do not know what will be done with me or you; I only follow what is revealed to me."[12]

Yet the same Qur'an, which did not tell much to Muhammad and his believers about their own future, did tell them, repeatedly, about something else: the stories of former prophets and believers who, just like the first Muslims, were abused and oppressed, only to prevail in the end.

That is why almost one-fourth of the Qur'an consists of *qasas*, or stories, of former prophets, with emphases that unmistakably resonate with the ordeal of the first Muslims. That is also why, as observed by the contemporary Jewish scholar Rabbi Reuven Firestone, "the Qur'an is less a literary work than it is a self-conscious scripture," and "is more straightforwardly didactic than the Hebrew Bible."[13] In other words, the Qur'an narrates history, not to be taken as a book of history but to tell stories to its believers in order to give them religious lessons, inspiration, and encouragement.

Most of these Qur'anic stories have heroes and villains. Most heroes are former prophets, some twenty-four of whom are mentioned by name. Except for two—the Arab prophets Hud and Salih—they are all Biblical figures.[14] Some are noted quite briefly, while a few are given a great deal of attention. Among the latter are Noah, Abraham, Lot, Joseph, and Jesus. Yet none of them even come close to the attention given to the most prominent figure of the whole Qur'an, who is, of course, Moses.

A SCHEME AGAINST THE PHARAOH

When you take a copy of the Qur'an and seek the story of Moses, you will find not one but many passages in different chapters.[15] Their dispersion may make them seem disconnected, but in fact there is an important connection between these passages: almost all of them are Meccan, as opposed to Medinan.[16] In other words, they were revealed in the Meccan phase of the Prophet Muhammad's mission, which was characterized by the oppression of the Muslim community, and not the Medinan period, when Muslims achieved political and military power.

Now, with this Meccan context in mind, let's read the opening of the most comprehensive Moses story in the Qur'an, which is in the Meccan chapter *al-Qasas* (28):

> We recount to you [Prophet] part of the story of Moses and Pharaoh, setting out the truth for people who believe.
>
> Pharaoh made himself high and mighty in the land and divided the people into different groups: one group he oppressed, slaughtering their sons and sparing their women—he was one of those who spread corruption. But We wished to favor those who were oppressed in that land, to make them leaders, the ones to survive, to establish them in the land, and through them show Pharaoh, Haman, and their armies the very thing they feared.[17]

Note that in the very beginning, we are told that this is a story of not one but two men: it is the "story of Moses *and* Pharaoh." The latter was the title given to the rulers of ancient Egypt, while the Qur'an seems to use it to refer to a specific Pharaoh—an arrogant and cruel one. The Qur'an also shows remarkable attention to this Pharaoh—the term appears seventy-four times in the Qur'an, second only to Moses himself. It shows how central the struggle between the two men is to the foundational story of Islam.[18]

The Qur'anic passage above also tells that Pharaoh oppressed a certain group of people in his land, and even slaughtered their sons. Those who are familiar with the Bible can easily recall here a theme from the Book of Exodus: the commandment by Egypt's Pharaoh that "all male Hebrew children born be killed by drowning in the river Nile."[19] The Qur'an seems to allude to this tragic story by giving little details, as typical, while emphasizing the theological lesson: yes, the Pharaoh was brutally powerful, but God "wished to favor those who were oppressed."

Meanwhile, the Qur'an does give an interesting detail: the Pharaoh seems to have an associate named Haman. Those who are familiar with the Bible, however, can recall a different Haman, narrated in the Book of Esther. This was a cruel vizier who indeed persecuted Jews—yet not in Egypt during the time of Moses (around the fourteenth century BC) but in the Persian Empire at the time of Xerxes the Great (fifth century BC)—in other words, almost "a thousand miles and years away."[20] This dissonance between the Biblical and Qur'anic figures of Haman has long been picked up by critics of Islam. They argue that Muhammad, whom they consider the author of the Qur'an, "mixed up sacred stories."[21]

In return, some Muslim scholars offer a very different explanation: the Qur'anic Haman has nothing to do with his Biblical namesake. Instead, it is a reference to the high priests in ancient Egypt called Ha-Amen.[22] Therefore, this is not a flaw of the Qur'an but rather a "miracle" of it, as the Prophet Muhammad could not possibly have known the ancient Egyptian terms that we know today thanks to the modern study of hieroglyphs.

Yet there is a third explanation, arguably a stronger one, that falls short of interreligious polemics, but which reflects a more complex interfaith connection: that Haman was not really a historical figure but an archetype. As recent scholarship has shown, "Haman was viewed in the pre- and post-Islamic Near East as an ahistorical character, who could dip in and out of literary contexts when a villain was required."[23] In rabbinic Jewish literature, too, "Haman could turn up wherever there was trouble."[24] In fact, his very presence in the Book of Esther could also be due to such preexisting archetypes in "Babylonian antecedents."[25]

Therefore, when the Qur'an was condemning Pharaoh and Haman, it was probably addressing a cultural milieu familiar with these typologies. Meanwhile, it was certainly giving its primary addressees, the first Muslims, an encouraging message: tyrants, their associates, and their armies could inflict all sorts of torment on innocent believers such as you. Yet those oppressors would ultimately lose, because God "wished to favor those who were oppressed."

FROM THE RIVER TO THE MOUNTAIN

After letting us know that the Pharaoh's regime would face "the very thing they feared," chapter *al-Qasas* gets to the story of Moses:

> We inspired Moses' mother, saying, "Suckle him, and then, when you fear for his safety, put him in the river: do not be afraid, and do not grieve, for We shall return him to you and make him a messenger."
>
> Pharaoh's household picked him up, later to become an enemy and a source of grief for them: Pharaoh, Haman, and their armies were wrongdoers. And Pharaoh's wife said, "Here is a joy to behold for me and for you! Do not kill him: he may be of use to us, or we may adopt him as a son." They did not realize what they were doing.[26]

Meanwhile, the sister of Moses, who watches all this from afar, comes onto the scene and offers the real mother as a wet nurse. "We restored him to his mother in this way," God tells us, "so that she might be comforted, not grieve, and know that God's promise is true, though most of them do not know."[27]

That is how Moses grows up in the Pharaoh's palace. When he kills an Egyptian to defend an Israelite, however, he gets into trouble and flees. When he reaches the place called Midian, on the other side of the Red Sea, he finds an old shepherd with two young daughters, whom he kindly helps. Soon, the shepherd makes an offer: to marry his daughter, and to work for him for eight years, at least, if not ten.

Moses accepts the offer and settles in Midian, but at the end of that period, he begins to move again. On the way he sees a "fire" on a mountain, and goes to just check it, only to experience the turning point of his life. He hears the Almighty God:

> Moses, I am your Lord. Take off your shoes: you are in the sacred valley of Tuwa. I am God; there is no god but Me. So, worship Me and keep up the prayer so that you remember Me.[28]

God then tells Moses to throw his staff, which miraculously turns into a snake. He also tells him to put his hand inside his shirt, which comes out "white but unharmed." Finally, he tells him to go to the Pharaoh, accompanied by his brother, Aaron, because the latter is "more eloquent."[29]

So far, the Qur'anic story of Moses closely parallels that of the Bible, only with some subtle nuances: in the Bible, we do not see any "revelation" to the mother of Moses; she rather seems to put the baby on the Nile on her own. Also, in the Bible, the baby is found by Pharaoh's daughter, not his wife as in the Qur'an. The story about the Egyptian killed by Moses is also slightly different in both scriptures: the killing seems less premeditated and less intentional in the Qur'an, presenting Moses as less blameworthy. The Qur'an doesn't name the shepherd in Midian, while the Bible names him as Jethro.[30] Also, in the Qur'an the shepherd seems to have two daughters, whereas in the Torah he has seven.[31]

Such differences between the Bible and the Qur'an are interesting, and are open to various interpretations. Yet still, it is hard to find in them any big theological significance. However, as we go further in the story, we come to a fascinating difference whose theological significance cannot be missed.

WHAT TO DO WITH THE PHARAOH?

This remarkable difference between the Bible and the Qur'an is in the call that Moses extends to the Pharaoh. In the Bible, we read that Moses goes to the Pharaoh and tells him:

> This is what the LORD, the God of the Hebrews, says: "Let my people go, so that they may worship me."[32]

This memorable phrase, repeated several times in the Book of Exodus as the divine call to the Pharaoh, has subtle messages: Moses represents "the God of the Hebrews"—not necessarily the God of the Egyptians and the Pharaoh himself as well. No wonder Moses asks for "my people" to go, so that *they*—the Hebrews—may worship God. The Pharaoh is guilty of oppressing the Hebrews, and not allowing *their* worship. He doesn't seem guilty of his own lack of worship, which is neither asked nor expected.

In the Qur'an, however, we have a remarkably different version of the same story. Moses, again, goes to the Pharaoh, and again asks for his people—the Hebrews—to be set free. But there is more than that. Now God is not just the "God of the Hebrews" but also the Lord of everyone, including the Pharaoh himself, who is invited to "right guidance":

> Go and tell him: "We are your Lord's messengers, so send the Children of Israel with us and do not oppress them. We have brought you a sign from your Lord. Peace be upon whoever follows the right guidance; it has been revealed to us that punishment falls on whoever rejects the truth and turns his back on it."[33]

In another Qur'anic chapter, *al-Shu'ara* (26), which gives another snapshot from the same story, we hear a similar message from Moses to the Pharaoh: "We bring a message from the *Lord of the Worlds*: let the Children of Israel leave with us." Then the two men engage in a theological discussion:

> Pharaoh asked, "What is this 'Lord of the Worlds'?"
>
> Moses replied, "He is the Lord of the heavens and earth and everything between them. If you would only have faith! He is your Lord, and the Lord of your forefathers . . . Lord of the East and West and everything between them. If you would only use your reason!"
>
> But Pharaoh said [to him], "If you take any god other than me, I will throw you into prison."[34]

So, in the Qur'an, God is not just the Lord of the Hebrews. Instead, he is the Lord of everything and everybody, the East and West, the living Egyptians and their forefathers. Pharaoh is condemned for denying this one true God—and, instead, deifying himself.

OF YAHWEH AND ALLAH

What do these nuances in the Biblical and Qur'anic stories of Moses exactly mean?

Jack Miles, an Episcopalian Christian, scholar of religion, and Pulitzer Prize–winning author, maps it well. In his book *God in the Qur'an,* he compares Allah with God in the Bible, or Yahweh. In particular, he examines how they differ on the story of Moses and Pharaoh. In the Bible,

> Yahweh does not want to convert Pharaoh into a Yahweh-worshipper. He does not want to tell Pharaoh anything through Moses. Very much to the contrary, Yahweh is going to see to it personally that Pharaoh remains stubborn so that He can show Pharaoh in no uncertain terms just who He is.[35]

Conversely, in the Qur'an, Allah invites Pharaoh to the true faith, even instructing Moses, "Speak to him gently so that he may take heed or show respect."[36] For the same reason, Moses gets into a theological discussion with Pharaoh, calling him to "use your reason."[37]

So, the key difference between the Biblical and the Qur'anic stories of Moses, as Miles puts it, is of two different divine goals: "Yahweh Elohim wants to defeat Pharaoh, Allah wants to convert him."[38]

The Pharaoh's rejection of Allah's call also has an interesting detail. While refusing to believe in the God of Moses, the Qur'anic Pharaoh's entourage says: "Have you come to us to turn us away from the ways we found our fathers following?"[39] Remarkably, in the same Qur'an, we also hear Arab polytheists rejecting Muhammad with a similar conservatism: "And when it is said to them, 'Come to what God has revealed and to the messenger,' they say, 'That on which we found our fathers is sufficient for us.'"[40]

The difference between the Biblical and Qur'anic narratives becomes even bolder when we go further in the story. This is the section about the "sorcerers" whom Pharaoh enlists to overshadow the miracles of Moses. In the Bible, we read,

> Pharaoh then summoned the wise men and sorcerers, and the Egyptian magicians also did the same things by their secret arts. Each one threw down his staff and it became a snake. But Aaron's staff swallowed up their staffs.[41]

Then what happens? The sorcerers, according to the Bible, seem silent. Only after another miracle, the plague of the mosquitoes, do they tell Pharaoh, "This is the finger of God."[42] So, they seem to admit that something divine is going on, but that is all we hear.

In the Qur'an, however, the same sorcerers go through a

dramatic conversion when they see the miraculous staff of Moses. They even defy Pharaoh, despite his cruel threats, with remarkable courage:

> But Moses threw his staff and—lo and behold!—it swallowed up their trickery, and the sorcerers fell down on their knees, exclaiming, "We believe in the Lord of the Worlds, the Lord of Moses and Aaron."
>
> Pharaoh said, "How dare you believe in him before I have given you permission? He must be the master who taught you sorcery! Soon you will see: I will cut off your alternate hands and feet and then crucify the lot of you!"
>
> "That will do us no harm," they said, "for we are sure to return to our Lord. We hope that our Lord will forgive us our sins, as we were the first to believe."[43]

So, again, the God of the Qur'an is not just the Lord of the Hebrews but "the Lord of Worlds." Moreover, anyone who comes with a clear heart can realize this truth. Even more, they should not fear to proclaim the truth, even if they are threatened with torture and death, because their courage will be rewarded in the afterlife.

The exact edifications, in other words, that Mecca's persecuted Muslims needed to hear.

DELIVERANCE FROM EGYPT

What about the Biblical theme of Moses leading the Israelites out of Egypt? The Qur'anic story of Moses, too, includes this theme—but not as the central theme. In the words of Miles,

> Allah [also] does intend that Moses should lead the Israelites out of bondage, out of Egypt, and on to a land that He has prom-

ised them, but this theme—so overwhelmingly central in the long, continuous story told by the anonymous narrator of the books of Genesis, Exodus, and beyond—is decidedly muted here as also in other parallel accounts in the Qur'an. . . . For Allah, the Egyptians' core offense is that they do not worship the one true God. Their oppression of the Israelites is just one instance of the wrongdoing expected of unbelievers.[44]

What all this really means is that in the Moses stories of the Bible and the Qur'an, we see two different visions of monotheism. One is monotheism that addresses, at least initially, a specific people, the Israelites. The other one is monotheism that explicitly addresses all peoples.

In fact, not just Moses but the second most prominent prophet of the Qur'an, Abraham, also comes across mainly as "the founder of a universal religion," unlike the Bible, where he comes across mainly as the forefather of Israelites.[45] In the words of the Christian theologian John Barton:

In the Bible, it is through Abraham and his son Isaac that God establishes the covenant with Israel which serves as a central theme throughout the entire biblical narrative. By contrast, the Qur'an makes no mention of the covenant with Israel at all, but rather prioritizes Abraham and his son Ishmael as universal prophets of monotheism and models of submission and faithfulness.[46]

No wonder the Qur'an also commands Muslims to follow "the faith of your forefather Abraham." Abraham, in other words, is the forefather of not just Jews but also all monotheists, who are explicitly called "Muslims" in the broad sense of the term: those who willingly submit to God.[47]

THE VICTORY IN THE SEA

After telling us about Moses' plea to Pharaoh, the Qur'an confirms another Biblical narrative: God's punishment of the Egyptians with disasters of "locusts, lice, frogs, blood." These disasters
are identical to four of the ten plagues narrated in the Bible.[48] But,
conversely, the Qur'an does not mention at all the most chilling
element in the Biblical story: the tenth plague, which is the killing
of all firstborn male children in Egypt.[49]

Yet none of these disasters convinces Pharaoh, who keeps per-
secuting the Israelites, and even pursues them once they begin to
flee. This brings us to a most dramatic scene in the Qur'anic story
of Moses, which is the parting of the sea. In the Meccan chapter
al-Shu'ara ("The Poets"), we read:

> Pharaoh and his people pursued them at sunrise, and as soon
> as the two sides came within sight of one another, Moses' fol-
> lowers said, "We shall definitely be caught." Moses said, "No,
> my Lord is with me: He will guide me."
>
> And We revealed to Moses: "Strike the sea with your staff."
> It parted—each side like a mighty mountain. And We brought
> the others to that place. We saved Moses and all his compan-
> ions and drowned the rest.[50]

This Qur'anic account of the parting of the sea is in parallel
with the Biblical account of the same story. But the Qur'an has
a detail that we do not find in the Bible: the Pharaoh, at his last
moment, regrets all his transgressions and repents from his sins.
In another Meccan chapter, *Yunus* ("Jonah"), we read:

> We took the Children of Israel across the sea. Pharaoh and his
> troops pursued them in arrogance and aggression. But as he
> was drowning, he cried, "I believe there is no God except the
> one the Children of Israel believe in. I submit to Him."

"Now? When you had always been a rebel, and a trouble-
maker! Today We shall save only your corpse as a sign to all
posterity. A great many people fail to heed Our signs."[51]

One interesting note about the passage above is that the Pharaoh's last words—"I submit to Him"—also translate as: "I am
from the Muslims." This reflects the Qur'anic teaching that being
a "Muslim" actually means being a monotheist who "submits" to
God. Another note is the discussion that Pharaoh's last-moment
faith sparked in the Islamic tradition. Was this a valid faith that
saved him in the afterlife? Most Muslim scholars say no, arguing
that faith in such a moment of no return is not meaningful—as
implied in the Qur'anic response to Pharaoh: "Now?" But others, especially masters of the Sufi tradition such as Ibn al-Arabi,
argue that the Pharaoh "died clean" and was probably saved. A
third group remains undecided.[52]

An interesting comment on this issue came from the Ottoman
polymath Katip Çelebi (d. 1657), who embraced Ibn al-Arabi's
view that last-minute conversion must have saved the Pharaoh.
And why should we argue otherwise, he said, unless we are Jews,
who had a legitimate grudge against the tyrant:

> Now that these two different planes of investigation are known,
> if any man disputes this matter is he not a fool? Would he
> withhold God's mercy from His creatures? What harm does
> it do him if Pharaoh is a believer? What good does it do him
> if Pharaoh is an infidel? Certainly if the Jews maintain the lat-
> ter thesis they have a right to do so, in revenge, because their
> forefathers suffered great wrong at Pharaoh's hands. But what
> reason is there for people of other creeds to follow them?[53]

Yet, such nuances aside, the gist of the Qur'anic story has
been undisputed in Islam: the Pharaoh, despite all his earthly
power, was defeated by Moses. God's will to uplift the Children of

Israel—"those who were oppressed in that land"—was fulfilled, as the Meccan chapter *al-A'raf* ("The Heights") clearly stated:

> We drowned them [Pharaoh's people] in the sea. And We made those who had been oppressed succeed to both the east and the west of the land that We had blessed. Your Lord's good promise to the Children of Israel was fulfilled, because of their patience, and We destroyed what Pharaoh and his people were making and what they were building.[54]

Commenting on this verse, as well as other relevant passages from the Meccan period, the Turkish theologian Mustafa Öztürk stresses that they are quite sympathetic to the Israelites: the latter are presented as the *mustad'afin,* or the oppressed, who were ultimately saved by divine grace—the exact kind of people with whom the first Muslims of Mecca would identify.[55]

Conversely, the Pharaoh was the exact kind of person that Muslims would identify with their Meccan oppressors. In fact, the Prophet Muhammad explicitly drew that analogy when he condemned the very leader of those oppressors, Amr ibn Hisham—whom Muslims called Abu Jahl, or "Father of Ignorance"—as "the Pharaoh of this community."[56]

THE GOLDEN CALF AND THE "SAMARITAN"

The Meccan story of Moses continues, in chapter *al-A'raf* quoted above, coming to themes where the Children of Israel also do wrong. The first instance is when, after being miraculously saved from the Pharaoh's army, they come across a people who worship idols, which they envy. "Moses, make a god for us like theirs," they say to their prophet. But Moses responds only with rebuke:

> You really are foolish people. [What] these people practice is doomed to destruction, and what they have been doing is use-

less. Why should I seek any god other than God for you, when
He has favored you over all other people?"[57]

This rebuke by Moses seems to bring the Israelites back to
their senses, but there comes another instance, which is one of the
most dramatic episodes in the Biblical story of Moses as well:
the golden calf. In the Qur'anic version of the story, Moses goes
up to a mountain for forty days, for an "appointment" with
God, leaving behind his brother Aaron to take charge. Up on the
mountain, Moses wants to see God, but God rather shows him a
mountain that crumbles at the sight of the divine, also knock-
ing Moses down. So, God cannot be seen—at least not on this
earth. Yet still, God gives Moses the exceptional honor of con-
versing with him: "Moses, I have raised you above other people
by My messages and speaking to you."[58] That is why, to date, the
Islamic tradition has praised Moses as *kalimullah,* or "to whom
Allah has spoken."

On the same mountaintop, God also gives Moses "tablets,"
which "taught and explained everything." He also commands:
"Hold on to them firmly and urge your people to hold fast to
their excellent teachings."[59]

Yet back on the plains, the people of Moses go astray. They
begin worshipping "a calf made from their jewelry." That is
why Moses returns to them "angry and aggrieved." "How foul
and evil is what you have done in my absence," he says; "Were
you so keen to bring your Lord's judgment forward?" With
wrath, he also throws the tablets down, and seizes Aaron "by
the hair."[60]

So far, the Qur'anic story again largely parallels the Biblical
account, but there is also a significant difference: in the Bible,
Aaron is the one who leads the Israelites astray in the absence of his brother. Yet in the Qur'an we see Aaron as purely
innocent—maybe just not strong enough. To the fuming Moses,
he says:

Son of my mother, these people overpowered me! They almost
killed me! Do not give my enemies reason to rejoice! Do not
include me with these evildoers!⁶¹

That is why the Qur'anic golden calf story has another culprit:
a man named al-Samiri who, according to the Meccan chapter
Ta Ha, leads Israelites to make the idol, and proclaims: "This is
your god and Moses' god, but he has forgotten."⁶² He also takes
pride in what he did, claiming, "I saw something they [Israelites]
did not." In return, Moses condemns him to permanent banishment:

Get away from here! Your lot in this life is to say, "Do not
touch me," but you have an appointment from which there is
no escape. Look at your god which you have kept on worshipping—we shall grind it down and scatter it into the sea.⁶³

Now, there is something curious about this al-Samiri, the
second villain of the Moses story after the Pharaoh: his name
may not be a personal name, but a designation of a group—
the "Samaritan." Muslim exegetes have often considered this
meaning, while differing on what exactly it refers to. One view is
that there was a tribe among Israelites called the "Samaritans,"
but their religion "differed from that of other Jews."⁶⁴ Some exegetes consider another possibility: the man was not a Jew at all but
perhaps an Egyptian who joined them during the Exodus, only
to revert to his native idolatry at the first chance. A twentieth-
century exegete of the Qur'an, the Pakistani scholar Abdul Majid Daryabadi, seems to have found this option compelling, as he
wrote:

Who was this al-Samiri? The word sounds more of an appel-
lation than of a personal name. If we look to old Egyptian, we
have Shemer, a stranger, and foreigner. As the Israelites had just

left Egypt, they might quite well have among them an Egyptian Hebrew bearing that nickname. And it is recorded by the
rabbis that the initiative in the matter of the calf worship was
taken not by the Israelites but the Egyptians who had joined
them at the time of the Exodus, and who were the source of a
great deal of trouble to Moses and Israelites.[65]

What this means is that in its own version of the golden calf
story, the Qur'an not only absolves Aaron, the Israelite prophet,
of any blame, it may even put the main blame, the making of the
calf and the seduction of the Israelites, on a non-Israelite.

"MERCY" FOR THE ISRAELITES

The Moses story of the Qur'an goes further in chapter al-A'raf,
where we read about the aftermath of the golden calf affair. We
hear of God's wrath: "Those who took to worshipping the calf
will be afflicted by their Lord's wrath, and by disgrace in this
life."[66] But, immediately after this condemnation, we also hear
of God's mercy: "Your Lord is most forgiving and most merciful
towards those who do wrong, then repent afterwards and truly
believe."[67]
    Then Moses, whose anger has "abated," takes the tablets that
he had thrown. Unlike in the Bible, the tablets don't seem to be
broken. Moreover, they include yet another message of compas-
sion: "Guidance and mercy for those who stood in awe of their
Lord."[68] Moses also chooses seventy men from his people for
an "appointment" with God. When these men are captured by
"trembling"—or perhaps an "earthquake"—Moses calls out to
God: "My Lord . . . will You now destroy us for what the fool-
ish among us have done?" God, again, reminds us of His Mercy:
"I bring My punishment on whoever I will," He says, "but My
mercy encompasses all things."[69]
    This theme of divine mercy is quite dominant in much of the

Qur'an, including the story of Moses and the Israelites. And as Jack Miles perceptively noted, this Qur'anic spirit of "forgiveness and reconciliation" is different from the "far more turbulent and violent" version of events in the Bible. The Bible, most notably, has a bloody episode that is absent in the Qur'an: the Israelites who prove loyal to Moses—the Levites—massacre about "three thousand men" who fell for the golden calf.[70] In the words of Miles,

> Yahweh, with Moses as His captain, punishes Israel with ferocious violence, including a slaughter whose scope bears comparison with the drowning of Pharaoh's army. Allah, by contrast, though He angrily condemns the faithless idolaters, forbears to punish them with any comparable severity. In the Qur'an, the Israelite idolaters immediately repent, and Allah never fails to answer repentance with mercy.[71]

Toward the end of its long narration of Moses and the Israelites, chapter *al-A'raf,* while wrapping up the story, also says something remarkably gracious about the Israelites: "There is a group among the people of Moses who guide with truth, and who act justly according to it."[72]

The verse is quite interesting, for it seems to tell something about not just the history of the Israelites but also the present time—that is, the time of the Qur'an. For the first Muslims who heard it in Mecca, it must have sounded like great news: that they were not the only righteous believers around, that there also exists "a group among the people of Moses."

However, this pluralist message would not go well in the later Islamic tradition, in which there developed an exclusivist claim to truth. That is why the verse above had to be explained away. So, as the authors of *The Study Qur'an* put it, "Despite the clear statement in this verse that among the people of Moses—that is, the Jews—are those who are just and rightly guided, commentators have often sought to limit the application of this statement."[73] Some said that those righteous Jews had "traveled eastward beyond China" and just disappeared there. Others said that this was only a reference to Jews who converted to Islam. However,

> these various attempts to qualify the reference to this righteous *ummah* among the people of Moses contradict the plain sense of the verse, which indicates that a group among the people of Moses, in the sense of being followers of Jewish Law and ritual, continue to live and worship righteously according to the teachings of the Torah. Other verses support the literal reading as well . . . which indicates that there were communities of righteous Jews still existing at the time of the revelation of the Qur'an.[74]

Back in Mecca, in the time of the Prophet Muhammad, Muslims may have well taken the verse in "the plain sense": that there were righteous Jews around them. Exactly when they heard this message is also worthwhile to note. Chapter *al-A'raf* is clearly Meccan, except a short passage that may be a later revelation from Medina.[75] Moreover, according to some exegetes, such as the twentieth-century Pakistani scholar al-Mawdudi, the chapter was revealed in the very last year before the Prophet's migration to Medina. The very year, in other words, that Mecca was becoming utterly unbearable, and Muslims were desperately seeking a way out.

So, could there be a connection between that way out of Mecca and the Qur'an's good news about righteous Jews?

"GOD PAVED THE WAY"—VIA JEWS

The question above begs us to revisit the turning point in Muhammad's prophetic mission: the *hijra,* or migration, to the city of Yathrib (later known as Medina) in the year 622. As is well known, this was made possible because while the Prophet was persecuted in Mecca by his own tribe, the Quraysh, two other Arab tribes in Medina, the Aws and the Khazraj, welcomed him to their city. In two subsequent pledges in a small valley called Aqaba, a few kilometers outside Mecca, delegations from these tribes both affirmed their belief in Islam and promised to protect the Prophet with all their might. That is how the Prophet and his believers envisioned a safe haven in Medina, to which they soon fled.

This is all common knowledge about Islam's beginnings, but there is a curious question about this story that is seldom asked: Why were these Medinan Arabs so ready, if not eager, to embrace Islam? Just like the Quraysh, they were longtime polytheists. Yet unlike the Quraysh, who knew that Muhammad was *al-Amin,* or "the Trustworthy," they didn't even know Muhammad. So, why were they so prone to believe in an unfamiliar prophet from a different tribe and a distant city?

One common answer to this question is that these two tribes of Medina, the Aws and the Khazraj, who had recently clashed swords in the bloody Battle of Bu'ath (617 CE), were seeking a fair arbiter to secure peace in their tense city. There may be some truth in this account, but it still does not explain why they embraced Muhammad as not just a political arbiter but also a religious leader.

Yet a little-noticed explanation already exists, in nowhere other than the earliest biography of Muhammad, *Sirat Rasul Allah,* or *Life of the Messenger of God,* written in the early years of the Abbasid Caliphate by Ibn Ishaq (d. 767) and available to us through the edited version of his student Ibn Hisham (d. 833). Here, while learning about the background of the first pledge at al-Aqaba, we read something interesting:

> When the apostle met [the delegation from Medina] he learned by inquiry that they were of the Khazraj and allies of the Jews. He invited them to sit with him and expounded to

them Islam and recited the Qur'an to them. Now God had prepared the way for Islam in that they lived side by side with the Jews who were people of the scriptures and knowledge, while they themselves were polytheists and idolaters. . . . The Jews used to say to them, "A prophet will be sent soon, His day is at hand."[76]

So, it seems that what really "prepared the way for Islam" was the presence of the Jews in Medina, who introduced their polytheist Arab neighbors to a monotheist tradition that deeply influenced them. In fact, this Jewish influence could be directly observed in the backgrounds of the very delegation that came from Medina to invite Muhammad to their city. As the historian Michael Lecker puts it:

> At the Aqaba meeting, twelve of the Medinan Arabs were designated as nuqabā or tribal representatives, nine of the Khazraj and three of the Aws. Seven out of the twelve nuqabā shared a common denominator: they were literate. Now since in pre-Islamic Medina literacy was acquired at the Jewish bayt al-midrās, this means that the literate nuqabā, while they possibly did not convert to Judaism, were educated by the Jews, and hence were prepared to accept Muhammad as the messiah expected by the Jews.[77]

There is another narration, shared by the great exegete of the Qur'an Fakhr al-Din al-Razi (d. 1210), that suggests Medina's Jews even tried to influence Mecca's polytheist Arabs, the Quraysh, in favor of Muhammad. Accordingly, during the Meccan phase of the Prophet, the polytheists sent a group to Medina to ask Jews what this new self-declared prophet is really talking about. The Jews reportedly responded by saying: "We find him on the attributes mentioned in the Torah." When the group returned to Mecca and shared the news, other polytheists were not impressed.

"As Muhammad is a sorcerer," they said, "Moses was a sorcerer, too."[78]

Razi reports this narration in his commentary on a Qur'anic passage in chapter *al-Qasas*. Here, after learning about the story of Moses, we hear God saying:

> Even now that Our truth has come to them, they [Meccan polytheists] say, "Why has he not been given signs like those given to Moses?"
>
> Did they not also deny the truth that was given to Moses before?
>
> They say, "Two kinds of sorcery, helping each other."[79]

"Two kinds of sorcery," or, rather, revelation, were "helping each other." Apparently, this is how Meccan polytheists perceived the messages of Moses and Muhammad. The former's struggle was an inspiration for the latter. Moreover, the former's followers, Jews, seemed like natural allies of the latter's followers, Muslims.

This fact on the ground was even verified by a journey to heaven—at least as Muslims believe. Islamic sources tell that about a year before the hijra, at a time of despair, God took Muhammad to a miraculous Night Journey (*Isra'*) from Mecca to "the furthest place of worship," which is largely believed to be Jerusalem.[80] Then, from there, from the very rock that today stands under the Dome of the Rock, Muhammad rose to the seven heavens, where he met the Biblical prophets who came before him: Adam, Jesus, Joseph, Enoch, Aaron, Moses, and Abraham. All greeted Muhammad, but his mentor proved to be Moses, advising him, repeatedly, to ask God to decrease the burdens of daily prayers on his people, which God indeed reduced from fifty times a day to just five.

This is how the first chapter of the Judeo-Islamic tradition looked like by the year 622. The Prophet was still in Mecca, but in early September, he received a sign from God to leave immediately, because a group of polytheist assassins was about to besiege his house. Leaving his beloved nephew Ali as a decoy, according to some reports, Muhammad secretly left his hometown with his close companion Abu Bakr, only to be pursued by Meccan cavalry. For three days, at first, they hid in a cave, then marched cautiously for about ten days.

In this perilous exodus, nothing as dramatic as the parting of the sea by Moses took place, but the Islamic tradition does narrate a small miracle of a spiderweb that saved the Prophet from being captured.[81] In its reference to the incident, the Qur'an also says, "God sent His tranquility down to him, aided him with forces invisible to you."[82] The word for tranquility is *sakina,* a word the Qur'an also uses while narrating how the Ark of the Covenant brought tranquility to the Israelites. It is also a word that unmistakably has a Hebrew precedent, *shekhina,* a term that denotes God's "dwelling" among men.[83]

The migration ended happily on September 24, 622, when Muhammad, recently joined by his family, arrived in Medina. Here he found his enthusiastic community of believers—both the "emigrants" from Mecca, and the "helpers" of Medina. He also found Jewish tribes, who had long settled in this agricultural oasis, and who were curious to know more about this new monotheist prophet. With them, the second chapter of the Judeo-Islamic tradition, a turbulent one, would begin.

2

WHAT REALLY HAPPENED IN MEDINA
(PART I)

Do not give me superiority over Moses.

—The Prophet Muhammad[1]

To Muslims their religion, to Jews their religion.

—The Covenant of Medina

MANY MUSLIMS KNOW OF THE BATTLE OF UHUD. IT WAS A war of swords that took place on March 23, 625, in the third year of the Prophet's migration to Medina, just outside that city, between Muslims and the polytheists of Mecca. The latter, as the belligerent side, came well prepared, and caused heavy losses to Muslims, with about seventy martyrs. Among them were some of the most legendary companions, such as Hamza ibn Abdul-Muttalib, the Prophet's paternal uncle. The Prophet himself, to whom the enemy came dangerously close, was wounded.

Yet there was an exceptional figure at the Battle of Uhud, who many Muslims may have never heard of, and may be surprised by: a Jewish rabbi named Mukhayriq, who fought on the Muslim side, quite heroically, and even fell as a martyr. We learn this from the earliest biography of Muhammad, penned by the aforementioned Ibn Ishaq, where we read:

> Mukhayriq . . . was a learned rabbi owning much property in date palms. He recognized the Apostle [Muhammad] by his description and his own learning, and he felt a predilection for his religion. Until on the day of Uhud, which fell on the Sabbath, he reminded the Jews that they were bound to help Muhammad. They objected that it was the Sabbath. "May you have no Sabbath," he answered, and took his weapons and joined the Apostle in Uhud. His parting testimony to his people was: "If I am killed today my property is to go to Muhammad to use as God shows him." He was killed in the battle that followed. I am told that the Apostle used to say, "Mukhayriq is the best of the Jews."[2]

This is quite a remarkable report, giving us fascinating details. One is that this wealthy rabbi in Medina admired Muhammad and "his religion" so much that he went to battle with him. The war took place on a Sabbath, which naturally became an issue for his fellow Jews. But apparently their explicit objection was to this particular problem—fighting on Sabbath—and not fighting on the same side with the Muslims. Finally, the fallen rabbi left his property to Muslims, leaving a great name for him among them as "the best of the Jews."

In Muslim sources, it is even reported that Mukhayriq's donation became the first Muslim waqf, or endowment, establishing a precedent that would soon flourish in the medieval Islamic civilization, creating a rich tradition of charitable civil society.[3]

Does this all mean that Mukhayriq was a convert from Judaism to Islam? Or rather only "a righteous Jew who had affection for Muhammad"? Ibn Ishaq's account seems to be "deliberately ambiguous on the question."[4] Later Muslim tradition often assumed that Mukhayriq was a convert to Islam, perhaps as a way of explaining why he would be so pro-Muslim. Yet the early Muslim historian Ibn Sa'd (d. 845) wrote that Mukhayriq had lived and died as a Jew, and therefore he was buried not at the Muslim cemetery in Medina but just next to it—as a sign of respect, but also religious distinction.[5] In this view, Mukhayriq's response to his fellow Jews—"may you have no Sabbath"—didn't imply abandoning Jewish law, but rather taking a legitimate exception for self-defense, which already had precedence in the Jewish tradition.[6]

Mukhayriq, therefore, could indeed be not a Muslim but the "first Jewish martyr of Islam," in the words of the modern Muslim academic Muqtedar Khan, who highlighted the little-known episode.[7]

Yet this surprising conclusion would only raise a more curious question: Why would a Jewish rabbi in early seventh-century Medina fight on the side of Muslims in their war against the polytheists of Mecca? What could be the story behind that story?

A NICE BEGINNING

To decipher the story behind the Mukhayriq affair, let's take a moment to visualize Medina at the time of the Prophet's arrival in September 622. It was a widely spread oasis, divided, both regionally and politically, on tribal lines. The two main Arab tribes were the Aws and the Khazraj, who were later to become the "helpers" to Muhammad and his fellow "emigrants" from Mecca. Besides them, there was also a large population of Jews, who were probably the descendants of the survivors of the Jewish revolt against the Roman Empire some five centuries earlier. They also were divided into tribes, and the greatest three we know by name were called Banu Qaynuqa, Banu Nadir, and Banu Qurayza. ("Banu," by the way, means "sons of.")

The relations among these tribes were tense. Just five years before the Prophet's arrival, in 617, they had indeed shed much blood at the aforementioned Battle of Bu'ath. It was fought primarily between the Arab tribes, but the Jews were involved, too, and on opposite sides: Banu Nadir and Banu Qurayza were allied with the Aws, while Banu Qaynuqa was allied with the Khazraj. Tribal alliances, apparently, could matter more than religious solidarity.

Due to the uneasy truce that followed this war, Medina was prone to finding a *hakam*, or "arbitrator," a well-established custom in Arabia. This seems to be a key reason why different groups in the city, including Jews, welcomed Muhammad to be just such a peacemaker. We learn this from our second historical source to the story, *The Book of Raids*, penned by the Muslim scholar al-Waqidi (d. 823), who writes:

> The Prophet arrived in Medina, and its people were a mix— among them were the Muslims who had come together to the call of Islam. With them were the people of weapons and fortresses, and among them were the confederates of the two regions, the Aws and the Khazraj. . . . The Messenger of God . . . desired to establish peace for them and he reconciled with all of them.[8]

The "people of weapons and fortresses" was a reference to Jews, who were known for their artisanship and good defenses, as well as religious literacy that always fascinated the Arabs. But how did the Prophet seek "peace and reconciliation with them"?

We learn this from Ibn Ishaq, who also writes in his biography that when the Prophet arrived in Medina, he made "a friendly agreement with the Jews and established them in their religion and their property, and stated the reciprocal obligations."[9] Then, more remarkably, Ibn Ishaq quotes this "agreement" in full, transmitting to us an earlier document that did not receive much attention through the long centuries of Islam, when egalitarian pluralism wasn't popular, but gained much interest in the modern era when values began to change. The Indian-born Muslim scholar Muhammad Hamidullah (1908–2002) highlighted the document as "the Constitution of Medina," and even as "the first written constitution in the world."[10]

The term "constitution" may be a bit anachronistic, but this *kitab* or *sahifa*, meaning "book" or "document," is indeed a remarkable political agreement both for its authenticity, which is accepted by virtually all experts, as well as its content.[11] It has two basic parts. The first part sets up terms between "Believers and Muslims of the Quraysh and Yathrib," which is a reference to the religious followers of Muhammad, of both Mecca and Medina. (Why "believers" and "Muslims" are noted separately is a good question. One answer, hinted at by the Qur'an, is that these terms designate "concentric circles": "believers" are devout followers of Muhammad, "Muslims" include both them and newer recruits.[12])

The second part of the document begins by adding "Jews" to the settlement:

> The Jews who join us as clients will receive aid and equal rights; they will not be wronged, nor will their enemies be aided against them. . . . The Jews share expenditure with the believers as long as they are at war.[13]

Then, at least in what is the most common reading, the document even proclaims that Jews are "one community with the believers."[14] This phrase has gained much interest in the modern era, as the term here for "community" is *umma*, which is today used only to designate the universal community of Muslims. The earliest usage in Medina, however, suggests that an *umma* could be a political community that included both Muslims and Jews.

Then, in the same article, the document proclaimed what has

become its most famous line: "The Jews have their religion, and the Muslims have theirs."[15]

Jews, in other words, were not compelled to become Muslims. They were not even called on to convert. Instead, their freedom to keep practicing their religion was affirmed.

In return, both Muslims and Jews had the obligation to defend their city from any attack from the outside—especially from the Meccan polytheists, or the tribe of Quraysh. The document put this point emphatically:

> Incumbent upon the Jews is their expenditure and upon the Muslims theirs. They will aid each other against whosoever is at war with the people of this treaty. There is among them sincere advice and counsel.
>
> No protection will be granted to Quraysh nor to whoever supports them. They [the participating parties] undertake to aid each other against whosoever attacks Yathrib [Medina].[16]

Due to this concern with possible threats to Medina, some modern-day scholars define the text not as a "constitution" but as a "pact" or "covenant," which may be more accurate terms indeed. We will call it the Covenant of Medina.

For our purposes, there is an important question: Who exactly were the Jews who joined this covenant? All Jews in Medina, or just some of them?

This question has raised different answers as the document, strangely, does not mention the three big Jewish tribes that we know from other sources: Banu Qaynuqa, Banu Nadir, and Banu Qurayza. Meanwhile, the document does name certain Jewish tribes: "the Jews of Banu 'Awf, Banu-an-Najjar, Banu-al-Harith," and more. So, different theories have been proposed to explain this gap: perhaps those three big tribes were included, and the specified groups—the Jews of so-and-so—were in fact clans within them. (Just like the case with the major Arab tribe of Khazraj, which is mentioned by its various clans such sons of 'Awf, Harith, and Jusham.) The other theory is that the three big tribes were not a part of this covenant, but separate non-belligerency agreements were nevertheless made with them.[17] Also, some scholars think that the document we have today is in fact a composite text, formed later by bringing a few different agreements together.[18]

What is quite noteworthy is that the document mentions Banu Tha'laba, which, as we learn from other sources, was the very tribe of Rabbi Mukhayriq, the martyr at Uhud.[19] This suggests that the "first Jewish martyr of Islam," besides sympathy for Islam, could have also been driven by his loyalty to the Covenant of Medina, which gave Muslims and Jews an equal responsibility to defend their city.

Furthermore, the story of Mukhayriq also suggests that, at the time of Uhud, which took place almost three years after the hijra, some Medinan Jews were loyal to the covenant. That may also be why one of the agitators of the Uhud campaign, the Meccan polytheist Hind bint 'Utbah, had insisted that the attack should be on a Saturday "to ensure that the Jews of Medina could not join [Muhammad.]"[20] So she thought, perhaps, that otherwise more Jews could join the Muslims for the defense of Medina.

A RELIGIOUS TENSION

The Covenant of Medina was a remarkably good beginning for the Judeo-Islamic tradition. It offered a political order where Muslims and Jews could be equal partners, both following their own religions. While Muslims were the founders of this political order, Jews had no subordinate status. In other words, they were not subject to the poll tax called *jizya*, and lesser rights before the law, as Muslim empires would later establish as the conditions of *dhimma*, or protection, offered to Jews and Christians.

Yet this remarkably good beginning did not last long, and it is important to understand exactly why and how.

From the very sources that tell us about the Covenant of Medina, as well as the Qur'an that guided the Prophet's mission, we understand that, despite the political settlement, there soon emerged a religious tension between the Muslims and the Jews. Now they were living next to each other, frequenting the same marketplace, visiting each other's circles, and coming face-to-face. Jews were inquisitive about this new monotheistic faith, and Muslims were eager to win their acceptance. So, religious conversations and disputes took place, both in the newly established mosque, where rabbis visited with curiosity, as well as Jewish schools, where the Prophet or his companions went to preach. One of the reports in the hadith literature gives a glimpse of the mood:

> When the Prophet arrived at Medina, the Jews were observing the fast on Ashura (tenth of Muharram) and they said, "This is the day when Moses became victorious over Pharaoh." On that, the Prophet said to his companions, "You [Muslims] have more right to celebrate Moses' victory than they have, so observe the fast on this day."[21]

The fast that the Medinan Jews observed on the tenth day of their holy month, Tishri, is what Jews still honor as Yom Kippur. In Islam, the tradition has also lived on, though not as an obligatory fast as in the month of Ramadan, which came soon with new verses of the Qur'an, but merely as a "recommended" fast.[22] It is an interesting relic from the first moment when Muslims claimed the right to celebrate "the day when Moses became victorious over Pharaoh."

Yet in this claim, there was also a challenge to Jews: that Muslims had "even more right" to the legacy of Moses. The Qur'an made a similar claim to the very first patriarch of the Jews: "Those who have the best claim to Abraham are . . . followers [of] *this* Prophet."[23] This didn't mean that the Jewish faith was declared illegitimate, as the Qur'an did not explicitly ask Jews to abandon their faith and convert to Islam.[24] Instead, the Qur'an promised salvation to all faithful monotheists, including righteous Jews, as we will see later in detail.[25] Nevertheless, the Qur'an asked from Jews something else: to recognize, and confirm, the truth of Muhammad's prophecy. "Believe in the message I have sent down confirming what you already possess," a verse called on the Jews. "Do not be the first to disbelieve in it."[26]

Such calls seem to have convinced a few Jews in Medina to convert to Islam, the most famous of whom was Abdullah ibn Salam. The moment he saw Muhammad, reportedly, he was moved. "He is really, by God, the 'brother' of Moses and follows his religion," he cried. "He was sent with the same mission as Moses."[27] A few other Jews, such as Rabbi Mukhayriq, may have preserved their ancestorial religion while still affirming Muhammad's prophecy.

For Muslims who were trying to prove the truth of their newborn faith to their fellow Arabs, this confirmation by Jews, the quintessential monotheists, was important. That is why the Qur'an turned it into an explicit argument: "Is it not proof enough for [the polytheists] that the learned men of the Children of Israel have recognized it?"—"it" being the Qur'anic revelation itself.[28]

Yet the overwhelming majority of Medinan Jews, apparently, did not "recognize" the new faith. They, in other words, refused to accept that Muhammad was a real prophet. They even publicly challenged him. In return, the Qur'an challenged them back.

This religious tension is evident in the longest chapter of the Qur'an, *al-Baqara,* which was revealed in the first two years in Medina, where dozens of verses take on "O, Children of Israel." The tone is quite different from the Meccan verses, where the Children of Israel are a distant people, persecuted by the Pharaoh, and empathized by the Muslims. Now the Children of Israel are rather a present rival, with whom Muslims engage in polemics. These include critical reminders of their past disobediences, including the golden calf story:

> When it is said to them, "Believe in God's revelations," they reply, "We believe in what was revealed to us," but they do not believe in what came afterwards, though it is the truth confirming what they already have. Say [Muhammad], "Why did you kill God's prophets in the past if you were true believers? Moses brought you clear signs, but then, while he was away, you chose to worship the calf. You did wrong."[29]

Why was this the case? Why did Jews not "believe in what came afterwards"? The standard answer in the Muslim tradition is to blame Jews for some kind of communal egotism: that they well knew a new prophet was about to come, but they could not accept that this time he came from the Arabs, not Jews.[30] They had seen the truth, in other words, but rejected it out of arrogance.

On the other hand, Jews themselves have argued, from those first days in Medina, that they rejected Muhammad's prophecy only out of their own religious convictions. According to the Babylonian Talmud, prophethood had ended centuries earlier with the last Biblical prophets: Haggai, Zechariah, and Malachi.[31] Meanwhile, Jews did expect a Messiah—as they still do today—and this may be what the Muslim tradition has referred to, saying, "they knew him." But this Messiah, by definition, would be a descendant of King David who would liberate his fellow Jews from exile—not a Moses-like prophet who would establish a new religion among the Arabs.

This dissonance is reflected in an interesting passage in Ibn Ishaq's biography of the Prophet. We hear Muslims telling Medinan Jews: "Fear God, for you know right well that [Muhammad] is the apostle of God and you used to speak of him to us before his mission." In return, we hear Jews saying: "We never said that to you, and God has sent down no book since Moses."[32]

Meanwhile, a Qur'anic verse that is often quoted to support the "they knew him" argument may be less obvious than it seems. It reads: "Those We gave Scripture know *it* as well as they know their own sons, but some of them hide the truth that they know."[33] The "it" (or "he") here is explained in most Qur'anic commentaries as a reference to the Prophet Muhammad. However, one of the earliest exegeses of the Qur'an, that of Muqatil ibn Sulayman (d. 767), explained the "it" as the Kaaba. Jews, accordingly, had asked Muslims why they were venerating the Kaaba, "as it is just a stone." In return, the Qur'an said they knew the sacredness of this shrine "as they know their own sons."[34] And those who hid this truth were not all Jews in Medina, in case we miss the reference, but only "some of them."

Today, to have a fair sense of the seventh-century Jewish rejection here, contemporary Muslims can perhaps consider comparing it with the way most of them see the Baha'i faith. The latter, born in the nineteenth century, is a monotheist religion that shows great respect to all messengers of God, including the Prophet Muhammad. Yet the Baha'i "confirmation" of Islam hasn't led Muslims to return the favor by recognizing this new religion as theologically legitimate. (Quite the contrary, Baha'is have faced political persecution in Iran, Egypt, and some other Muslim states.) It seems that every newborn religion somehow honors the traditional ones while adding something new, but this very addition proves hard to accept for the traditional ones.

With this insight, Muslims and Jews today can develop a more empathic view of the religious tension in Medina. Perhaps we can all consider what Rabbi Reuven Firestone, a fair interpreter of the history of Islam and Judaism, puts as the view from both sides:

From the honest and authentic standpoint of the Jews . . .
Muhammad was a false prophet who could not be accepted
nor even trusted. But from the honest perspective of Muhammad and his followers, who absolutely believed in his status of
prophet, the Jewish rejection was tantamount to the rejection
of God.[35]

And yet, there was a way, in fact, to bridge this seemingly
unbridgeable gap: a certain interpretation of Jewish sources
could have led to the acceptance of Muhammad as a legitimate
prophet—not for Jews themselves, but for the gentiles. There is
basis for this in the Midrash: "Just as He [the Almighty] placed
angels and sages and prophets in Israel, so did he do similarly for
the nations of the world."[36] With such inspiration, the twelfth-
century Jewish scholar Nethanel ben al-Fayyumi indeed explicitly argued that Muhammad must have been such a gentile
prophet. "God sent different prophets to the various nations of
the world," he reasoned, "with legislations suited to the particular temperament of each individual nation."[37] In fact, even much
earlier, the Islamic scholar Muhammad al-Shaybani (d. 805), a
student of Abu Hanifa, the eponymous founder of the largest legal Sunni school, was reporting that there were "Jews in the areas
of Iraq . . . who recognize that there is no god but God and Muhammad is the Prophet of God, but they claim that he was sent
as a prophet to the Arabs, and not to the Jews."[38]

So, back in Medina, both Jews and Muslims could have considered each other's religion as fully legitimate: they were the
same monotheist creed, just for different peoples. Yet such mature perspectives hardly appear at the heat of first encounters,
and the encounter in Medina seems to be one such heated case.

There is one more point to consider: Medinan Jews may
have seen Islam, whose scripture was still in the making, as an
enigma. They could have had suspicions about where this new
religion would end up exactly. A question that Ibn Ishaq quotes

from a rabbi who visited Medina in 631—only a year before the Prophet's passing and the culmination of Qur'anic revelation—is quite telling in this regard: "Do you want us, Muhammad," the rabbi asks, "to worship you as the Christians worship Jesus, Son of Mary?"[39] The Prophet, of course, resolutely says no. But the question itself reflects a stage when Islam was yet not well known to outsiders, including Jews. It even suggests that the latter may have seen Islam as alarmingly akin to Christianity—an interesting point to which we shall soon return.

"ARGUING IN THE BEST WAY"

For all these reasons, a religious tension in Medina between the two self-confident versions of monotheism was probably unavoidable. Yet still, this religious tension could have been managed peacefully if it remained merely as religious polemics. We see evidence for this in our earliest and most authentic guide to the story, which is none other than the Qur'an. Here, in one of the latest verses in Mecca, we hear God commanding Muslims:

> Argue only in the best way with the People of the Book, except with those of them who act unjustly. Say, "We believe in what was revealed to us and in what was revealed to you; our God and your God are one [and the same]; we are devoted to Him."[40]

When the Prophet arrived in Medina, "arguing in the best way" seems to have continued, despite "hurtful" words. We learn this from the Prophet's early biographer, al-Waqidi, who reports:

> The polytheists and Jews among the people of Medina hurt the Prophet and his companions grievously, but God most high commanded His prophet and the Muslims to be patient and forgiving. About them it was revealed [in the Qur'an]: "You

are sure to hear much that is hurtful from those who were given the Scripture before you and from those who associate others with God. If you are steadfast and mindful of God, that is the best course."[41]

Our third important source for the life of Muhammad, al-Wahidi (d. 1075), the exegete who wrote about the "occasions of revelation," also reports an incident in Medina that reflects patience against "hurtful words." Accordingly, one of the most prominent Muslims, the future caliph Umar ibn al-Khattab (d. 644), became enraged when he heard a Jewish rabbi named Finhas making fun of a Qur'anic verse. But then, Umar's anger was curbed by the highest authority ever imaginable:

> When Umar ibn al-Khattab heard [the mockery by Finhas], he got his sword and went looking for him. [Angel] Gabriel went to the Messenger of Allah, and said to him: "Your Lord says to you, 'Tell those who believe to forgive those who hope not for the days of Allah.'" The Prophet said: "Certainly, by Him Who has sent you with the truth, anger will not show on my face!"[42]

Another interesting incident comes to us through the hadith literature. A holier-than-thou dispute broke out in Medina between a Muslim and a Jew. But the Prophet himself intervened:

> Two persons, a Muslim and a Jew, quarreled. The Muslim said, "By Him Who gave Muhammad superiority over all the people!" The Jew said, "By Him Who gave Moses superiority over all the people!" At that time the Muslim raised his hand and slapped the Jew on the face. The Jew went to the Prophet and informed him of what had happened between him and the Muslim. The Prophet sent for the Muslim and asked him

about it. The Muslim informed him of the event. The Prophet said, "Do not give me superiority over Moses."[43]

From this early Medinan period, there are also reports showing that Muslims paid respect to Jews as neighbors and fellow human beings. One is an incident where Muhammad stood up for a passing funeral, and when his companions told him it was the coffin of a Jew, he said, "Is it not a soul?"[44] In another moment, when one of his companions was served meat, Muhammad asked: "Have you given any to our Jewish neighbor?"[45]

There is even a remarkable case of the Qur'an admonishing the Prophet himself in order to defend the rights of a falsely accused Jew. The story began when a hypocritical Muslim named Tu'mah ibn Ubayriq stole a suit of armor, and then accused Zayd ibn Samin, a Jewish man in Medina, of stealing it. Ibn Ubayriq even brought his family to the Prophet to advocate for himself, to convince him in his libel. However, when the Prophet was indeed about to rule against the innocent Jew, a new revelation came to correct him:

> We have sent down the Scripture to you [Prophet] with the truth so that you can judge between people in accordance with what God has shown you. Do not be an advocate for those who betray trust. Ask God for forgiveness: He is most forgiving and merciful.[46]

After this verse, exegetes report, the Prophet cleared the innocent Jew from charges. Escaping from justice, Ibn Ubayriq renounced Islam, went to Mecca to join the idolaters, and died there when a wall in which he carved a hole to steal something fell on him.[47]

All this suggests that Medinan Jews, despite their rejection of Islam, could have remained in their home. Their religion would still have been respected, and their rights would still have been protected. That was true even after the famous change of *qibla*, or direction of prayer, which took place some sixteen or seventeen months after the hijra. Before this moment Muslims were praying toward Jerusalem, following the Jewish way. But, with a Qur'anic revelation, they began to pray toward Mecca, setting the standard for the whole Islamic civilization to date.[48] It was a sign of the parting of ways between Islam and Judaism. Yet this parting didn't need to escalate into political war, as the Covenant of Medina had already ruled that "the Jews have their religion and the Muslims have theirs." And the Qur'an, right after changing the qibla, reaffirmed this pluralism: "Each community has its own direction to which it turns, so compete with one another in doing good."[49]

Yet, unfortunately, a political war is exactly what happened. And it is important to figure out why.

A POLITICAL COLLAPSE

As the biographers of the Prophet tell us, the Covenant of Medina began to collapse gradually after the Battle of Badr, which took place in March 624, about a month after the change of qibla. That battle, which Muslims gallantly won, was between them and their archenemy, the Meccan polytheists, who continued to threaten them even after the hijra. Yet, back in Medina, it seems to have initiated a process where the Muslim community not only grew militarized but also began to suspect that Medinan Jews were taking sides with the Meccan enemy—a political treachery, in other words, and not merely a religious dispute.

A passage in al-Waqidi's biography of Muhammad hints at how this suspicion may have arisen. It is about how Ka'b ibn al-Ashraf, a prominent Jewish poet from the tribe of Banu Nadir, responded to the Muslim victory at Badr:

When Zayd b. Haritha arrived with tidings from Badr about the killing of the polytheists and the capture of prisoners from them, and when he informed them that he saw the prisoners chained, Ibn al-Ashraf was dejected and made low, and he said to his people, "Woe unto you! By God, the bowels of the earth are better for you than its surface today! The best of these people have been killed and taken prisoner. . . . But I will go out to the Quraysh and incite them, and I will mourn their dead so they will, perhaps, authorize me to go out with them."[50]

Then, Ibn al-Ashraf really went to the Quraysh and "incited them" for a new war with Muslims, paving the way for the Battle of Uhud. There are even reports that he went to Mecca with forty of his men and made a secret deal with Abu Sufyan, the then leader of the anti-Muslim campaign.[51] Soon after his return to Medina, Ibn al-Ashraf would be assassinated by Muslims—an incident that continues to be used to date to justify the death penalty for blasphemy. However, he seems to have been targeted not merely for his offensive poetry but also for his agitation for war.[52]

Ibn al-Ashraf was of the Banu Nadir, but his pro-Meccan stance seems to reflect the souring relations between Muslims and most Jews in Medina after the Battle of Badr. With one of them, Banu Qaynuqa, soon the first conflict would break out. Ibn Ishaq reports that after the Battle of Badr, the Prophet called on them to accept Islam, which they refused and said: "By God, if we fight you, you will find that we are real men!"[53] Waqidi adds that while such signs showed "enmity and breach of the agreement," the real deal-breaker came when a Muslim woman in the marketplace was humiliated by some men of the Banu Qaynuqa, followed by mutual killings.[54] Muslims then besieged the Banu Qaynuqa's fortress for two weeks, and after their surrender, expelled the whole tribe from Medina.

The pattern seems to have continued after every battle with

the polytheists. Following the Battle of Uhud (625), the Banu Nadir, long suspected of secret dealings with the Meccans, were similarly besieged for two weeks, and then also expelled from Medina. When they settled in the northern Jewish city of Khaybar, to "prepare for war against Muhammad and to recruit the aid of Arab tribes," the seeds for a second conflict were sown.[55] This was the Battle of Khaybar of 628, when Muslims besieged the city and, after some fighting, the Jews surrendered. They were given the right to stay in the land and to cultivate it, but only on the condition that they give half their produce as tax to the Muslim state based in Medina.

Two interesting details in the conflict with the Banu Nadir are worth noting, as they indicate that despite the bitter conflict, Muslims didn't give up their recognition of the legitimacy of the Jewish religion. The first one is that copies of the Torah seized during the siege of Khaybar were given back to Jews, as Muslims didn't want to desecrate them.[56] The second one, which is even more remarkable, is reported by the prominent Qur'anic exegete Ibn Kathir (d. 1373):

> When (an Ansar [Medinan Muslim]) woman would not bear children who would live, she would vow that if she gives birth to a child who remains alive, she would raise him as a Jew. When Banu An-Nadir (the Jewish tribe) were evacuated from Al-Madinah, some of the children of the Ansar were being raised among them, and the Ansar said, "We will not abandon our children."[57]

On this incident, Ibn Kathir continues to write, God revealed verse 2:256, which declared, "There is no compulsion in religion."[58] It is the very verse that has become, especially in the modern era, the Islamic motto for religious freedom. The fact that it was about allowing converts to Judaism to remain in Judaism, even at a young age, is remarkable. (An alternative narration connects the verse to another dispute about children who converted to Christianity, but the lesson is the same: Jews and Christians cannot be forced to convert to Islam.[59])

Again, all this suggests that, despite the political conflict, Jews could have survived in Medina.

Yet the political conflict only got more bitter. This is evident in the fate of the third major Jewish tribe in Medina, Banu Qurayza. As reported by the earliest biographer of the Prophet, Ibn Ishaq, the drama began with the Battle of the Trench (627), when Medina's Muslims survived, with much hardship, a twenty-seven-day siege by a huge army of polytheist tribes—the *ahzab,* or "parties," as addressed in the Qur'an.[60] These polytheist aggressors were also supported by the Banu Nadir, who had been exiled from Medina just two years earlier. Reportedly, in the middle of the siege, the leader of Banu Nadir secretly reached out to Banu Qurayza, who were still in the city, to betray the Muslims. Banu Qurayza's leader was reluctant, as he didn't know how the war would end, but he seems to have entered into secret negotiations about supporting the besiegers.[61] Therefore, when the siege finally collapsed and the enemy retreated, Muslims were convinced of Banu Qurayza's treason. Muslims may even have thought that "they might try to persuade the enemy to return."[62]

This was the end of the pact between Muslims and Banu Qurayza, which could have led to the expulsion of the tribe, as was the case with the two other major Jewish tribes. Yet Muhammad's biographers, as well as hadith sources, report a much harsher verdict, decreed by the chief of the Arab tribe of Aws but also approved by the Prophet: the execution of all the men, and the enslavement of the women and children. Ibn Ishaq also narrates that the mass killing took place in the marketplace of Medina, where all Banu Qurayzan males who had reached puberty were beheaded and then buried in a mass grave. "There were 600 or 700 in all," he adds, "though some put the figure as high as 800 or 900."[63] Differing to some extent, one of the earliest exegetes of the

Qur'an, Muqatil ibn Sulayman, gives the number of the executed men as 450.[64]

In any case, this is a shockingly violent story. And, as the bloodiest episode in the whole biography of the Prophet Muhammad, it begs some consideration. In traditional Islamic sources, it is often conveyed with little concern, seen as a fitting sentence for an unforgivable treachery that could have extinguished Islam at its birth. Contemporary Muslim traditionalists also often note that the grim sentence—execution of males, enslavement of women and children—was exactly what the Torah, in Deuteronomy 20, commanded Israelites to do to their own enemies in the land of Canaan.[65] Western scholars who try to be fair to Muhammad also note that such brutalities were quite common in the ancient world, and thus "Muhammad's crude power politics" should not be judged by our modern standards.[66]

Placing the birth story of Islam in its historical context is indeed necessary, for both non-Muslims and Muslims themselves. However, we the latter also believe that Islam introduced moral progress to that context, which seems hard to argue in the face of the Banu Qurayza story, because it is not easy to justify the extermination and enslavement of a whole tribe just to punish a political wrongdoing by the tribe's leadership.

REVISITING THE BANU QURAYZA STORY

Due to this moral problem, some modern-day Muslims have sought an alternative way to look at the fate of Banu Qurayza—to question whether such a mass killing really happened. A first attempt was made by Walid N. Arafat in his 1976 article "New Light on the Story of Banu Qurayza and the Jews of Medina."[67] He argued that such a collective punishment would be against the Qur'an, as well as the Covenant of Medina, both of which stressed individual responsibility for crimes. He then noted that our earliest version of the story was written "145 years after the event in question," and its author, Ibn Ishaq, was discredited by some prominent scholars. Moreover, some details of the story—such as the detention of hundreds of captives in a single house in Medina—did not seem plausible. What really happened, according to Arafat, was that only "a few specific persons" of Banu Qurayza were executed for treason, but the story was later blown out of proportion.

This article was followed by Barakat Ahmad's 1979 book, *Muhammad and the Jews: A Re-examination,* where similar arguments were raised to conclude, "the whole story of this massacre is of a very doubtful nature."[68] More recently, prominent Muslim scholars in the West, such as Shabir Ally and Hamza Yusuf, also voiced doubts about the standard story.[69] The latter stated, for example:

> When you actually go back to check the account of the massacre, it says that all the Jews were held in the house of Umm Haram. And I thought, "How big was that house?" So, I asked my friend, Shaykh Abdullah Alkadi, who's probably the most learned person I've ever met, about the sirah [biography] of the Prophet. I asked, "How many people could Umm Haram's house hold?" He said, "A maximum of ten." And yet the literature says that three hundred to nine hundred Jewish men were executed. That's a huge disparity![70]

Most recently, a 2021 biography of the Prophet, *Muhammad, the World-Changer* by the Canadian imam Mohamad Jebara, repudiated "the notorious 'Medina Massacre' myth," going as far as to consider it as a "character assassination leveled against Muhammad."[71]

Among Western scholars, Fred Donner, who emphasizes Islam's inclusive beginnings, also doubts the accuracy of the Banu Qurayza story and even the conflicts with the two other tribes. These "stories about Muhammad's clashes with the Jews of Medina," he suggests, could be "greatly exaggerated (or perhaps invented completely) by later Muslim tradition—perhaps as part of the project of depicting Muhammad as a true prophet, which involved overcoming the stubborn resistance of those around him."[72] The British historian Tom Holland also notes that the stories about the "annihilation" of Medinan Jews are "all suspiciously late." They all come from "the heyday of Muslim greatness," when "the authors would have had every interest in fabricating the sanction of the Prophet for the brusque slapping down of uppity infidels."[73] Their primary aim, in fact, could be the "cowing of the Christians of the Middle East."[74]

In a most recent work, *Muhammad's Military Expeditions: A Critical Reading in Original Muslim Sources*, Ayman Ibrahim, a scholar of Islamic studies, himself a Christian, also raises doubts about the Banu Qurayza story, as well as some other unnerving reports in the early biographies of Muhammad that were written more than a century after the fact. He shows that these stories, which include a narration that Muhammad was fatally poisoned by a Jewish woman, are full of contradictions and implausibilities.[75] Even more telling, they often have little or no basis in the Qur'an, our earliest source to Muhammad's life, as others have noted.[76] Hence, Ibrahim suggests, these antagonistic stories in their imperial context may have been authored to assert "Islam's superiority and militaristic hegemony," by portraying Muhammad as "strong, unyielding, superior, and, to some extent, harsh and unforgiving with his enemies."[77] Today, he adds, "Our world can benefit greatly from the critical approach of treating these traditions as figurative and hyperbolic."[78]

Personally, I believe that the truth about Banu Qurayza may never be fully known, but questioning the traditional story, both historically and morally, is a step forward in Islam today.

POLITICS VERSUS RELIGION

Nevertheless, even if we doubt the massacre story and certain details of other episodes, it seems undeniable that the Jewish-Muslim coexistence in Medina, which began with a remarkable pluralism that we see in the Covenant of Medina, failed, leaving a dark shadow on the Judeo-Islamic tradition. So, it needs some consideration.

A key point that many Muslim commentators rightly note is that the three major Jewish tribes in question were targeted not because of their religion but because of their politics: their collaboration, real or perceived, with the Meccan polytheists. The Qur'an stresses this point in a relevant passage. It condemns those "with whom you made a covenant, but then they break their covenant every time."[79] Then it commands Muhammad: "And if you learn of treachery on the part of any people, throw [their covenant] back at them, for God does not love the treacherous."[80] Which means that if this treachery issue weren't a concern, then the Covenant of Medina could have survived, as noted by various commentators of the Qur'an.[81]

No wonder, as also stressed by Montgomery Watt, one of the towering Western scholars on Islam, that even after the Banu Qurayza affair there actually remained some Jews in Medina, "perhaps quite a number." This indicated that Muhammad did not adopt "a policy of clearing all Jews out of Medina just because they were Jews."[82] As long as Jews "ceased to be actively hostile," Watt added, "they were unmolested."[83]

Beyond Medina, too, various Jewish groups seem to have survived under the nascent Muslim state. Muslim sources write that the Jewish community in Khaybar resided in the area until the time of Caliph Umar, who reportedly expelled them in 642 to Syria, supposedly based on a hadith of the Prophet: "Let there be no two religions in the Arabian Peninsula." However, this hadith may be a later invention, and there may never have been such a policy to expel all non-Muslims from the heartlands of Islam, as historical records indicate their continued presence: while narrating the events of the late ninth century, the prominent Muslim scholar al-Tabari mentions a "Jew from Khaybar."[84] In the tenth century, the Muslim geographer al-Maqdisi describes a settlement at Wadi al-Qura, a valley a little north of Medina, as a "splendid, flourishing" town with merchants and crops, only to add: "It is dominated by Jews."[85] Jewish legal writings from the medieval period also indicate that Jewish communities lived in both Wadi al-Qura and Tayma, another oasis in today's northern Saudi Arabia, well after the birth of Islam.[86] Such historical evidence calls into question whether there was really "ever an historical attempt to remove non-Muslims from the Hijaz."[87]

Even more remarkable is the story of the Jews of Yemen, a country that was incorporated into Islamic rule in the year 628, when the Prophet Muhammad was still alive. Just like the Christians of the nearby Najran region, these Jews were given *dhimma,* or protection, which remained intact all the way to the mid-twentieth century. As the Israeli historian Yosef Tobi puts it in *The Jews of Yemen*:

> The Jews of Yemen themselves, like their brethren in north and central Arabia, did not incline towards this new faith of Muhammad. Yet no religious or political tension arose between them and the Muslims that might have resulted in the imposition of Islam on them or their expulsion from the country, as happened to Jewish tribes around Madina [*sic*].[88]

There is even a narration that Muhammad explicitly ordered his commanders in Yemen: *La yuftanu yahudiyyun 'an yahudiyyatihi,* or "A Jew will not be induced to abandon his Judaism."[89]

So, we can safely argue that the interreligious conflict in Medina was more political than religious.

Yet this still leaves us with an important question: Why did such a bitter political conflict emerge between the first Muslims and their first Jewish neighbors?

In Muslim sources, the answer is sometimes found in some quintessential Jewish arrogance and perfidy. In this view, the Prophet Muhammad had done his best to reach out to Medinan

Jews, had offered them religious freedom, yet they betrayed this goodwill by collaborating with bloodthirsty polytheists out of mere malice, only to receive the punishment they deserved.[90]

In contrast, in Jewish and most Western sources, the moral weight of the story is sometimes reversed: Jews had welcomed the Prophet Muhammad to Medina as a political arbiter, but he soon also demanded their religious recognition, and when Jews refused him, he created pretexts to expel or annihilate them. And if the Jews really sided with Arab polytheists, it was only because Muslims presented a greater menace.

Admittedly, these two opposite narratives are hard to bridge. Yet, inadvertently, they have something in common: while judging what happened in Medina, they look into just Medina. They, at most, focus on the Jews and Muslims of the Hijaz, or western Arabia, seeing their encounter as an isolated story. Yet if we do something rarely done by both sides, by zooming out and seeing the broader context in which this story may have unfolded, a more nuanced picture begins to appear.

WHAT REALLY HAPPENED IN MEDINA
(PART II)

Some Muslims have a strange habit of imagining that
the formative era of Islam was exempt from history . . .
that Muhammad, his family, his companions, and his
opponents made decisions in an environment possessed of
no memory, no context, or no basic human calculation,
as if everything was manufactured somewhere far away,
and only dropped down in western Arabia for reasons
God only knows.

—Haroon Moghul, American Muslim writer[1]

IF AN ALIEN FROM OUTER SPACE WERE TRANSPORTED TO EARTH in the early seventh century to observe what we today call the Middle East, the Arabian Peninsula would actually not catch his immediate attention. Because just outside this barren region, which had never impacted world affairs, there was the real drama that defined the known world: the long and brutal conflict between the two greatest powers of the time. One was the Eastern Roman Empire, also known as the Byzantine Empire, which was centered in Constantinople and held Christianity as its official religion. The other was the Sassanid Empire, which was centered in Persia and held Zoroastrianism as its official religion.

These empires had fought a series of wars over a few centuries, but the one that lasted from AD 602 to 628 was the most devastating and spectacular. In the early stage, the Sassanids had a major advance, capturing huge territories including the Caucasus, Armenia, Central Anatolia, Syria, and Egypt. In 614, they even seized Jerusalem, which had been a Roman town since the first century, and the Christian holy city since the fourth century when Rome adopted Christianity. That is why the Byzantines were horrified to see Jerusalem fall in heathen hands. Christians were killed, churches were ruined, and the sacred True Cross—believed to be the actual cross on which Jesus Christ was crucified—was carried as war booty to the Sassanid capital, Ctesiphon. However, the tide would soon turn, and the Christians would rejoice when the Byzantine emperor Heraclius, with a surprise attack in 627, crushed the Sassanid armies at the Battle of Nineveh, reconquered Jerusalem, and even took back the True Cross.

Now, what is interesting for our story is that in this big clash of empires, Jews had taken a side: the Sassanids. They even actively supported the Sassanid conquest of Jerusalem in 614, "with all the men they could muster."[2] Their hope was that the Zoroastrians, who didn't see any religious significance in Jerusalem, could give them control of the city, and even allow the reestablishment of an autonomous Jewish state.[3]

But why would Jews side with the Sassanids? The answer was reasonably simple: this Zoroastrian empire was tolerant of their faith, at least by premodern standards. Thanks to a settlement with Shapur I (242–272), the second king of the dynasty, Jews were given autonomy in their religious affairs, in return for accepting the principle "the law of the king is law."[4] This hierarchal tolerance would suffer some interruptions, but at the time of King Chosroes Parwiz (591–628), Jews felt secure with the Sassanids and hence "joined forces" with them.[5]

In contrast, the Byzantine Empire was a nightmare for the

Jews. John Chrysostom (d. 407), the archbishop of Constantinople, had condemned them as "killers of Christ," ascribing to them "every imaginable evil."[6] His writings and sermons set the tone for Byzantine rule, whose long history reflected a "consistent fanaticism" against Jews. Implications included conversion of synagogues to churches, the banning of the Mishna, anti-Jewish riots, and forced conversions to Christianity.[7]

Meanwhile, all this Christian persecution of Jews provoked a bitter response—and in nowhere other than the Arabian Peninsula. This was the Himyarite Kingdom in today's Yemen, which was initially a pagan state but adopted Judaism—or at least a "Judaizing monotheism"—around the year 380.[8] Around 523, the last monarch of the kingdom, Yusuf As'ar Yath'ar—nicknamed Dhu Nuwas, or "the one with sidelocks"—seeking "a reprisal for the persecution of his co-religionists in Christian countries," attacked the Christians in Najran, a city on modern Saudi Arabia's border with Yemen.[9] He forced these Christians to convert to Judaism, and when they refused, he threw them alive into burning ditches, while also killing Byzantine merchants in the region. Alarmed by these atrocities, the Christian kingdom of Abyssinia, an ally of Byzantium, gathered a fleet and invaded Yemen, killing King Dhu Nuwas and destroying the Jewish monarchy "with fire and sword, plundering, massacring."[10]

This was how the "Judeo-Christian" nexus looked in the early seventh century, at the dawn of Islam. It was a far cry from the cordial interfaith relations that emerged in the modern liberal West. Christianity was deeply infested with religious antisemitism, and Jews were quite suspicious of Christians, throwing their lot rather with theologically more distant groups such as the Zoroastrians.

So, Islam was born in such a schismatic time and milieu. With its dedication to Abrahamic monotheism and its relentless campaign against idolatry, the Qur'an often honored both Jews and Christians, equally, as "the People of the Book." But these people of the Book themselves could rightly wonder on whose side this new religion was. And Medinan Jews had good reasons to think that it was on the other side.

THE ROMAN CONNECTION

To see how nascent Islam might have looked to Medinan Jews, let's recall that when the Prophet Muhammad met them with his hijra in 622, a big portion of the Qur'an was already revealed and proclaimed. It included long narrations about Moses and the Pharaoh, as we have seen in the first chapter, which could only be music to Jewish ears. But the same Meccan Qur'an also sang the praises of Jesus, in a long chapter named after his mother, Maryam, or Mary. The nativity story presented in this Qur'anic chapter, which has strong parallels with the Gospel of Luke, confirmed one of the key Christian doctrines: the virgin birth of Christ. For Medinan Jews, it could have sounded only too "Christian."

Islamic sources tell us that chapter *Maryam* was revealed quite early on, in the fourth year of the first revelation. The following year, it seems to have helped solidify a strategic friendship between Muslims and Christians. This was the first hijra from Mecca, by the weakest members of the Muslim community, to the Christian kingdom in Abyssinia, which then ruled today's Ethiopia, Eritrea, and neighboring lands. "Go to Abyssinia, for the king will not tolerate injustice and it is a friendly country," the Prophet reportedly told these Muslim refugees. They were indeed welcomed by the king, or the "Negus," Najashi, who only asked what this new religion of theirs teaches about Jesus. Muslims told him that Jesus is "the servant of God, and His apostle, and His spirit, and His word, which He cast into Mary the blessed virgin."[11] Moved to tears, King Najashi told the Muslim refugees that there was little difference between them, and they could live in his kingdom safely and freely.

In case you missed it, this was the very Christian kingdom that destroyed the Jewish kingdom of Himyar about a century earlier. What is even more significant is that the Qur'an, in another early Meccan revelation, praised the Christian victims of this Jewish kingdom. In chapter *al-Buruj,* or "The Constellations," in a passage broadly thought to be a reference to the persecution of Najran Christians by Dhu Nuwas—"the one with sidelocks"—the Qur'an read:

Damned are the makers of the trench.
The makers of the fuel-stoked fire!
They sat down to watch what they were doing to the believers.
Their only grievance against them was their faith in God, the Mighty, the Praiseworthy.[12]

Just by hearing this, and by knowing the recent history of ancient Arabia, Jews of Medina could have well thought that this new religion of Muhammad was on the same side as Christians.

Yet, alas, the Qur'an itself would soon leave no doubt about that. In chapter *al-Rum,* or "Romans," which came toward the end of the Meccan period, the Qur'an declared:

The Romans have been defeated in a nearby land.
But after their defeat they will prevail within a few years.
God is in command, first and last.
On that day [of Roman victory] the believers will rejoice.[13]

This extraordinary passage is quite remarkable for a few reasons. First, throughout the whole Qur'an, it is the only reference to actual world events outside the Arabian Peninsula—indicating how important this particular event must have been. Second, there is little doubt it refers to the battles between the Byzantine and Sassanid Empires. Third, it clearly hints that Muslims were in favor of the Byzantines, to the level of "rejoicing" in their victory.

Why would the tiny Muslim community in Mecca be so sympathetic to the Christian superpower of the time? The well-known answer in the Islamic tradition is what the Muslim exegete al-Wahidi wrote:

> The Persians defeated the Byzantines. The Prophet and his Companions heard this while in Mecca and felt sad about it. . . . The disbelievers of Mecca, on the other hand, were exultant and spiteful. When they met the Companions of the Prophet, they said to them: "You are people of the Book and the Christians are people of the Book. We are without a revealed Scripture and our brothers, the Persians, have defeated your brothers, the Byzantines. If you ever fight us, we will defeat you too."[14]

This story makes sense, but it also has a blind spot: the "people of the Book" also included Jews, whose position did not fit into the neat picture of monotheists versus pagans. Instead, as we have seen, the vicious antisemitism of the Byzantines had been a great threat to them, making them understandably pro-Sassanid. Which also means that, despite their religious aversion to idolatry, Jews of Arabia must have found themselves politically close to Arab polytheists, who were allies of "our brothers, the Persians."

Now, this political nexus can give us a new way to understand the famous line in the Qur'an that lumped "Jews and polytheists" together as the fiercest enemies of Muslims, while singing the praises of Christians:

> You are sure to find that the most hostile to the believers are the Jews and polytheists. And you are sure to find that the clos-

est in affection towards the believers are those who say, "We are Christians."[15]

The verse went on to add that Christians had "priests and monks among them" who "are not arrogant." Yet this does not rule out that there could be other factors at play, such as the geopolitics of the early seventh century, which puts Muslims and Christians on the one side, and Jews and pagans on the other.

Muslims, historically, seeing the story of Islam in often purely theological terms, have not paid much attention to this political nexus, but it has been recently highlighted by some secular historians. Among them is the Israeli scholar Michael Lecker, a leading expert on early Islam whose work has also been referenced by the historians G. W. Bowersock and Juan Cole, as well as the Muslim author Haroon Moghul.[16] All think that the pro-Christian themes in the early years of Islam may be glimpses of a political connection between Muslims and Byzantium. Lecker even suggests it was no accident that the Prophet's arrival in Medina in 622 was preceded, just months earlier, by the beginning of the Byzantine emperor Heraclius' successful military campaign against the Sassanids. He also shows connections between the tribes who joined the Covenant of Medina and the Christian Arab tribe of the Ghassanids, allies of Byzantium. The implication is that, from a purely political point of view, the Medinan state led by the Prophet Muhammad could initially be "a political entity friendly to Byzantium." And for Jews, this could only have been alarming news.[17]

For our own story, the Judeo-Islamic tradition, this political background puts the Jewish distrust of early Islam in context: that it was not the result of some inherent and eternal tension between Islam and Judaism. It was rather the result of the politics of the time, when Medinan Jews understandably feared Byzantine encroachments, and may have perceived nascent Islam similarly.

A DISPUTE OVER JESUS?

In fact, Medinan Jews may have perceived nascent Islam as not just pro-Christian but also Christian-like.

Why? First, as noted earlier, beginning in its Meccan period, the Qur'an praised Jesus in terms reminiscent of Christianity: he was miraculously born of the virgin Mary, he himself performed miracles, and he was "an example for the Children of Israel."[18] In Medinan verses, the terminology got even more assertive: in eleven different instances, the Qur'an called Jesus *al-Masih,* or "the Messiah."[19] The term was used without any explanation, but Medinan Jews probably didn't need one. Here was a new religion telling them, once again, that the Messiah they awaited had already come, and they had erred terribly by rejecting him. In other Medinan verses, the Qur'an praised Jesus even as "Word" of God, which sounded all too similar to Christian theology.[20]

To be sure, the same Qur'an also denied the divinity of Jesus and condemned the doctrine of the Trinity. So, it distanced itself from both the Christian divinization of Jesus, as well as the Jewish rejection of him. By this middle position, Islam appeared as a rebirth of "Jewish Christianity"—a "heresy" in the early church, which followed Jesus not as the Christian Christ but the Jewish Messiah. How this theological rebirth, which astonished some modern scholars of religion, came to be is a curious question that I probed in an earlier book, *The Islamic Jesus: How the King of the Jews Became a Prophet of the Muslims.*[21]

Yet back in early seventh-century Arabia, in the eyes of Medinan Jews who were trying to make a sense of Islam, Jewish Christianity would appear Christian enough—and heretical enough, too. That is why they seem to have engaged in disputes about Jesus and Mary, whose praises the Muslims were singing. We see this in the Qur'anic chapter *al-Nisa,* reportedly revealed in the fourth year of the hijra, where a certain "People of the Book" are condemned for uttering "a terrible slander against Mary." They are even condemned for boasting, "We have killed the Messiah, Jesus, son of Mary."[22]

The Qur'anic answer to this latter statement—"They had not killed him, nor crucified him, but it appeared to them as such"—has been traditionally taken by Muslims as a denial of the Crucifixion, a tenet of Christianity. However, as Montgomery Watt once put it,

> A careful reading of the passage about the crucifixion of Jesus shows that it is not intended as a denial of Christian doctrine, but as a denial of a Jewish claim to have triumphed over the Christians, and it goes on to assert the superiority of the Christian hope.[23]

To be sure, "a Jewish claim to have triumphed over the Christians" may sound bizarre to many modern-day Jews. Even more bizarre may be the idea that Jesus and Mary were insulted by Jews. But premodern views among Jews and Christians about each other could be quite acrimonious, and there are indeed medieval Talmudic texts that do throw accusations of indecency against Mary, and even a narrative that "proudly proclaims Jewish responsibility for Jesus' execution."[24] That is why some scholars suggest that the Qur'an's take on the Crucifixion is actually a response to "a Talmudic counter-narrative to the New Testament."[25]

And all this means that the "Christian" tone in the Qur'an may have added to the tension between the Muslims and Jews of Medina, making Jews fear that Islam would follow the same course with the Christianity of the time—anti-Jewish, both politically and theologically. A contemporary Jewish source, *Jewish Unpacked*, makes the same point:

> It was also unacceptable to the Jews that Muhammad viewed Jesus as a prophet. . . . The Jews were concerned that, like Jesus,

Muhammad would be deified, and they would once again experience terrible persecution.[26]

The American rabbi Allen S. Maller, who has written extensively about early Islam, agrees:

> I think most Jews were afraid that after the death of Prophet Muhammad, his ex-pagan polytheist followers would turn him into a son of God and worship him, just as the followers of Jesus had turned him into a Son of God; and not only worshipped him, but persecuted Jews who would not worship Jesus.[27]

This Jewish anxiety can be seen in the question that we have already heard from a rabbi visiting in Medina in AD 631: "Do you want us, Muhammad, to worship you as the Christians worship Jesus, Son of Mary?"[28] It suggests that the tension between the first Muslims and their contemporaries in Medina may have been exacerbated, if not caused, by the bitter experience Jews had long had with Christianity, to which nascent Islam may have looked both politically close and theologically similar.

THE LESSON FROM MEDINA

As we have seen in this chapter, the story of Muslims and Jews in Medina began with a remarkably pluralist "constitution." It proclaimed a principle that is still admirable in the modern world: "The Jews have their religion, and the Muslims have theirs." Yet, as we have seen, this pluralism collapsed gradually, with distrust, hostility, war, expulsion, perhaps even mass execution.

What both Muslims and Jews should agree about today is that this conflict was not an archetype of a permanent conflict between Islam and Judaism. Instead, it was a historical episode, which could have played out differently if the historical conditions had been different. One key to realizing this is seeing the larger geostrategic conflict of the time: the great war between the Byzantine and Sassanid Empires. If Muslims and Jews had found themselves on the same side in this drama instead of falling into opposite sides, the story in Medina could have been less confrontational.

A great late scholar who studied this story, Montgomery Watt, had pondered on this road not taken. In his seminal book, *Muhammad at Medina,* published in 1956, he wrote:

> It is interesting to speculate on what would have happened had the Jews come to terms with Muhammad instead of opposing him. At certain periods they could have secured very favourable terms from him, including religious autonomy, and on that basis the Jews might have become partners in the Arab empire and Islam a sect of Jewry. How different the face of the world would be now, had that happened![29]

To be sure, the suggestion that Islam could have been "a sect of Jewry" would be theologically unacceptable for Muslims. Islam, we the latter believe, was destined to be the distinct universal religion that it is. Yet still, we should consider that Islam's relationship with Jews could have begun quite differently from the way it did. If the Covenant of Medina didn't collapse, for example, the legal status of Jews under Islam could have been more elevated than the *dhimmi* status, which we will see in the next chapter.

Meanwhile, seeing the conflict in Medina as a historical accident is crucial today for understanding the Qur'an's approach to Jews because the conflict has found echoes in many Qur'anic verses, especially in the long chapters of *al-Baqara, al-Nisa,* and *al-Maida.* Due to the unchronological ordering of the Qur'an, these chapters even appear at its very beginning—as the second, fourth, and fifth suras—puzzling some new readers about why the Muslim scripture opens with such heated polemics against Jews.

In fact, as we have seen, the Qur'an rather began with its own proclamation of monotheism, with great admiration for Moses and unmistakable sympathy for the Israelites. This Meccan spirit changed only in Medina, and only due to the new theological and political clash Muslims unexpectedly faced. The Turkish theologian Saime Leyla Gürkan describes this textual evolution as follows:

> When looking at the Qur'anic verses on the Jews/people of Israel and the people of the book overall, there are two points that need to be emphasized: (1) Firstly, the content and style of these verses change, somewhat gradually, from the ideal and neutral, even positive, to the actual and negative; this is due to the experience Muslims had with Arab idolaters as well as Jews in the Meccan and Medinan periods, respectively. . . . The Jews who are mentioned negatively in the Qur'an are not a peaceful group who, though they do not recognize the prophethood of Muhammad, nevertheless accept the call of conciliation with Muslims and remain faithful to it; rather, they are a group who wage a theological and political campaign against Muslims and ally with Arab idolaters with whom the former has been at war. Thus, the emphasis of the Medinan verses on the betrayal of the people of Israel of their covenant with God in the past should be understood in this vein.[30]

In this contextuality of the Qur'an, there is also an important lesson for Muslims today: when Qur'anic verses speak of *al-Yahud,* or "the Jews," they often do not speak about the totality of the Jewish people from the distant past to the active present. They rather speak about the specific Jews the Qur'an faced in its own historical context.

QUR'ANIC "JEWS" IN CONTEXT

Unfortunately, despite the contextuality of the Qur'an, which was realized and noted by its earliest exegetes, a later trend that became all too popular in the modern era began to read the Qur'an's isolated verdicts on "Jews"—and "Christians," as well—as universally applicable definitions. For example, today some Muslims quote the Qur'anic verse "Never will the Jews or the Christians approve of you until you follow their religion" as an affirmation of a permanent enmity to Islam by Jews and Christians—or "the West."[31] However, according to one of the earliest Qur'anic commentators, Muqatil ibn Sulayman, "the Jews" in this verse referred to those in Medina, and "the Christians" referred to those in Najran.[32]

Quite similarly, when the Qur'an says, "They kindle the fire of war" and "spread corruption in the land," one needs to realize that it speaks about the role of the Banu Qaynuqa, Banu Nadir, or Banu Qurayza in the battles of Uhud or the Trench—and not some universal Jewish conspiracy behind global conflicts, as asserted in the 1998 charter of Hamas.[33]

This contextuality of the Qur'an also explains why some of the views it ascribes to "the Jews" cannot be found anywhere in the Jewish world outside the Qur'an's own time and milieu. One of these reads, "The Jews say, 'God's Hand is shackled.'"[34] As the great medieval Qur'anic exegete Fakhr al-Din al-Razi (d. 1210) had also acknowledged, there is really no such common belief among Jews and it is against their own understanding of God.[35] So, it must have been an isolated and rhetorical polemic in Medina.

Similarly, the Qur'an condemns "the Jews" for calling "Uzair," who is probably the Biblical Ezra, as "the Son of God"—just like Christians calling Jesus the Son of God.[36] Yet there is no such known belief among Jews, either in history or today. So, the only explanation is that this, too, was an isolated case. In fact, according to the prominent Sunni exegete al-Tabari (d. 923) it was only one single Jew, Finhas of Medina, who claimed, "Uzair is the Son of God."[37] Meanwhile, some current scholars think it is possible that the Qur'anic Uzair could be the Biblical Enoch, who was elevated to a quasi-divine figure in some apocryphal Jewish texts, which may have been influential among Medinan Jews.[38]

In any case, the divinization of Uzair seems to be a very exceptional case among Jews. However, for centuries, some Muslims missed this point, resulting in unnecessary doubts about the monotheist nature of Judaism. This has understandably annoyed some Jewish scholars who conversed with the Islamic tradition, one of whom was the great medieval rabbi and philosopher Moses Maimonides. In a passage where he affirms that Muslims are certainly monotheists, he adds, irritably but also fairly: "Because they lie about us, and falsely attribute to us the statement that God has a son, is no reason for us to lie about them and say that they are idolaters."[39]

We will see the appreciation of Islamic monotheism by Moses Maimonides—and his son, Abraham—in the chapters ahead. Back to the Qur'an's view of Jews, the importance of contextuality can't be stressed enough, but there is something more: in the midst of all its polemics against Medinan Jews, the Qur'an also warned Muslims against seeing them all in the same light. After a passage condemning those from "the People of the Book" who "transgressed," the Qur'an adds:

> But they are not all alike. There are some among the People
> of the Book who are upright, who recite God's revelations
> during the night, who bow down in worship, who believe in
> God and the Last Day, who order what is right and forbid
> what is wrong, who are quick to do good deeds. These people
> are among the righteous.[40]

So, taking the Qur'anic criticisms of Jews as sweeping characterizations would be misleading, *even in the Qur'an's own con-*

text. It would be much more misleading to take them out of that context and turn them into universal stereotypes.

No wonder that, soon after Medina, the change of context would soon dramatically alter the nature of the relationship between Muslims and Jews. Muslims coming out of Arabia would create a huge empire stretching from Spain to India, in which many Jews would find the chance to live safely, worship freely, and even flourish exceptionally.

Whatever happened in Medina, in other words, would stay in Medina. In the broader world, the Judeo-Islamic tradition would begin to thrive.

UNDER THE KINGDOMS OF ISHMAEL

Islam saved Jewry. This is an unpopular, discomforting claim in the modern world. But it is a historical truth.

—David J. Wasserstein, professor of Jewish studies[1]

ON JUNE 8, AD 632, PROPHET MUHAMMAD PASSED AWAY IN Medina. His successors, or caliphs, assumed the political leadership of the Muslim community and kept spreading the faith by way of *futuh,* or conquests. The campaign began with the Rashidun Caliphate (632–661)—the "rightly guided" first four caliphs—and continued under the Umayyad dynasty (661–750). With astonishing successes and speed, in just a century Muslims had conquered a large part of the known world. Their "promised land" seemed limitless, until they were constrained by geostrategic facts.[2]

One of the observers of this burgeoning Islamic empire was a Jewish scribe from the middle of the seventh century who wrote the text known as *The Secrets of Rabbi Shimon bar Yohai.*[3] That famous rabbi himself, Shimon bar Yohai, lived back in the second century, and he had witnessed the terrible persecution of Jews by the Roman Empire. Yet, as the legend goes, the rabbi had also seen a vision about a brighter future, which our seventh-century Jewish scribe reported to us:

These are the secrets that were revealed to Rabbi Shimon b. Yohai while he was hiding in a cave on account of Caesar king of Edom [Rome]. And he stood in prayer for forty days and forty nights and he began thus: "Lord God, how long will you spurn the prayer of your servant?" Immediately the secrets and hidden things of the eschaton were revealed to him. . . .

When he understood that the kingdom of Ishmael would come upon [Israel], he began to say, "Is it not enough, what the wicked kingdom of Edom has done to us that [we must also endure] the kingdom of Ishmael?"

And immediately [Angel] Metatron the prince of the Presence answered him and said:

"Do not be afraid, mortal, for the Holy One, blessed be He, is bringing about the kingdom of Ishmael only for the purpose of delivering you from that wicked one [i.e., Edom/Rome]. He shall raise up over them a prophet in accordance with His will, and he will subdue the land for them; and they shall come and restore it with grandeur."[4]

So, Jews had suffered a lot from "the kingdom of Edom," that is, the Roman Empire. Yet God would save Jews from this wickedness, by raising "the kingdom of Ishmael," that is, the Arab Empire. The latter would be led by "a prophet," whose victories would be a blessing for Jews.

But how? According to our document, Rabbi Shimon bar Yohai asked the same question of the angel who had brought him the good news: "How will they [Arabs] be our salvation?" The angel responded:

Did not the prophet Isaiah say: "When he sees riders, horsemen in pairs" [Isa. 21.7]? [So] when the one who rides on the camel comes, through him the kingdom of the one who rides on a donkey [Zech. 9.9] has emerged."[5]

This means that "the one riding a camel," which seems to refer to the Prophet Muhammad, would herald the "one who rides on a donkey," which is how Jews typically imagine their much-awaited Messiah.

In other words, *The Secrets of Rabbi Shimon bar Yohai* shows that some Jews who witnessed the rise of Islam saw it as "a messianic deliverer divinely chosen to liberate the Jews and their Promised Land from Rome's oppressive yoke." Stephen J. Shoemaker, an expert scholar on early Islam who makes this comment, also adds:

> Such direct identification of Muhammad as the fulfillment of Jewish messianic hopes as expressed in these biblical traditions is extraordinary. . . . Whether or not Muhammad was actually proclaiming the Messiah's advent, this apocalypse certainly affords evidence that there were in fact Jews who understood the appearance of Muhammad and the rise of his new religious movement as realizing this eschatological promise.[6]

But why would some seventh-century Jews see Islam in such a positive light? The story of the Jews of Medina, which we saw in the previous chapter, was rather bleak. So, how could things have changed so remarkably?

THE TURN WITH BYZANTIUM

As we saw in the previous chapter, the first Muslims were sympathetic to the Christian powers of their time, including Byzantium. In contrast, they saw the latter's archenemy, the Sassanid Empire, as the allies of their own enemies.

This honeymoon with Byzantium seems to have continued until the summer of 629—about three years before the Prophet Muhammad's passing. We get a sense of this in the story about the letters the Prophet sent in that year to three *muluk,* or kings: the Byzantine emperor Heraclius, the Sassanid emperor Chosroes, and the Abyssinian king Najashi. In all these letters, carried by envoys, "Muhammad, the servant of God and His messenger" extended an audacious call: "I invite you to Islam, so that you will be saved." In return, Chosroes got infuriated, tore the letter apart, and told one of his governors to march on Medina, take Muhammad prisoner, and bring him to the Persian capital. In contrast, as Muslim historians tell us, Heraclius read the letter respectfully and placed it on his chest. Later legends among Muslims would even suggest that the Byzantine emperor actually believed in the Prophet, but could not make his people, the Romans, accept him. For centuries, Heraclius would enjoy "overwhelming approval of Muslim chroniclers and historians," who attributed to him sincere piety and good morals.[7]

Yet something unexpected took place in July 629, when a Muslim envoy who was carrying yet another letter from the Prophet to a governor in Syria was arrested, tortured, and killed by the very chief of the Ghassanids, the Christian Arab tribe that controlled today's Jordan. Muslims took this provocation as a cause for war and sent a large army of three thousand troops to fight the Ghassanids. But in the meantime, the Ghassanids had secured help from their allies, including, most crucially, Byzantium. The result was the Battle at Mut'a in September 629, at a place east of the Jordan River, at which heavily outnumbered Muslims sustained significant losses, only to gradually retreat to Medina.

This first bloodshed at the hands of Byzantine forces was followed by the Expedition of Tabuk the next year, in October 630, which was the Prophet's last and largest military campaign. It began when he received news of a Byzantine attack on Medina, which led him to prepare a huge army to face the enemy in Tabuk, a location about 350 miles north of the Muslim capital. The nice surprise was that the Byzantine army never showed up and the anticipated battle never happened. Yet still, the expedition had an everlasting impact: it presented the tense context for chapter *al-Tawba*, or "Repentance," the last major chapter of the Qur'an and also the only one that does not begin with the iconic phrase "In the name of God, the Compassionate, the Merciful." The reason, as noted by many Muslim scholars, was that the chapter gave an ultimatum to the Arab polytheists who had broken their recent peace treaty with Muslims: they would either convert to Islam or face the sword. It also gave a second ultimatum, to "the People of the Book," who were treated with more lenience, but still domination. Muslims were commanded to fight them "until they pay the *jizya* [poll tax] and agree to submit."[8]

These two verses in chapter *al-Tawba*—much later dubbed "the Verse of the Sword" and "the Verse of the Jizya"—could have been taken as contextual, only applicable to specific non-Muslim groups who were aggressive against Muslims in the first place.[9] But mainstream Islamic tradition took them rather as permanently valid, and even as "abrogating" the earlier Qur'anic verses that called for restraint and nonaggression. The consequence was somewhat limited with the Verse of the Sword, as it was often narrowed to Arab polytheists who ceased to exist soon after the genesis of Islam. But the Verse of the Jizya proved universally consequential, as it became the basis for the conquests of territories that were formerly ruled by Christians and Zoroastrians, and later by other groups such as Hindus.

That is how Byzantium, to which Muslims initially looked with sympathy, became their prime target once they left the Arabian Peninsula. Under the definitive rule of Caliph Umar (634–644), the second successor to the Prophet, Muslim armies conquered much of Syria, Palestine, and Egypt—which all used to be Byzantine territories. A key event was the Battle of the Yarmuk in 636, where the Muslims devastated the Byzantine forces, opening the way for them to take Jerusalem only months later. The Byzantine Empire still survived in Anatolia and the Eastern Balkans, but it lost much of its grandeur.

The Sassanids, meanwhile, were not even that lucky. The armies of the Rashidun Caliphate conquered them as well, in subsequent waves, putting an end to the ruling dynasty, and the empire itself, by 651.

In other words, with the rise of the Islamic Empire, the world that Jews had known had dramatically changed. The Sassanid Empire, which the Jews had supported against the Byzantines, completely disappeared. But Jews also realized that the safety they had found under the Sassanids—communal autonomy, in exchange for political loyalty—was also offered by Islam, and on even better terms.[10]

That is why the political matrix that the Qur'an defined between the three Abrahamic faiths—that Christians are "nearest" to Muslims, while Jews are "strongest in enmity"—disappeared once Muslims left Arabia. The new geostrategic facts of western Asia, North Africa, and southern Europe would make Christendom the main adversary of Islam for many centuries to come. They would also make Jews "nearest" to Muslims.

The Secrets of Rabbi Shimon bar Yohai is the earliest document that hints about this Judeo-Islamic axis. It shows that some seventh-century Jews, who had suffered greatly under the "kingdom of Edom," or Rome, put their hopes in the "kingdom of Ishmael." They even saw the advent of Islam as the beginning of a Messianic age.

And we can see that they had reason to think so when we look at what happened then at the epicenter of any Messianic hope, which is, of course, Jerusalem.

THE JEWISH RETURN TO JERUSALEM

The conquest of Jerusalem by Muslims in 638 is a famous story one can often find in discussions on religious tolerance. It shows how Muslims conquered a holy city dominated by Christians, yet, to the latter's surprise, didn't destroy their lives or harm their churches. Instead, they granted Christians a level of religious freedom that was remarkable for the age.

The heroes of the story are two men: Caliph Umar, whose commanders put the city under siege for six months, and Saint Sophronius, the Patriarch of Jerusalem, who finally negotiated a peaceful surrender. Accordingly, the Patriarch insisted on giving his city not to any Muslim commander but to the very "Commander of the Faithful." Hence Caliph Umar came all the way from Medina to Jerusalem, surprising the inhabitants with his shabby appearance in modest clothes. Then, as reported by the Christian chronicler Eutychius (d. 940), the caliph visited the holiest of all Christian shrines: the Church of the Holy Sepulchre. When the prayer time came, Umar said to Sophronius: "I want to pray." The latter responded, "Commander of the Faithful, pray in the place where you are now."[11] Umar politely declined, and instead prayed outside, on the steps east of the church. Then he explained why: "If I had prayed inside the Church, you would be losing it and it would have gone from your hands because after my death the Muslims would seize it saying: 'Umar has prayed here.'"[12] Later, right on the spot where he prayed, Muslims would build the Mosque of Umar, which still rises next to the Church of the Holy Sepulchre in the Old City of Jerusalem. (This small mosque should not be confused with the much larger Al-Aqsa Mosque, which can also be called Mosque of Umar.)

This interfaith encounter also left behind a covenant between the caliph of Islam and the Christians of Jerusalem, which we know thanks to the medieval Muslim scholar al-Tabari. It is a pleasantly tolerant text, which only comes with an unpleasant exception at the very end:

> In the name of God, the Merciful, the Compassionate. This is the assurance of safety (aman) which the servant of God, Umar, the Commander of the Faithful, has granted to the people of Jerusalem. He has given them an assurance of safety for themselves, for their property, their churches, their crosses, the sick and the healthy of the city, and for all the rituals that

belong to their religion. Their churches will not be inhabited
[by Muslims] and will not be destroyed. Neither they, nor the
land on which they stand, nor their cross, nor their property
will be damaged. They will not be forcibly converted. No Jew
will live with them in Jerusalem.[13]

So, Christians would keep living and worshipping in Islamic
Jerusalem, but Jews were not welcome.

But who was it exactly that unwelcomed them? The Christians or the Muslims?

The Christians, apparently. First, the text above lists the exclusion of Jews in line with concessions given to Christians, such
as assurances of their churches and properties. The Israeli historian Moshe Gil also makes this point, adding that the exclusion of
Jews seems to reflect "the Christians' demands and their hatred of
the Jews."[14] This hatred had religious roots, but it was also exacerbated by the Jewish support for the Sassanid invasion of Jerusalem
some twenty-three years earlier. The latter was an incomparably
bloodier affair compared with Caliph Umar's conquest, whose
memories must have been still vivid among the city's Christians.
Conversely, when they retook Jerusalem from the Sassanids in
628, just a decade before the Muslim conquest, their emperor,
Heraclius, had ordered an "indiscriminate slaughter of Jews and
ultimately their expulsion from the city."[15] The feelings between
Christians and Jews, there, must have been quite inimical.

Yet, in fact, we don't even need to guess who was really uneasy
about Jewish presence in Jerusalem, thanks to a finding from the
Cairo Genizah, a huge collection of medieval Jewish documents, of
about a quarter-million leaves, discovered by two British scholars
in 1896 in the *genizah,* or storeroom, of an ancient synagogue in
Cairo. A document in this precious collection, written in Judeo-
Arabic, tells about a bargain between Caliph Umar and Patriarch
Sophronius about the status of Jews in Jerusalem. Umar, accordingly, asks for some two hundred Jewish families to be allowed to

settle in the city. The Patriarch opposes "strongly," so the caliph reduces the number to seventy families.[16] Then he returns to the Jews and asks them where they want to be settled:

> Then [Umar] said: "Where in the city do you want to live?" And they said: "In the south of the city," that is, the market of the Jews, for their aim was to be near the holy place and its gates. . . . The commander of the faithful granted them that, then from Tiberias and its environs seventy households transferred with their women and children, and they rebuilt their area with buildings that had lain destroyed for generations until grown old.[17]

The area given to these Jews was southwest of the Temple Mount, just next to their sacred Western Wall. This was the origin of the "Jewish Quarter," which is still one of the four sections in Jerusalem's Old City—besides the Muslim, Christian, and Armenian quarters. Other documents show that these Jewish settlers were allowed to pray in the Temple area, build a synagogue, and establish a *beit midrash,* or religious school.[18]

So, it appears that Caliph Umar carved a space for Jews in Jerusalem, despite the Christians who did not want to see them there. The assurance given to Christians—that "no Jew will live with them in Jerusalem"—seems somehow attenuated, through negotiations, by giving Jews a quarter of their own.

Now, the historic significance of this settlement cannot be overstated: ever since the Roman emperor Hadrian crushed the Bar Kokhba revolt in AD 135, Jews had been banned from settling in Jerusalem, even from approaching it. This banishment continued, first under the pagan and then the Christian phase of the Roman Empire, "more or less consistently for slightly more than five hundred years."[19] It ended only thanks to the triumph of Islam. Salmon ben Yeruham, a tenth-century scholar from the Karaite sect of Judaism, had earnestly appreciated this fact, writing:

As we know, the Temple remained in the hands of the Romans for more than 500 years and they [Jews] did not succeed in entering Jerusalem; and anyone who did and was recognised [as a Jew] was put to death. But when the Romans left it, by the mercy of the God of Israel, and the kingdom of Ishmael was victorious, Israel was permitted to come and to live.[20]

For the centuries to come, Jewish life in Islamic Jerusalem, just like Christian life, would continue in peace. These two religions even dominated the populace. Hence, at the end of the tenth century, the Muslim geographer al-Maqdisi, who was a Jerusalemite himself, was complaining that there were no Muslim theologians in the city and nobody was interested in Islamic sciences, whereas "the Christians and the Jews were numerous."[21] He would also add that there were always "strangers" in the city, most of whom must have been pilgrims—Muslims, Christians, and Jews.[22]

JEWS ON THE TEMPLE MOUNT

After their conquest of Jerusalem, Muslims also showed proper respect to its holiest ground for Jews, the Temple Mount, which the Christians were using for centuries only as a dumpster. Right after taking the city, Caliph Umar cleaned up the rubbish and strengthened the structure. His advisor was Ka'b al-Ahbar, a Yemenite Jewish rabbi who had converted to Islam several years before and gained prominence in the Muslim community as *dhul kitabayn,* or "owner of two books," meaning the Qur'an and the Torah.

It is remarkable that Jews appreciated these changes on the Temple Mount, as we see in *The Secrets of Rabbi Shimon bar Yohai.* Its author, besides praising the Prophet Muhammad as a Messianic deliverer, also praises "the second king" of the Ishmaelites, who seems to be none other than Caliph Umar:

The second king who will arise from Ishmael will be a friend to Israel. And he will repair their breaches and the breaches of the Temple. And he will shape Mount Moriah and make it completely level. And he will build for himself there a place for worship over the Foundation Stone [Even Shtiyya], as it is said, "and your nest is set in the rock" [Num. 24.21]. . . . And he will die in peace and with great honor.[23]

The Jewish author was mistaken about just one detail: the "place for worship over the Foundation Stone," which is the splendid Dome of the Rock that still crowns Jerusalem, was built not by Caliph Umar but some fifty years after him by the Umayyad caliph Abd al-Malik ibn Marwan. The latter also appointed some Jewish families as guardians and servants of the Temple Mount, and charitably exempted them from the poll tax.[24]

There is even a report from Salmon ben Yeruham that in the early phase of Muslim rule in Jerusalem, Jews could pray on the Temple Mount—a very controversial issue today. Yeruham wrote:

When by the mercy of the God of Israel the Rum [the Romans] departed from us and the kingdom of Ishmael [the Arabs] appeared, the Jews were granted permission to enter and reside there. The courts of the (House of the) Lord were handed over to them, where they prayed for a number of years.[25]

But later, Yeruham adds, news that some Jews were drinking wine at the site angered the Muslim caliph, who expelled them "from all but one of the Temple compound gates." Sharing "this extraordinary report," the historian F. E. Peters suggests:

Then, the Jews of Jerusalem were at one time permitted, and availed themselves of the opportunity, to pray on the Temple

mount itself. This was in the earliest days of the Muslim occupation of the city, perhaps before Abd al-Malik's construction
of the Dome of the Rock and the subsequent consecration of
the entire Temple mount as the "Noble Sanctuary." Once the
Dome was constructed, the character of the area must have
changed substantially.[26]

Nevertheless, the construction of the Dome of the Rock may
not have been seen as bad news by the Jews of the time, as we saw
in *The Secrets of Rabbi Shimon bar Yohai*. There is also a remarkable Midrash passage that says that an Arab ruler "shall build the
house of the God of Israel."[27] Commenting on this report, which
"appears somewhat strange to us today," Moshe Gil reasoned that
it probably meant that an Arab ruler "shall build on the site where
the house of the God of Israel stood."[28] But even if that is the case,
it shows that Jews did not see the Dome of the Rock as an abom-
ination, as they would see a pagan temple or any other profanity.

THE PACT OF UMAR—REAL OR PROJECTED

Caliph Umar, the second successor to Muhammad, is a crucial
figure in Islamic history not only for his conquests, which included Jerusalem, but also for establishing some fundamental
laws and institutions. Among them was the so-called Pact of
Umar, a document that defined the terms between the new Islamic empire and "People of the Book," in particular Jews and
Christians. In fact, today many historians, both Muslim and
non-Muslim, think the text—or at least parts of it—actually
appeared much later, at the time of the Umayyad caliph Umar
ibn 'Abd al-Aziz (r. 717–720), only to be projected back to the
more prestigious second caliph.[29] It may have taken its fullest
form even during the time of the Abbasid caliph al-Mutawakkil,
who is known for having taken a decisive turn against rationalist

theologians (Mu'tazilites) in favor of dogmatists (Hanbalis), as well as imposing harsh measures on Jews and Christians.[30]

Nevertheless, for more than a millennium, the Pact of Umar has defined the nature of the relationship between Muslims and *dhimmi*—the "protected," yet inferior, non-Muslims under Islamic rule. So, it deserves some attention.

As reported by the Muslim historian Ibn Asakir (d. 1176), it is an interesting document, as it appears as a letter by the conquered Christians themselves to Caliph Umar, listing the conditions they accept for themselves, in order for "safe-conduct for ourselves, our descendants, our property, and the people of our community." Some conditions are quite reasonable, such as "We shall not give shelter in our churches or in our dwellings to any spy nor hide him from the Muslims." But others are certainly designed to reflect the supremacy of Muslims:

> We shall not manifest our religion publicly nor convert anyone to it. . . . We shall show respect towards the Muslims, and we shall rise from our Seats when they wish to sit. . . . We shall not display our crosses or our books in the roads or markets of the Muslims.[31]

Most of these conditions were symbolic, while another condition imposed on non-Muslims under Islamic rule was tangible: the *jizya*, or poll tax, that all adult, able, and free non-Muslim males had to pay to the Islamic state, unlike Muslims who enjoyed the status of first-class citizens. It was a financial burden whose weight varied over time—but it also exempted non-Muslims from military service.

Were such discriminatory conditions really Islamic—in the sense of being defined by the two scriptural sources of Islam, the Qur'an and Sunna? It depends on interpretation. As mentioned before, the Qur'an did command Muslims to fight the People of the Book "until they pay the *jizya* with their hands, and they are subdued."[32] But it wasn't clear whether this was universally applicable. It was also not clear what "subdued" meant.

No wonder Muslims, as seen in the Pact of Umar, defined "subdued" by looking at mundane sources: the preexisting laws of the Byzantine and Sassanid Empires, which also imposed strict legal hierarchies. Among them were "Byzantine curbs on Jews," such as not building new synagogues, not giving testimony against Christians, and not defaming Christianity—which show up in the Pact of Umar, but with "Christian" being replaced with "Muslim." Similarly, "Sasanian regulations for distinguishing between nobles and commoners," such as not wearing the same headgear, overcoats, belts, shoes, and hairstyles of the superior group are also copied in the Pact of Umar, with "nobles" being redefined as "Muslims."[33]

In fact, even the Qur'anic notion of *jizya* was a preexisting custom: it seems to be the Arabicized version of *kizyat,* a levy the Sassanid rulers used to collect to finance the affairs of war.[34] Moreover, the original targets of the Verse of the *Jizya* were already "accustomed to payment of tribute to Byzantine and Sassanian overlords."[35]

What all this means is that like much of the rest of Islamic law, the Islamic laws on non-Muslims were "historical"—shaped by existing historical practices rather than being new inventions. Nevertheless, Islamic law's adaptation of these practices—as also seen in the status of women or slaves—came with remarkable improvements. Because while inheriting the supremacist elements of Sassanid and Byzantine laws, Islamic laws also gave the *dhimmi* guarantees that they never explicitly and reliably enjoyed: "physical security, religious and economic liberty, and autonomy for their community," as the Israeli historian Eli Barnavi once summarized. Therefore, Barnavi added:

> The legal status accorded to non-Muslims made the Arab conquest seem far more benevolent towards vanquished peoples

than the previous rule of Persians, Byzantines. . . . The Jews, formerly "tolerated," now become "protected."[36]

To be sure, this hegemonic "protection" was quite short of equal citizenship that we have in the liberal democracies. Hence it should not be idealized. But for its time, it was quite ideal, and Jews seem to have had little doubt about that.

THE JEWISH-ARABIC CABAL

Since Islam appeared as a great improvement on the Jewish condition, Jews kept welcoming Islamic conquests in what used to be Christian lands. A Christian manuscript from the fifteenth century tells how this worked in Hebron, which held out longer than other Byzantine cities in the region. Moshe Gil quotes it with helpful explanations:

> When they [the Muslims] came to Hebron they were amazed to see the strong and handsome structures of the walls and they could not find any opening through which to enter; then Jews happened to come, who lived in the area under the former rule of the Greeks [that is, the Byzantines], and they said to the Muslims: give us [a letter of security] that we may continue to live [in our places] under your rule [literally, amongst you] and permit us to build a synagogue in front of the entrance [to the city]. If you will do this, we shall show you where you can break in. And so they did.[37]

Similar support for Muslim conquerors seems to have happened in Caesarea, a coastal town some twenty miles south of modern-day Haifa. The Muslim historian al-Baladhuri writes that it was a Jew in town who "revealed to the Arabs a secret entry into the town," thus enabling the conquerors to take over the city.[38]

Could these reports be reflections of ancient anti-Jewish tropes—myths about "Jewish conspiracy"? The modern historian Stefan Leder grants that this is possible, but, comparing both Muslim and Christian reports, he concludes that "a Jewish community with markedly pro-Arab sentiments" clearly existed.[39]

Jews seem to have aided Muslim conquests not only by helping them begin but also helping them endure. This was the case in Tripoli, a northern coastal city in Lebanon, which was seized by armies of the first Umayyad caliph, Muawiya (d. 680). The interesting point, noted by Muslim chroniclers, is that to secure the city, the caliph stationed in its citadel Jewish troops, who would also be the only inhabitants of the town in the next few decades.[40] "The Muslims trusted the Jews," since the latter were "unlikely to betray them."[41]

Besides Muslim sources themselves, some Christian writings of the era also speak about the cooperation between Jews and Muslims, only to see it as a conspiracy against the true faith. The first among them is *Doctrina Jacobi*, or *Teaching of Jacob*, a Greek text composed sometime between 634 and 640. It has long intrigued Western scholars as it is the earliest known account of Islam by outsiders—and not a very friendly one, as it calls Muhammad "a false prophet." What is most significant is that the document also speaks about the danger of "Jews who are mixed up with the Saracens," the latter being an ancient Christian term for Arabs and Muslims.[42] It also tells how Jews "rejoiced" with the victories of Saracens. When the *candidatus*, or the commander of the Byzantine army in Palestine, was felled by Muslims, our Christian author says:

People were saying "the candidatus has been killed," and the Jews were overjoyed. And they were saying that the prophet had appeared, coming with the Saracens, and that he was proclaiming the advent of the anointed one.[43]

The second Christian text from the same era is an Armenian chronicle attributed to a Bishop Sebeos, and seems to have been written at the beginning of the 660s. While telling the story of the Byzantine emperor Heraclius, the author pauses to give a brief account of the rise of Islam. Remarkably, he describes it as a new Abrahamic movement among the "sons of Ishmael," inspired by the story of Moses:

> At that time a man appeared from among these same sons of Ishmael, whose name was Muhammad, a merchant, who appeared to them as if by God's command as a preacher, as the way of truth. He taught them to recognize the God of Abraham, because he was especially learned and well informed in the history of Moses. Now because the command was from on high, through a single command they all came together in unity of religion, and abandoning vain cults, they returned to the living God who had appeared to their father Abraham.[44]

Furthermore, Sebeos tells us about Jews who actively participated in this new Abrahamic movement. First, he tells about a Jewish group from Edessa, who traveled across deserts to reach "the sons of Ishmael" to ask for their help against the Byzantine Empire—even before the rise of Islam.[45] Then, when Arab armies indeed moved against Byzantium, Sebeos mentions "the plots of the seditious Jews, who . . . secured an alliance with the Hagarenes."[46] (The term, coming from Hagar, the mother of Ishmael, was then used by Eastern Christians to refer to Arabs.) Sebeos even writes that Muhammad "loved Israel," and that he proclaimed: "God promised this land to Abraham and his descendants after him forever."[47]

Stephen Shoemaker summarizes Sebeos's view of Islam as follows:

> At the heart of Muhammad's message . . . was a call for his followers, sons of Isaac and Ishmael together, to rise up and

reclaim the promised land of their Abrahamic patrimony in the biblical Holy Land. Muhammad enjoins here the "sons of Abraham" collectively, and not only the sons of Ishmael, to take back their land from the occupying Romans.[48]

Moshe Gil, too, thinks that the chronicle of Sebeos reveals a very peculiar perception of Islam: "a sort of cabal between the Jews and the Arabs against the Christians."[49]

This "cabal" seem to have become mainstream in many parts of what we today call the Middle East. As the historian Maurice Harris wrote a century ago in *History of the Medieval Jews,* while the "Mohammedan faith had spread with great strides," in not just Syria but also Iraq, "Jews gladly settled under their sway."[50] No wonder Baghdad, the capital of the Abbasid dynasty, soon "became a center of commerce and learning and housed a thousand Jewish families, with a college." Harris added:

> Though the first Caliphs were somewhat masterful in forcing forward the new Faith they were, on the whole, both tolerant and broad. More than that, they were lovers of culture. . . . They became patrons of literature and helped to usher in a new era of scholarship and letters that may be compared with the Alexandrian era of Greek culture, some eight centuries earlier. As the Jew had contributed toward the former, so likewise he shared in the latter. . . . These solemn days offered opportunities for a grand survey of Israel's past and for hopeful visions of God's enduring providence.[51]

At this point, let me note that the purpose of reviewing this history is not to glorify Islamic conquests, which caused bloodshed, enslavement, and misery, as have all wars in human history. But these conquests took place in an age of empires, and empires can be compared to each other based on the values that have further flourished in the modern world—such as freedom, justice, and tolerance. I should also note that not all Jews welcomed the conquests or benefited from them. There are accounts from Egypt showing that Jews, as well as Christians, suffered at the hands of the Muslim conquerors.[52] Yet if a general pattern can be defined, it is what the historian Robert G. Hoyland outlined in his study of early Islam through the eyes of non-Muslim accounts: "Whereas Christians regarded the invading Arabs as God's rod for their chastisement, many Jews saw them rather as God's instrument for their deliverance."[53]

And nowhere was this deliverance more obvious than in the southwestern end of Europe, where lies the Iberian Peninsula.

THE LIBERATION OF IBERIA

Throughout the seventh century, when Islam was gradually dominating today's Middle East and North Africa, the Iberian Peninsula was a nightmare for Jews. Called Hispania, it was ruled by Visigoths, a Germanic people who embraced Catholicism in the late sixth century, only to soon dictate it to all their subjects. In 612, King Sisebut forced all Jews to convert to Christianity. Many Jews fled, but most others, more than ninety thousand of them, chose to stay, some of them just pretending to be Christian. Yet this apparent conversion only brought more persecution. Children of baptized Jews were taken from their parents, while those found to be "secret Jews" were sold as slaves. A later king, Receswind, even ordered that Jews who secretly practiced their faith "should be beheaded, burned, or stoned to death."[54] As the historian R. Dykes Shaw put it more than a century ago, the whole "Catholic period of the Visigothic dominion" was a tale of "relentless persecution." Jews were "despoiled of their goods, robbed of their children, compelled to apostasize." They were forced not to "act, or speak, or think, in any way that would offend the true faith."[55]

Yet this nightmare would begin to end in the fateful year of

711, when Tariq ibn Ziyad, a commander of the Umayyad Caliphate, crossed the strait between the Atlantic Ocean and the Mediterranean Sea from the North African coast. His troops first camped at a majestic coastal peak, which became known as the Mountain of Tariq, or Jabal al-Tariq. The Spanish derivation of the term, Gibraltar, is still the name of both the rock and the strait that separates Spain from Morocco.

These Muslim conquerors soon crushed the Visigothic army at the Battle of Guadalete, only to invade much of Iberia over the next few years. The invasion would continue for the next two decades, well into France, until it was stopped at the Battle of Tours (732), where the Frankish ruler Charles Martel defeated the Muslim army. This decisive Christian victory has remained a memorable event in European history, hailed by some Western historians as the turning point that saved all of Europe from being Islamized forever. Among them was Edward Gibbon (1737–1794), who famously wrote that if the Muslim advance were not halted at Tours, "perhaps the interpretation of the Koran would now be taught in the schools of Oxford, and her pulpits might demonstrate to a circumcised people the sanctity and truth of the revelation of Mahomet."[56]

What is less known is where the other "circumcised people," namely Jews, stood in this conflict. "When Tarik b. Ziyad in 711 crossed the Straits of Gibraltar, and overran the Visigothic Kingdom," Encyclopaedia Judaica tells us, "there were no communities of openly professing Jews in Spain." However,

there remained in the country many secret Jews who welcomed the Muslims as their saviors from long oppression and flocked to join them. According to reliable Arabic sources, the Muslim invaders made it their custom to call together the Jews wherever they found them and to hand towns which they had conquered over to them to garrison. . . . This happened at

Córdoba, Granada, Toledo, and Seville. Since the number of Muslim soldiers was relatively small, there can be no doubt that they appreciated the military help of the Jews who enabled them to continue their campaigns without having to leave behind them sizable units.[57]

There is even a report that in Toledo, the Visigothic capital, the gates of the city "were opened by Jews at a time when the Christians were assembled in their churches on Palm Sunday."[58]

In fact, even long before the Muslim conquest in 711, a Church Council held in Toledo in 694 had accused the Jews of plotting against the Christian kingdom in collaboration with "their co-religionists overseas," only to demand that the severest measures be taken against them: all Jews were to be enslaved, their possessions confiscated, and their children under the age of seven given to Christians to be raised as Christians.[59]

This accusation by the Council of Toledo has led to speculations about whether the Jews of Iberia really had secret connections with Muslims—and even possible Jews among the latter—long before Tarik ibn Ziyad's invasion.[60] It is not impossible, as we know that Jews had joined Muslim conquests in North Africa as well: in Tunisia, the Arab conqueror of the Maghreb, Uqba ibn Nafi (622–683), had invited Jews to settle in the newly founded town of Qayrawan and exempted them from taxes to foster economic growth.[61]

Some of these Christian accounts about "Jewish treachery" could be myths reflecting the anti-Jewish stereotypes of the time. But the Iberian Jews' support for Muslim conquerors against the ruling Christians seems to have been real. It also presents an ever-valid lesson: if a political order oppresses a minority, it is only normal for that minority to look to foreign powers as liberators. Therefore, instead of condemning that minority for "treachery," that political order first should question its own tyranny.

A GOLDEN AGE

After the Muslim conquest, much of Iberia became Al-Andalus, a Muslim state that lasted for more than seven centuries, despite various political upheavals within and the relentless campaigns of *Reconquista,* or "reconquest," by Christians. It also became the home to a vibrant civilization marked by economic prosperity and cultural flourishing. The cities of Córdoba, Sevilla, and Granada became centers of architecture, science, and learning, fascinating Christian visitors from Europe, who had never seen such beautiful cities with great libraries and bookshops, clean, paved streets with lights, beautiful gardens, public baths, running water, aqueducts, and sewage systems. One of them, a tenth-century Saxon nun and playwright, even called Córdoba *decus orbis,* or "the ornament of the world."[62]

A key feature of this brilliant civilization was *convivencia,* or coexistence, of Muslims, Jews, and Christians, as defined by a modern Spanish scholar. Muslims were clearly dominant, but the space they opened to both the Christians and the Jews under their rule was quite tolerant for its time. For Iberian Jews, the fruit of this tolerance was an exceptional flourishing, as the historian Leon Sachar described in his 1940 book, *A History of the Jews*:

> For the Jewish population in Spain the coming of the invaders was a godsend. The Moslem was more concerned about poll taxes than about converts and therefore most of the old restrictions disappeared. Jews entered fully into the life of the country and soon rose to wealth and power. Many of them became leading landowners and financiers; others, prominent physicians and statesmen. They took advantage of the exceptional cultural opportunities and added to the glories of the age. . . . The happy union of Hebrew and Moslem culture produced a renaissance in literature and philosophy, in science and religion.[63]

About a decade before Sachar, another Jewish historian, Maurice Harris, had also praised the Jewish experience in Muslim Spain. This was a new era in history, he wrote, when Jews found "blessings of religious liberty, personal security, and social esteem." As a result,

> Hand in hand, the Moor and the Jew made explorations in the realms of knowledge, and their united achievements kindled a light in the Peninsula that shone the more brilliantly in contrast with the sombre background of Europe's Dark Ages.[64]

With such poetic words, the Jewish experience in Muslim Spain was wholeheartedly praised by quite a few Jewish authors in the late nineteenth and early twentieth centuries. (We will see the reasons for this affinity in a later chapter, "The Good Orientalists.") More recently, other historians argued that these accounts are too rosy, as Iberian Jews had also faced some dark episodes under Muslim rule, which is true. One was the terrible massacre in Granada in 1066, when the Muslim population violently rose up against the Jewish vizier Joseph ibn Naghrella, who they believed had conspired against the kingdom. They not only killed the vizier but also attacked the Jewish population, killing "more than 1,500 householders."[65]

The other dark episode, which lasted much longer, was the forced conversion campaign launched by the Al-Muwahiddun, or the Almohads, the Berber dynasty that invaded Muslim Spain and imposed its unusually intolerant brand of Islam. They had a peculiar doctrine that held that their leader, Ibn Tumart (d. 1130), was the awaited Mahdi—Islam's own version of the Messiah—so the end was near, and the "protection" given to the People of the Book was now invalid. They initiated a forced conversion campaign of Jews and Christians that began in the 1170s and lasted for a few decades. Many Jews were killed, others had to pretend to convert to Islam, and many others fled Muslim Spain.

Yet these episodes of Jewish persecution by Muslims were exceptions, not the rule. No wonder that, while some Jews who escaped the Almohads headed to the Christian kingdoms in northern Spain, Sicily, and Italy—which were now much preferable to Muslim Spain—others simply headed to other lands of Islam where the usual "protected" status of Jews and Christians remained intact. Among them was the towering Jewish scholar Moses Maimonides, who, with his family, first moved to Morocco and ultimately settled in Fustat, the then capital of Egypt.

The fact that the Almohads didn't represent mainstream Islam can also be seen in a fascinating detail in a Jewish manuscript that was preserved for centuries in the Cairo Genizah: a letter penned in 1148 by Shelomo ha-Cohen, an Egyptian Jew, to his father, who was based in Yemen. In his Judeo-Arabic text, while relating the terrible news of the persecution of their coreligionists in Spain, ha-Cohen refers to the Almohads as *khawarij*.[66] This was the name of a fanatic sect in early Islam that religiously condemned and even violently attacked other Muslims, giving themselves a very negative image for centuries to come. So, the fact an Egyptian Jew saw the Almohads as *khawarij* stresses how far away they were from mainstream Islam.

As for Maimonides, it should not be missed that he found the freedom to profess his true faith in Egypt, again a land of Islam. There, soon he became the personal physician to the Muslim ruler al-Fadil, a vizier of Salah ad-Din, and later probably also Salah ad-Din himself.[67] A legend even grew that he rejected an offer to join the court of Salah ad-Din's archenemy, the Crusader king Richard the Lionheart.[68] He still felt "more at home with the Moslems than with the Christians."[69]

That is all why it is still meaningful to speak of a Jewish "golden age" in Muslim Spain. In fact, Eli Barnavi wrote about the "golden age of the Jewish communities in Muslims lands," meaning "a period of brilliant economic prosperity and cultural

creativity" that lasted for centuries after the first Muslim conquests.[70] Another historian, Rabbi Joseph Telushkin, wrote that
"the Golden Age of Spanish Jewry" spanned the tenth to twelfth
centuries, and found it the "closest parallel in Jewish history to
the contemporary golden age of American-Jewish life."[71]

This bright epoch was disrupted in the twelfth and thirteenth
centuries, due to three forces: the rise of the Almohads in North
Africa and Spain; the brutal destruction of the Abbasid Caliphate
in the East by the Mongols; and the Mamluk kingdom in Egypt,
which created an extremely centralized state, suffocating the urban middle classes, including Christians and Jews.[72]

Yet there was another calamity that placed Jewish life in
Muslim lands in jeopardy—but only alongside Muslim life
itself. This was the Christian military expeditions called the Crusades, which put Jews and Muslims, once again, on the same
side.

UNITED AGAINST THE CRUSADERS

The Crusades began when Pope Urban II gave a historic speech
at the Council of Clermont, held in 1095, calling all Christians
in Europe to go to war against Muslims in order to reclaim the
Holy Land. "*Deus vult!*" the Pope famously said, "God wills it!"
which soon became a battle cry. Those who obeyed the call af-
fixed crosses to their outer garments, hence the name *croisés,*
or "crusaders." They included kings, noblemen, knights, priests,
soldiers, and ordinary peasants. For the next two centuries, in
eight major waves, they would target the Muslim Middle East,
causing much destruction and horror, and leaving a very dark
legacy in Muslim memory.

One thing that Muslims should see, though, is that the Crusades didn't come out of nowhere. They were provoked by continuous Muslim advances on Christian states, the latest of which
was the gradual conquest of Anatolia by the Seljuk Turks after

their victory against the Byzantine armies at the Battle of Manzikert in 1071. Also, the persecution of Christians and the destruction of the Church of the Holy Sepulchre in Jerusalem under
the Fatimid caliph al-Hakim (d. 1021)—an unusually cruel ruler,
in fact an outright mad one—sent shock waves through Europe,
which culminated in the Christian response. Therefore, those
who see the Christian crusade as a response to Muslim advances
have a point.

Yet there is another aspect that made the Crusades more savage
than the Muslim campaigns: unlike Muslims, medieval European
Christians did not have a sense of the "People of the Book," with le-
gally recognized rights. Also, Islam had a well-developed doctrine of
war, or military jihad, which made the crucial distinction between
enemy combatants and noncombatants, thanks to the Prophet Muhammad's instructions to his military commanders: "Do not kill
any children or women, or any (farm) laborer."[73] In Christianity,
the "just war" theory developed by Saint Augustine and others
included similar ethical constraints, but Crusaders seem to have
found a way out of it: in his call for the First Crusade, Pope Urban
defined Muslims as "Amalek," for whom the verdict in the Hebrew
Bible is notoriously ruthless: "Now go, attack Amalek. . . . Spare no
one, but kill alike men and women, infants and sucklings."[74]

The irony is that the Crusaders' "Amalek" would include not
just their primary targets, Muslims, but also Jews. As the hordes
of the First Crusade began their long and chaotic march from
Western Europe to Jerusalem, some of them thought that the
worst of all "infidels" were already too close to miss.[75] One of their
leaders, the French nobleman Godfrey of Bouillon, had sworn to
avenge "the blood of the Crucified with the blood of Israel," and
to leave not "a remnant or residue among those bearing the name
Jew."[76] Jews appealed to saner Christian leaders and bribed some
Crusaders to be left alone, but they could not avert the disaster.
One after another, Jewish communities in France, Germany, and
Bohemia became the first victims of the First Crusade, suffering

huge massacres, forced conversions, and mass suicides to avoid the
conversions.⁷⁷ "They slaughtered the women also," wrote Albert of
Aix, the famous chronicler of the Crusades, "and with the point
of their swords pierced young children of whatever age and sex."⁷⁸

Finally, after four years of marching, pillaging, and killing,
the Crusader army reached Jerusalem. After a siege, Godfrey of
Bouillon breached the city walls from the Jewish Quarter, where
"inhabitants defended themselves alongside their Muslim neighbors."⁷⁹ What followed was a horrific bloodbath, described by
one of the Crusaders with a chilling sense of joy:

> But now that our men had possession of the walls and towers,
> wonderful sights were to be seen. Some of our men (and this was
> more merciful) cut off the heads of their enemies; others shot
> them with arrows, so that they fell from the towers; others tor-
> tured them longer by casting them into the flames. Piles of heads,
> hands, and feet were to be seen in the streets of the city. . . . But
> these were small matters compared to what happened at the
> Temple of Solomon, a place where religious services are ordi-
> narily chanted. What happened there? If I tell the truth, it will
> exceed your powers of belief. So let it suffice to say this much,
> at least, that in the Temple and porch of Solomon, men rode in
> blood up to their knees and bridle reins. Indeed, it was a just
> and splendid judgment of God that this place should be filled
> with the blood of the unbelievers, since it had suffered so long
> from their blasphemies.⁸⁰

These slain "unbelievers" were Muslims, of course. But Jews
were also among them, sharing the same tragic fate. As the
Lebanese French author Amin Maalouf describes in *Crusades
Through Arab Eyes*:

> The fate of the Jews of Jerusalem was no less atrocious. During
> the first hours of battle, some participated in the defence of

their quarter, situated on the northern edge of the city. But when that part of the city walls overhanging their homes collapsed and the blond knights began to pour through the streets, the Jews panicked. Re-enacting an immemorial rite, the entire community gathered in the main synagogue to pray. The Franj barricaded all the exits and stacked all the bundles of wood they could find in a ring around the building. The temple was then put to the torch. Those who managed to escape were massacred in the neighbouring alleyways. The rest were burned alive.[81]

Note that the Crusaders are called the Franj, or "the Franks." That was how Muslims called them. They did not call them "Christians," because they already knew many Christians—Greeks, Nestorians, Armenians, Copts, and other Eastern communities—who had lived peacefully with Muslims for centuries, including in Jerusalem. But these Franks from Europe were a different breed. They were exceptionally violent and, as Muslims saw them, exceptionally crude. "The warm humor is lacking among them," wrote the Abbasid writer al-Masudi in the tenth century, "their natures gross, their manners harsh, their understanding dull."[82] They represented a part of the world that, at the time, looked less civilized.

And as people of a more cultured civilization, Muslims and Jews of Islam defended themselves against the Franks. After the fall of Jerusalem, the next line of defense was Haifa, which was besieged in the summer of 1101 by the forces of the Norman prince Tancred. With reference to the chronicles of Albert of Aix, Moshe Gil tells us what happened there:

It appears that it was mainly the Jewish inhabitants of the city who defended the fortress of Haifa. In his rather strange Latin style, [Albert] mentions that there was a Jewish population in Haifa, and that they fought bravely on the walls of the city. He explains that the Jews there were protected people of the Muslims (the Fatimids). They fought side by side with units of the Fatimid army, striking back at Tancred's army from above the walls of the citadel . . . until the Crusaders overcame them and they were forced to abandon the walls. The Muslims and the Jews then managed to escape from the fortress with their lives, while the rest of the population fled the city en masse. Whoever remained was slaughtered, and huge quantities of spoils were taken.[83]

After the First Crusade, the Franks established four Crusader states, dominating the Eastern Mediterranean coast from Jerusalem to Edessa (Urfa in modern-day Turkey). Later Crusades would be launched to fortify or revive these kingdoms, which would gradually shrink in the face of Muslim campaigns of jihad. The latter would lead to a major Muslim victory in 1187, with the reconquest of Jerusalem. Yet the war with Crusaders would continue for another century, until the last Crusader stronghold in Acre fell to Muslim armies.

And guess where Jews stood in this prolonged conflict between the Christian Crusade and Muslim jihad? With the latter, of course.

JEWS FOR JIHAD

We see this pattern in Muslim reports from the time that tell of various episodes of Jewish support or sympathy for Muslim victories against the Crusaders. One comes from the time of Imad al-Din Zangi, the Muslim ruler who is well known for giving the Crusaders their first serious setback by taking back Edessa in 1144. What is less known is that, after his conquest, "to strengthen the anti-Franj party within the population, he moved in three hundred Jewish families of whose indefectible support he was certain."[84]

In 1146, Zangi was assassinated, and both part of his kingdom and his campaign of jihad were inherited by his second son,

Nur ad-Din. The latter's armies had to fight the Second Crusade, and even challenge local Muslim rulers in Damascus who colluded with the enemy. That tension led Nur ad-Din to take over Damascus in 1154, with a curious detail Muslim historians mention in passing: It was a "Jewish woman" who let down a rope to the soldiers of Nur ad-Din, helping them seize the city.[85]

When Nur ad-Din died in 1174, he was succeeded by the greatest champion of the anti-Crusader campaign: Salah al-Din. He was the one who crushed the Franks at the historic Battle of Hattin in 1187, then captured Jerusalem a few months later. In a striking contrast to the Crusader savagery some ninety years prior, Salah al-Din took the city peacefully, sparing civilians, respecting local Christians, and expelling only the Franks. Even to these he showed remarkable clemency, which would create great respect for him in Christian Europe for centuries to come. Among many Muslims, especially Sunnis, he would turn into a timeless hero of Islam.[86]

But Salah al-Din was a hero for Jews, too. Because once he reconquered Jerusalem—just like Caliph Umar did some 550 years earlier—he invited Jews back to the holy city, which had been forbidden to them by the Crusaders since their savage invasion in 1096. Among those who were moved by this moment was Judah al-Harizi, a Jewish traveler from Toledo who had settled in the Islamic East. He wrote a poem where he embraced "the restoration of Islamic sovereignty over Palestine as a sign of the approaching messianic age."[87] He even went as far as to compare Salah al-Din to the Persian king Cyrus, who had allowed the exiled Jews to return to Jerusalem after the Babylonian exile.[88] The Muslim ruler, according to al-Harizi, had called back "all seed of Ephraim"—apparently meaning scattered Jews—to Jerusalem:

> Then he [Salah al-Din] commanded that in every city there sound a call to both great and small, saying: "Bid Jerusalem take heart in rebirth, that all seed of Ephraim who desire shall

return in mirth, who are left in Mosul and Egypt's dearth, and those dispersed to the uttermost ends of the earth. From all sides let them gather unto her and settle within her border."[89]

Indeed, when al-Harizi visited Jerusalem decades later, in 1216, he would find a sizable Jewish community composed of immigrants from France, the Maghreb, and former inhabitants of Ashkelon.[90] So, the pattern had continued: when Islam was in Jerusalem, Judaism was as well.

MUSLIMS AS JEW-ISH

The episodes mentioned so far in this chapter may be seen as anecdotal, but they do reflect a consistent pattern, as the scholars Allan Harris Cutler and Helen Elmquist Cutler highlighted in their 1987 book, *The Jew as Ally of the Muslim*.[91] As they observed, throughout medieval times, "Jews usually rejoiced when Christian territory fell into Islamic hands." In return, medieval Christians, especially in Europe, perceived the two religions as wicked allies working together against the true faith. Hence the image of the Jew as "the fifth column of the Muslim" appeared in many religious texts or literary fictions of premodern Europe— from the writings of Martin Luther to William Shakespeare, to Christopher Marlowe.[92]

In a more recent book, *Jewish Muslims*, the scholar David M. Freidenreich shows that many premodern European Christians saw Islam as simply a form of Judaism. They believed that "Muslims are Jewish—or, if you prefer, 'Jew-ish.'"[93]

This medieval European perception also included an interesting legend about the origins of Islam, which said that Muhammad, not having personally received any divine revelation, could have turned out to be a good Christian. Because he was "educated" by Bahira, an Arab Christian monk whose early encounter with the child Muhammad is indeed narrated in Islamic sources—

but only as a sign of his prophethood, not as its source. In the Christian version of the story, Bahira, now renamed Sergius, was the source of Muhammad's new religion, but later Jews "had corrupted the originally true doctrines of Islam," making it "different from Christianity, and in various ways similar to Judaism."[94] Originally developed among Eastern Christians, this narrative found another echo in medieval Europe in the writings of the Benedictine monk Peter the Venerable (d. 1156). "Lest he become a true Christian, the Jews whispered to Mohammad," he claimed, "especially of that execrable book of the Jews, the Talmud."[95] A few centuries later, some Protestant reformers also criticized Islam as "a patchwork religion," which had taken "many of its worst ideas from the 'wrong religion' (i.e., Judaism)."[96]

Such conspiracy theories about the origin of Islam, I believe, are no more credible than conspiracy theories about the origin of Christianity—such as that Saint Paul was a "Roman agent" who distorted the true teachings of Christ. Yet still, they cover some truth: Islam, as the third great branch of the Abrahamic tree, had elements that resembled both Judaism and Christianity. But, in the final analysis, it was clearly more similar to Judaism than to Christianity.

And no one knew this better than medieval Muslim and Jewish scholars, who didn't shy away from learning from each other's religious tradition. Their mutual borrowings were quite remarkable, which may come as a surprise to some Jews and Muslims today who imagine their faiths as much more insulated, and others as well who may share the same illusion of clear-cut religious traditions with no diffusions.

That is why we will now pause examining the political history of the Judeo-Islamic tradition, and look closer to the theological side of it. We will see how aspects of Judaism became "halal" for Islam, and how aspects of Islam became "kosher" for Judaism—in fascinating ways that influenced their historical trajectories.

HALAL JUDAISM, KOSHER ISLAM

Judaism and Islam are not identical twins, they are fra-
ternal twins. The differences take on weight, because the
similarities so impress.

—Jacob Neusner and Tamara Sonn,
professors of religious studies[1]

Probably most Jews in the world today know Moses
Maimonides (d. 1204). As the towering rabbi, jurist, and philosopher of the twelfth century, he left behind an intellectual legacy
that has been revered to this day. His *Mishneh Torah*, or "Repe-
tition of the Torah," is a monumental compilation of Jewish law,
while his *Guide for the Perplexed* is a masterful synthesis of Jewish theology with Aristotelian philosophy. For all these achieve-
ments, he has been highly revered. Some even called him "the
Second Moses."

It would be unfair, though, to recall the great Maimonides
while neglecting his similarly brilliant son, Abraham Maimonides (d. 1237). The latter was born in Egypt, his family's second
home after the flight from the oppressive Almohad rule in Al-
Andalus. Like his father, he also became a jurist, a theologian,
a physician, and even *rais al-Yahud*, or "the leader of the Jews."
His fame quickly spread as one of the major rabbinical authorities of the time, so he began to receive correspondence from as

far away as Syria, Yemen, and Jerusalem. Meanwhile, also following his father's example, he became the private physician of the Muslim ruler of the time, the Ayyubid al-Malik al-Kamil (r. 1218–1238).

Yet Abraham Maimonides also took a new direction in religion, which proved too controversial to some of his contemporaries: he sought to introduce unforeseen reforms to Judaism, the inspiration for which he found in nowhere other than Islam—and especially in its mystic tradition, Sufism.

This interesting story has been uncovered by the modern scholar Elisha Russ-Fishbane in *Judaism, Sufism, and the Pietists of Medieval Egypt: A Study of Abraham Maimonides and His Times.* Abraham's affinity for Islam, we learn here, was based on an insight he owed to his father: Islam was based on the same pure monotheism that Jews themselves followed. In a letter addressed to the Jews of Provence in the year 1235, Abraham Maimonides put it as follows:

> The children of Ishmael have, for their part, adopted this [monotheistic] faith from the children of Israel and have built the foundation of their religion upon it. They have rejected the error and folly of their ancestors, who used to worship idols and did not affirm the unity and exaltedness of [God's] name, as it is written, "Nations shall come to You from the ends of the earth and say, Our ancestors have inherited lies, [vanity] that is of no avail" (Jer. 16:19). This was also expressed by one of the prophets, "From the rising of the sun to its setting, My name is great among the nations" (Mal. 1:11).[2]

Abraham even wrote that "because their worship is characterized by pure monotheism," it is similar "to the sacrificial rite [in the Temple] offered for His name."[3] It was an insight that today can perhaps help Muslims and Jews overcome their tensions around what they respectively call al-Haram al-Sharif, or the Temple Mount.

But Abraham didn't stop at merely appreciating Islam's theological correctness. This, he thought, allowed Jews to learn from Islam. At a time when the Islamic civilization was at the zenith of its power, he was feeling that Judaism was at "a crisis point, a spiritual nadir in its age-old exile."[4] Jews needed a religious revival, a new spirit, which Abraham found in the Sufi *tariqas,* or orders, that were then an established part of Islamic life in Egypt and much of the rest of the Muslim world.

So, Abraham began frequenting Sufi orders, observing their teaching and rituals, and recommending them to his own Jewish community. In his 2,500-page book *Kitab Kifayah al-Abidin,* or *Comprehensive Guide for the Servants of God,* written in Judeo-Arabic, he praised Sufi values such as "sincerity, mercy, generosity, gentleness, humility, faith, contentedness, abstinence, mortification and solitude." Even more controversially, in his own synagogue, where he was the head rabbi, he introduced new practices that were all unmistakably Islamic: ablutions before prayer, the raising of the hands in supplication, standing in rows, and prostrations during prayer.

But how could Jews follow the practices of another religion? Wasn't this heresy?

Against these questions, which he seems to have faced, Abraham first argued that the Talmud indeed banned "imitating the ways of the gentiles" (*hukkot ha-goyim*), but these "gentiles" were only the idolaters. In contrast, Islam was a reliably monotheist religion. So, Jews could be more comfortable with the ways of the Muslims.[5]

Second, Abraham made an argument common to most religious reformers, both in the past and the present: the novelties that he advocated were in fact not alien to his faith. Instead, they were ancient and authentic Judaic practices wrongly abandoned by Jews themselves, while wisely adopted and preserved by Muslims. "The ways of the ancient saints of Israel," as he put it, had "now become the practice of the Sufis of Islam."[6]

Were these wishful thoughts and exaggerations? According to Shelomo Dov Goitein, the twentieth century's towering scholar on Jewish life in medieval Islam, Abraham's "Jewish Sufism" included some exaggerations, but also some truth:

> He was right in the matter of worship by prostration. This was indeed an old Jewish custom, as many passages of the Bible indicate. As late as the second century A.D. it must have been quite common, for it was said of Rabbi Akiba, one of the most famous sages of that time, that at the beginning of prayer he was found in one corner of the synagogue and at the end in another, because of his incessant bowings and prostrations. Later on, however, prostrations were banned from the service of the synagogue, possibly because they had become so prominent in the practices of both the Christian monks and the Jewish sectarians, the latter calling their place of service an outright "House of Prostration." Muhammad, following either Christian or Jewish sectarian example, enthusiastically adopted bowings and prostrations; and subsequently the Muslim pietists adhered to this practice with particular fervor.[7]

Nevertheless, Abraham Maimonides's reform project didn't achieve much success. Some of his fellow Jews, scandalized by his "unlawful changes," even appealed to the Muslim ruler of the time to block this confusing effort. Abraham himself passed away at a young age. Yet, some of his close associates preserved their mystical practices for several generations, until the rise of the Kabbalah as the main source of Jewish mysticism. They were, in the words of Elisha Russ-Fishbane, "unapologetic in their respect (at times, even admiration) for the good found in the Islamic religion."[8] And their "Jewish Sufism" was only one of the various facets of interaction within the Judeo-Islamic tradition, as we will now see.

COMMON THEOLOGY, COMMON LANGUAGE

As noted, Abraham Maimonides's sympathy for Islam was rooted in a fact that was also acknowledged by his father: unlike most other religions of the world, Islam was a sister faith that shared the very core of Judaism: a pure, staunch, unadulterated monotheism.

Moses Maimonides had made this clear in a letter he wrote to a certain Obadiah the Proselyte, a rare convert from Islam to Judaism, who still honestly defended Islam against the accusation that it was an idolatrous religion. The latter view was based on a myth among some Jews (as well as Christians) of the time that the Kaaba in Mecca was in fact home to an idol, making Muslims idol-worshippers. Refuting this myth, Rabbi Moses forthrightly wrote:

> The Ishmaelites are not at all idolaters; [idolatry] has long been severed from their mouths and hearts; and they attribute to God a proper unity, a unity concerning which there is no doubt.[9]

"Their error and foolishness is in other things," added Rabbi Moses, mincing no words against this rival faith, whose zealots had recently persecuted his own family. "But," he concluded, "as regards the unity of God they have no error at all."[10]

This Jewish affirmation of Islamic monotheism had legal consequences, which have survived. A contemporary website that shares the religious rulings of Ovadia Yosef, the Sephardi Chief Rabbi of Israel from 1973 to 1983, explains some of them as follows:

> We are therefore lenient and sell our lands in Israel to Muslims during the Shemitta (Sabbatical) year based on the "Heter Mechira" process although it is forbidden to sell land in Eretz

Yisrael to an idol-worshipper; this is because Muslims are not considered idol-worshippers. Based on this, mosques are not considered actual houses of idol worship and one may enter them according to the letter of the law.[11]

Meanwhile, the same Jewish affirmation has not been extended to churches, which, due to the concerns with the doctrine of the Trinity as well as religious iconography, has not been considered impeccably monotheist. That's why for centuries, the rabbinic consensus, based on the Talmud, has been that it is forbidden to enter a church, "even if just to admire the architecture or artwork."[12]

The common grounds between Islam and Judaism also include the primacy of law in both religions—the Halakha and Sharia, respectively, which have many similarities. Both have dietary laws, such as the strict prohibition on pork. Both prescribe circumcision for all males. Both prescribe modest dress for women, which, in their traditional interpretations, include head coverings—for all women in Islam, for all married women in Judaism.

These similarities between the two religions have practical results. In Western countries, Muslims who cannot find food that is certified halal can often safely opt for food that is kosher. Asked for a fatwa, or religious verdict, on this question—"Can Muslims eat kosher?"—a staunchly conservative Muslim source responds: "There is nothing wrong with the Muslim eating Jewish foods on which is written the word 'kosher,' unless it is known that they have added any alcohol to it."[13] Sharing the same opinion, the prominent American Muslim cleric Yasir Qadhi adds: "It is important that stronger ties be developed between observant Muslims and Jews so that we benefit from each other's experiences, unite against Islamophobic and anti-Semitic efforts to ban ritual animal slaughter."[14]

The religious terminologies of both religions are also analogous. In Islam, the very pillar of the faith, or *iman,* is the proclamation

"There is no god but God."[15] In Judaism, the pillar of the faith, or *emunah,* is a similar proclamation: "Hear, O Israel, Our Lord is God, Our Lord is One."

Many other terms in the two traditions are unmistakably common:

> The Islamic term for almsgiving is *sadaqah.* In Judaism, it is *tzedakah.*
>
> Another Islamic term for almsgiving is *zakat.* In Judaism, it has a parallel in *zekhut,* or merit.
>
> The Islamic term for ritual purity is *tahara.* In Judaism, it is *taharah.*
>
> The Islamic term for fasting is *sawm.* In Judaism, it is *tzom.*
>
> The Islamic term for pilgrimage is *hajj.* In Judaism, it is *hag.*
>
> The Islamic term for daily prayers is *salat.* In Judaism, it has a parallel in *tzolata.*
>
> The Islamic term for school is *madrasa.* In Judaism, it is *beit midrash,* meaning house of study.
>
> The Islamic term for religion is *din.* In Judaism, it is also *din,* only with an emphasis on its legal aspect.[16]

And while Muslims greet each other by saying *as-salamu alaikum,* which means "peace be upon you," Jews say *shalom aleykhem,* which means the exact same thing.

The similarity between the two religions is also visible in the role of clergy, which is quite different from the role of the priesthood in Christianity, especially in its Catholic form. As the late historian Bernard Lewis once observed:

> There are indeed certain resemblances between the position of the ulema in Islamic life and that of the rabbinate in orthodox Jewish communities. Neither the alim (the singular of ulema) nor the rabbi is an ordained priest; neither has any sacerdotal

office. Neither Judaism nor Islam has sacraments, altars, or or-
dination, or priestly mediation. There is no religious office that
an alim or a rabbi can perform that any ordinary adult male
believer, possessing the necessary knowledge, cannot perform
equally well. Both are professional men of religion, but neither is
in any sense a priest. They acquire their status through knowledge, through learning, and through recognition, which becomes a form of certification—the semikha of the rabbi closely
resembling the ijaza a new alim receives from his teacher. In
all these respects as well as some others, there are striking resemblances in training, qualification, and function between
the orthodox rabbi and the Sunni Muslim alim.[17]

Such remarkable similarities between Judaism and Islam have
led some even to ask whether they are "the same religion." My
answer is no, they are not, but mainly due to a matter of audience:
Judaism is Abrahamic monotheism for Jews; Islam is Abrahamic
monotheism for gentiles. Christianity is Abrahamic monotheism
for gentiles, too, but with a distinct theology and antinomianism
of its own, which are alien to both Judaism and Islam.

THE RISE AND FALL OF ISRA'ILIYYAT

The parallels between Islam and Judaism, as well as the tolerance Jews often found under Muslim rule, allowed for the rise
of a "creative Jewish-Arab symbiosis, lasting 800 years [ca. 500–
1300]," as Shelomo Dov Goitein wrote half a century ago. In the
first half of this "symbiosis," Islam developed "under Jewish impact," while in the second half, Judaism "received its final shape
under Muslim-Arab influence."[18]

Today, some Muslims may find this idea of a "Jewish impact"
unacceptable, thinking that Islam has been a self-contained tradition all along, based on the Qur'an and the example (*sunna*) of
the Prophet, both of which are divinely revealed or guided. But

the Islamic tradition itself reveals a Jewish impact, which even has a specific name: *Isra'iliyyat.* Literally "of the Israelites," the term refers to the early Islamic practice of incorporating religious knowledge from Jewish sources into Qur'anic exegesis and other religious writings. (A similar term, *Masihiyyat,* refers to borrowings from Christian sources; but this was a less significant strain and was often subsumed under *Isra'iliyyat.*)

Why did Muslims need to learn anything from Jews and Christians? The great Muslim historian of the fourteenth century Ibn Khaldun offered an answer in his magnum opus, *The Muqaddimah*:

> The reason is that the Arabs had no books or scholarship. The desert attitude and illiteracy prevailed among them. When they wanted to know certain things that human beings are usually curious to know, such as the reasons for the existing things, the beginning of creation, and the secrets of existence, they consulted the earlier People of the Book about it and got their information from them. The People of the Book were the Jews who had the Torah, and the Christians who followed the religion of (the Jews).[19]

However, there were more grounds to *Isra'iliyyat* than mere intellectual curiosity. The Qur'an itself repeatedly honored the *Tawrat* (Torah) and the *Injil* (Evangel, or Gospel) as previous revelations of God that Muslims should respect: "He has sent the Scripture down to you [Prophet] with the Truth, confirming what went before: He sent down the Torah and the Gospel."[20] Another verse reads: "Before this was the Book of Moses as a guide and mercy, and this [Qur'an] is a Book confirming it in Arabic."[21]

Moreover, the Qur'an explicitly told Muslims to *learn* from these ancient scriptures and their followers: "Bring the Torah and read it"; "Ask those who read the Scripture before you"; and

"Ask the Children of Israel."[22] Furthermore, a narration (hadith) from the Prophet Muhammad also justified *Isra'iliyyat*: "Relate the traditions from the Children of Israel; there is no restriction on that."[23]

Based on such premises, many Muslim scholars in the formative centuries of Islam freely engaged in *Isra'iliyyat*, as noted by the contemporary academic Sadreddin Berk Metin:

> Muslim writers in the pre-modern period were comfortable with consulting and citing Jewish sources—indeed they did so liberally. . . . Referring to Jewish sources or holding them legitimate, at least to some degree, was not unusual, let alone being regarded as highly problematic. Muslims openly inherited narrations from the Jewish tradition as early as the 7th century and held them as legitimate sources of religious knowledge lest they "openly" contradicted the Qur'an.[24]

However, this trend did not go unchallenged. The first serious challenge to *Isra'iliyyat* appeared in the works of Ibn Taymiyya (d. 1328) and his disciple Ibn Kathir (d. 1373), both of whom lived at a time when Muslim attitudes to non-Muslims had turned more hostile, partly in response to the carnage caused by the Crusades and Mongol invasions. It is in their writings that *Isra'iliyyat* clearly appears as a term with negative connotations, and to imply traditions that "had nothing to do with Islam but were of Jewish origin."[25]

Then, *Isra'iliyyat* faced an even stronger rejection in the modern era and, perhaps surprisingly, among reformists who are often called "Islamic modernists."[26] They were critical of the many problems they saw in the Islamic tradition—often sensibly so—but they found an all-too-easy scapegoat in *Isra'iliyyat*, which had supposedly corrupted a more pristine Islam. And just like their medieval predecessors, they were influenced by the politics of their day:

they were on the Arab side of the Arab-Israeli conflict, and the now-stigmatized term *Isra'iliyyat* reminded them of "the State of Israel more than of the ancient Israelites."[27]

The Muslim view of *Isra'iliyyat* is ultimately related to a criticism that the Qur'an repeatedly raises against the Jews in its historical context: that they "distorted" the Torah to serve their mundane goals. The Arabic word for "distortion" is *tahrif,* which became a well-known term among Muslims to argue that all the Bible is distorted, so it is unreliable. However, from the earlier centuries onward, some Muslim scholars, such as Ibn Khaldun and al-Maqrizi (d. 1442), argued that the "distortion" was not in the text of the Bible but in its interpretation.[28] In other words, some Jews had simply misinterpreted the Torah—just like Muslims themselves can misinterpret the Qur'an.

The contemporary Muslim academic Joseph Lumbard agrees with this second view, and explains why it is more coherent from a Qur'anic perspective:

The notion that previous scriptures have been abrogated in the sense of being nullified or excessively distorted to such an extent that their message no longer reflects the particularity of the original teachings, as some Muslims maintain, would seem to be contradicted by verses such as 5:43: "And how is it that they come to thee for judgment, when they have the Torah, wherein is God's Judgment?" and 5:68: "Say, 'O People of the Book! You stand on naught till you observe the Torah and the Gospel, and that which has been sent down unto you from your Lord.'" In this same vein, 5:47 says of Christians: "Let the people of the Gospel judge by that which God has sent down therein." It would be contradictory for the Qur'an to speak of the efficacy of judging by the Torah and the Gospel if it were to also maintain that these scriptures have been abrogated or excessively distorted.[29]

Therefore, one could argue that the early Muslim scholars who borrowed from Jewish sources, especially the Bible, were not doctrinally wrong. Historically, too, their engagement with *Isra'iliyyat* expanded Muslim knowledge, which otherwise would have been much more limited. How would Muslims know about the story of Job, for example, which the Qur'an mentions briefly in a few verses, but the Bible narrates in a whole book?[30]

Meanwhile, Muslim engagement in *Isra'iliyyat* had a positive impact on the other side of the Judeo-Islamic tradition. "The fact that the new religion of Islam assimilated many Jewish elements at the time of its origin and during the years of its consolidation," observed Hava Lazarus-Yafeh, a twentieth-century scholar, helped many Jewish sages to adopt "a much more lenient attitude toward it than toward other religions." Lazarus-Yafeh also added, echoing Goitein:

> Two periods can be clearly distinguished in the interrelationship of Judaism and Islam. During the first period—the 7th and maybe also the 8th centuries—Judaism, more than any other religion and culture, left a decisive impact on Islam, a new religion in the process of consolidation. In the second period—probably from the 8th century, and in particular from the 9th century onward—Islam, which had become a rich and variegated culture, profoundly influenced Jewish culture. Consequently, the interrelationship of these two cultures may be regarded as a closed circle, a rare phenomenon in cultural relationships.[31]

In the next chapter, we will focus on the second period, which is the time when Islam "profoundly influenced Jewish culture." The phenomenon of Jewish *Islamiyyat,* so to speak.

But before that, there is one more theme we need to tackle on how "halal" Judaism is for Islam, and how "kosher" Islam is for

Judaism. It is the question of whether the two religions see each other as eternally blessed or eternally damned. It is, in other words, the important question of salvation.

SALVATION MATTERS

All three major Abrahamic religions—Judaism, Christianity, and Islam—teach that there is life after death. They also teach that in this "hereafter," the good people will be rewarded while the bad people will be punished. But who is "good" and who is "bad"? In other words, who will be "saved" and who will not?

A common answer is to claim that only "our people" are saved. In Christianity, this view was expressed for centuries with the famous maxim *extra ecclesiam nulla salus,* or "there is no salvation outside the church." This view is also called "salvific exclusivism," meaning that its promise for salvation excludes the out-group.

Quite remarkably, the Qur'an took an issue with salvific exclusivism as expressed by Jews and Christians in its historical context. In the long chapter of *al-Baqara,* it read:

> They also say, "No one will enter Paradise unless he is a Jew or a Christian." This is their own wishful thinking. [Prophet], say, "Produce your evidence, if you are telling the truth." In fact, anyone who direct themselves wholly to God and do good will have their reward with their Lord: no fear for them, nor will they grieve.[32]

Based on this Qur'anic verse, many Muslims have assumed that Jews and Christians are salvific exclusivists. However, in both religions, more inclusivist views developed over time.

This is especially true for Judaism. Though not as pronounced as in Christianity and Islam, it bears a faith in *olam ha-ba,* or "the world to come," in contrast to *olam ha-zeh,* or "this world." The interesting point is that while initially "gentile nations [were] denied entry into the world to come,"[33] the rabbis ultimately developed a more inclusive view: those who have a place in the "world to come" are not only Jews themselves who follow the Laws of Moses but also gentiles who follow the laws of Noah, which are the "minimal moral duties enjoined by the Bible on all men."[34] They are these seven rules:

1. Not to worship idols.
2. Not to curse God.
3. Not to commit murder.
4. Not to commit adultery or sexual immorality.
5. Not to steal.
6. Not to eat flesh torn from a living animal.
7. To establish courts of justice.[35]

These "Noahide Laws," which offer a moral framework much broader than Judaism itself, have also been pointed to as the Judaic basis for natural law—"the common rational, ethical ground of Israel and mankind."[36] Non-Jews who follow them are called "righteous gentiles," and they "have a portion in the world to come," as Moses Maimonides put it clearly centuries ago.[37] He added that righteous gentiles are also "entitled to full material support from the Jewish community and to the highest earthly honors."[38]

Now, there is something important about this common ground of Israel and mankind: it is shared by Islam. Any Muslim who reads the seven laws of Noah will find them very familiar, because they are all elements of Islamic law. In fact, the Qur'an seems to be decreeing a version of them in chapter 17, *al-Isra,* in a passage that commands, soon after mentioning Noah: "Set up no other god beside God," "Speak respectfully (to parents)," "Do not go anywhere near adultery," "Do not take life, which God has made sacred," "Do not go near the orphan's property, except with the best," and "Give full measure when you measure."[39]

No wonder, then, that from the earliest centuries of Islam, Jews had little doubt that Muslims were among the righteous gentiles who honor the Noahide Laws. A contemporary Jewish source puts this unequivocally: "Since Islam is strictly monotheistic, Muslims have always been considered Noahides."[40] (Jews have been less sure about Christians, due to Christianity's complex theology. However, "since the later Middle Ages, Jews have acknowledged that the Christian doctrine of the Trinity was not the same as idolatry, and they were also recognized as Noahides."[41])

This also means that, according to Judaism, Muslims will be saved in the hereafter. A contemporary rabbi puts this plainly in response to a question:

> Since Islam follows the seven Noachide laws, yes, Muslims have a place in the world to come. Obviously, there are individuals that will not have a place, terrorists, slave traders, etc. but the general populace who follow the Seven Noachide laws within the framework of Islam, yes.[42]

What about Islam? Does it return the favor, and offer a good place to Jews in the world to come—or *akhira,* as it is called in Islam?

In the Qur'an we can find a remarkably magnanimous answer to this question. We already saw it in the verse that criticized Jewish or Christian salvific exclusivism. Against them, the Qur'an said, "Anyone who direct themselves wholly to God and do good will have their reward with their Lord." Any ethical monotheist, so to speak, will be saved.

But the Qur'an didn't leave it there. In two separate Medinan verses that are almost verbatim, it explicitly promised salvation to other monotheists:

The [Muslim] believers, the Jews, the Christians, and the Sabians; all those who believe in God and the Last Day and do good will have their rewards with their Lord. No fear for them, nor will they grieve.[43]

For the [Muslim] believers, the Jews, the Sabians, and the Christians; those who believe in God and the Last Day and do good deeds, there is no fear: they will not grieve.[44]

The exact identity of the "Sabians" in these verses is unclear, and many scholars think that they are the Mandeans, a monotheist religion in Mesopotamia that considers John the Baptist as the final and most definitive prophet. There is no doubt, however, about who Jews and Christians are. It also seems quite clear that the Qur'an promises them a place in its world to come.

However, this is not what most Muslims think today, because both the Sunni and Shiite traditions explained away the two verses above by taking another Qur'anic verse as more definitive: "If anyone seeks a religion other than Islam, it will not be accepted from him: he will be one of the losers in the Hereafter."[45] The salvation of Jews and Christians, in this view, was possible before the arrival of Islam—but once "the call" reached the people, Islam superseded former monotheisms. Some nuanced scholars, such as al-Ghazali, added that "the call" must come properly and fairly, and those who heard about Islam only disparagingly would be excused. Yet still, salvific exclusivism—which the Qur'an criticizes when held by Jews and Christians—became a predominant belief among Muslims. Many of them turned it even more extreme, by narrowing salvation to their specific sect within Islam.[46]

Nevertheless, it is possible to read the Qur'anic verses on salvation in a more pluralist sense. The "Islam" that the Qur'an defines as the only religion acceptable to God may well not be the historical religion that began with the Prophet Muhammad but the pristine monotheism that was also preached by Noah, Abraham, and Moses. A contemporary Muslim scholar, Mohsen Kadivar, among others, puts it plainly: "Islam is the name of all the Abrahamic religions and has no meaning other than submission to God."[47] Moses Mendelssohn, whom we will meet later in this book, would agree with him, as he wrote:

> "I am the Eternal, your God, the necessary, independent being, omnipotent and omniscient, that recompenses men in a future life according to their deeds." This is the universal religion of mankind, not Judaism.[48]

With this conceptualization of Islam simply as monotheism, the Qur'an's promise to "Jews, the Christians, and the Sabians"—in fact, all ethical monotheists—must still be valid. This argument, which has some precedents in early Islam, is defended today by "a relatively small but vocal group of Muslim scholars."[49] It is also gaining ground among "growing contingents of Muslim pluralists."[50]

Which brings us to an interesting conclusion to this chapter on what is "halal" about Judaism and "kosher" about Islam. Besides all the remarkable similarities they share on earth, the two religions may also share a common place in heaven—the *olam ha-ba* or the *akhira*. Surely, it is up to God to rule on the fate of any individual Jew or Muslim, as they would both believe. But their own beliefs suggest that they may both be "saved."

HOW ISLAMIC RATIONALISM
ENRICHED JUDAISM

*Contact with Muslim rationalism forever transformed
the way in which Judaism was both approached and
defined.*

—Aaron Hughes, professor of Judaic studies[1]

Both Judaism and Islam are "legalistic" religions. The revealed law, in other words, is their central concern. Hence, scholars of religion often define them as religions of orthopraxy, or correct behavior. The other concern, orthodoxy, or correct belief, has been more fundamental to Christianity.

However, this doesn't mean that correct belief is unimportant in Islam and Judaism. Quite the contrary, they both developed their own traditions that study belief. In Islam, it was called *kalam*, which literally means "speech" but is often translated as "theology." And it had a profound impact on Islam itself, and, well, more than that, as we will now see.

Kalam flourished in the early Abbasid Caliphate, during the eighth and ninth centuries, in its cosmopolitan cities in Iraq, where some Muslim scholars began to produce systematic ideas on new questions that did not bother their earlier coreligionists. Some of these problems, such as the status of the "grave sinner," or belief in predestination versus free will, were provoked by internal tensions within Islam. Others were sparked by the intellectual challenges posed by long-established traditions, such as Christianity, Zoroastrianism, Manichaenism, and, most important, Greek philosophy.

What is remarkable about kalam for our story is that it had an everlasting impact on not just Islam but also Judaism. Bernard Lewis stressed this fact, noting, "The emergence of a Jewish theology took place almost entirely in Islamic lands."[2] Aaron W. Hughes agrees:

> The development of rational theology in Judaism took place in Arabic and under Islam. Prior to this, with the exception of Philo of Alexandria, there was little or no systematic engagement with theology. Since Philo had very little impact on subsequent Jewish thought—his biggest influence seems to have been among the early Church fathers—and since Jews in late antiquity used other models and genres to articulate their theological concerns, the development of rational theology is intimately connected to the Jewish immersion in Arabophone culture. As Jews adopted Arabic and as they began to think in Arabo-Islamic categories, it was only natural that they would begin to try to connect the themes of rationalist theology to Judaism. If they did not, Judaism would appear to be intellectually obsolete. The result was the rise of what we may call Jewish Kalam.[3]

Some thought that this Islamic influence on Judaism may have begun with the Karaites, a Jewish sect that flourished in the Islamic Middle Ages, with a "Protestant" approach—accepting the Torah, but not the "Oral Torah."[4] There is even an interesting story that the very founder of Karaism, Anan Ben David (d. 795), shared a jail cell with Abu Hanifa, the founder of the most rationalist Sunni school, whose practical advice helped to get Anan released.[5] Yet, in fact, both the Karaites and mainstream rabbinic Jews seem to have been exposed to Muslim influence "more or less at the same time," and "gradually through the spread of the Arabic language and culture."[6]

Besides this natural diffusion, there was a specific institution that seems to have facilitated this exposure: *majlis al-kalam,* or the "salon of theology." These were regular gatherings held at the very court of the Abbasid caliphs, where theologians of all faiths came together to speak without censorship or fear using the universal language of reason. It was an exceptionally liberal environment that shocked more orthodox Muslims. We learn this from an account by such a Muslim, a Hanbali visitor to Baghdad who was appalled by the open rationality he saw in the salons of theology. As reported later by the eleventh-century Muslim historian al-Humaydi, this visitor wrote:

> At the first meeting there were present not only people of various [Islamic] sects, but also unbelievers, Magians, materialists, atheists, Jews and Christians, in short, unbelievers of all kinds. . . . One of the unbelievers rose and said to the assembly: "We are meeting here for a discussion. Its conditions are known to all. You, Muslims, are not allowed to argue from your books and prophetic traditions since we deny both. Everybody, therefore, has to limit himself to rational arguments." The whole assembly applauded these words. So you can imagine . . . that after these words I decided to withdraw. They proposed to me that I should attend another meeting in a different hall, but I found the same calamity there.[7]

As a side note, and a sad one, let me add that it would be hard to see such free debates in today's Baghdad—or Riyadh, or Tehran, or Islamabad—because the Islamic civilization has long lost that remarkable openness, which was the very secret of its golden age. Those who were shocked by this "calamity" ultimately succeeded in narrowing its scope, with unfortunate consequences that are still with us today.

THE JEWISH MU'TAZILITES

Coming back to our story, those who engaged in this cosmopolitan culture in early Islam included two Jewish thinkers who proved to be of historic significance: Dawud al-Muqammis (d. ca. 937) and Saadia Gaon (d. 942). Both writing in Arabic, they engaged in theological and philosophical discussions of the day, following "the basic structure, techniques, and topics of those found among their Muslim colleagues."[8] The only major difference, as one would expect, was that while Muslim theologians were articulating the truth of Islam, Jewish ones were articulating the truth of Judaism.

In this story, Saadia Gaon, or Saadia ben Yosef al-Fayyumi to use his full name, deserves special attention. Born in Egypt in 882, and having lived and studied in Palestine, he ultimately settled in Sura, a city in southern Iraq, where he became the head the Jewish academy that preserved the great tradition of the Babylonian Talmud. Here he was given the honorific title "gaon," meaning an exceptional scholar with a great knowledge of the Torah. Among many other accomplishments, he penned *The Book of Beliefs and Opinions,* which represents the first systematic attempt to integrate Jewish texts with philosophy. "It helped to shape much subsequent rabbinic thought," wrote Hughes, and "remains today at the heart of traditional Judaism."[9]

Now, here is a significant detail—and remarkable irony—in this phenomenon of Jewish kalam: the brand of theology embraced by Saadia Gaon and other Jewish theologians who followed his path was that of a particular school known as the *Mu'tazila.* Its adherents, the Mu'tazilites in English, are often called the "rationalists" of Islam because of the independent authority they granted to human reason, besides divine revelation, in discerning moral truths. However, because of Islam's own internal war of ideas, Mu'tazilites would ultimately be condemned as heretics—by the bluntly dogmatic Hanbalites and their more sophisticated kin, the Ash'arites. Consequently, the Mu'tazilite influence on Islamic thinking would be largely curtailed, with fateful consequences, as I discussed in an earlier book, *Reopening Muslim Minds: A Return to Reason, Freedom, and Tolerance*.[10]

So, the irony is that the Mu'tazilite "heresy" got marginalized in Islam, but it survived and even flourished in Judaism.

A modern-day academic who highlighted this much-forgotten connection was Alexander Altmann (1906–1987), an Austrian-born rabbi and scholar who fled Nazi Germany to ultimately teach at Brandeis University in America. In his 1944 article, "Saadia's Conception of the Law," he first notes that this conception "must be viewed against the background of Islamic *Aufklärung* [Enlightenment] in the tenth century."[11] Then Altmann demonstrates Saadia's incorporation of certain Mu'tazilite ideas. For example, while arguing that moral values are "planted by God in our intellects," Saadia had given the example of "gratitude," which is the standard example in Mu'tazilite texts.[12] This was quite remarkable, in the words of Altmann,

> not only because it illustrates the extent to which Saadia is under the spell of Mu'tazilite thought, but also because it sheds light on the meaning of this multicoloured term, "Reason" ('aql). Reason demanding gratitude can only mean a natural moral instinct, not Reason in any sense of logic. This is exactly the Mu'tazilite conception of Reason as an organ of moral judgment. It denotes man's natural gift, his mental equipment by birth (fitra), and is tantamount to the Stoic notion of man's nature of Reason.[13]

We see an early account of this theological transmission from Islam to Judaism in a source no less authoritative than Moses Maimonides. In *The Guide for the Perplexed,* he mentions the influence of the *"mutakallimun* of Islam" or Muslim theologians, on Jewish scholars—both "the Geonim" such as Saadia Gaon, and "the Karaites." Then, adds Maimonides:

> Also it has so happened that Islam first began to take this road [of theology] owing to a certain sect, namely, the Mu'tazila, from whom our coreligionists took over certain things walking upon the road the Mu'tazila had taken. After a certain time another sect arose in Islam, namely, the Ash'ariyya, among whom other opinions arose. You will not find any of these latter opinions among our coreligionists.[14]

The Mu'tazilite influence on Jewish scholars was so deep that one can speak of "Jewish Mu'tazila," as Sabine Schmidtke, professor of Islamic intellectual history at the Institute for Advanced Study at Princeton, calls it:

> It was Mu'tazilism in particular that was adopted to varying degrees from the 9th century onwards by both Rabbanite and Karaite authors, so that by the turn of the 11th century a "Jewish Mu'tazila" had emerged. Jewish scholars both composed original works along Mu'tazilite lines and produced copies of Muslim Mu'tazilite books, often transcribed into Hebrew characters. The influence of the Mu'tazila found its way to the very centres of Jewish religious and intellectual life in the East.[15]

Meanwhile, one of these Jewish Mu'tazilites, the Karaite scholar Levi ben Yefet, also felt enough affinity with Islam that he "implicitly recognized Muhammad as a friend of God endowed with prophethood, though ranking below Moses."[16]

This theological transmission is so remarkable that some

Mu'tazilite manuscripts, which have been lost or destroyed in Islamic lands, survived among Jews. Often transcribed into Hebrew for Jewish scholars' own use, they were preserved for centuries in the genizahs of Egypt and elsewhere, and some of them ultimately ended up it the Abraham Firkovich collection at the National Library of Russia in Saint Petersburg.[17] In 2003, a Mu'tazilite Manuscripts Project Group was founded by Sabine Schmidtke and David Sklare of the Hebrew University in Jerusalem to study these ancient texts. Despite remarkable work over the years, as Schmidtke noted in 2019, "The scholarly investigation of the Jewish Mu'tazila, its historical connection to Muslim counterparts, and a systematic exploitation of the Islamic primary materials preserved in Jewish collections, are still in their infancy."[18]

Yet some of the perspectives that the Mu'tazilites advocated within Islam but proved to be more influential within Judaism are already traceable. And they are quite interesting, as we will now see.

SHARIA, HALAKHA, AND HUMAN REASON

In Islam, Mu'tazilite theologians were affiliated with the early juristic trend known as *ahl al-ray,* or "people of reason," that emerged in Iraq in the eighth century. What separated them from the rival trend, *ahl al-hadith,* or "people of tradition," was the larger authority they granted to human reason in interpreting Sharia, the religious law. This rationality was reflected in their legal concept of *istihsan,* which means "to consider something good." Since the human mind is capable of discerning "good" and "bad," they believed, it could give legal judgments even without basis in revealed texts. However, the ascendance of the "people of tradition" would lead to a strict textualism in Islamic legal theory, turning *istihsan* into an "underutilized tool."[19]

In these early centuries of Islam, Jewish law, which had many

similarities to Islamic law, didn't seem too rationalist. If anything, Muslims perceived Jewish law as "rigid and uncompromising," while being proud that Islamic law was "easier, more lenient
and flexible."[20] In this early Muslim self-perception, Islam was
"a moderate religion," whereas Judaism was a "stern religion."[21]
Even the later Qur'anic commentator Fakhr al-Din al-Razi (d.
1210) would proudly argue that while "the Sharia of Jesus" is all
too permissive and "the Sharia of Moses" is all too strict, the Sharia of Muhammad follows a moderate middle path.[22]

To project modern terminology, Islamic law was even more
feminist than Jewish law. For example, according to the Torah,
when a father dies, all his inheritance would be received by his
sons. Daughters would get nothing, unless there were no sons
in the family.[23] In contrast, the Qur'an ruled: "Men shall have a
share . . . and women shall have a share."[24] Women's share was
half men's, so it was short of equal rights that many women have
in the modern world.[25] Yet, in a social setting where the financial
responsibility for the family was unilaterally on men, it was remarkably pro-female legislation.

Islamic laws on divorce were also more advantageous for
women than were Jewish laws. That is why some medieval Jewish
women began appealing to Muslim courts, as Gideon Libson, a
rare scholar of comparative Jewish and Islamic law, puts it:

> A third factor influencing the absorption of Muslim usages
> was the lenience of Islamic law in certain areas, in regards to
> both substance and procedure, compared to the corresponding
> provisions of Jewish law. . . . Accordingly, there was a growing
> tendency among Jews to turn to Muslim courts, furthering an
> appreciation among Jews of the Muslim court system and its
> regulations. There is ample evidence, for example, of women
> in the category known as "rebellious wife" (ishah moredet) ap-
> pealing to Muslim courts in order to circumvent Jewish law,
> which would not readily grant them a divorce.[26]

However, having an advanced start is one thing; having the conceptual tools to keep advancing is another. On the latter front, the Islamic legal tradition seems to have lost its cutting edge by the decline of "the people of reason." In comparison, Jewish law, having more rational tools for its renewal, seems to have caught up with Islamic law, and at times even surpassed it.

Gideon Libson demonstrates these different trajectories both conceptually and historically.[27] Conceptually, Jewish law included rational tools—similar to the early Islamic *istihsan*—that allowed rabbis to make new legal decisions on purely rational grounds, without scriptural basis, and at times even overriding scripture. The first of these tools is *sevarah,* which literally means "reason," and which refers to "a law which can be arrived at by a process of reasoning," with "no Scriptural warrant."[28] In fact, in the words of the modern-day rabbi Eliezer Berkovits, a ruling by *sevarah* may be "so convincing that it may compel one's conscience to suppress the plain meaning of a Biblical injunction."[29] And this is due to the conviction that there is "complete congruence between the clear reason of man and the purpose and spirit of the Torah."[30] A very Mu'tazilite conviction, so to speak.

This rationality in Judaism justified *takkanah,* or enactment, by rabbis, which is defined as "the addition of a new norm to the overall halakhic system."[31] It also justified *minhag,* or custom, "as a formal source of law and as a basis for the creation of new legal norms."[32] Meanwhile, in Islam, custom, or *urf,* was also considered as a formal source of law by some early Hanafis—the "people of reason"—but its authority was later reduced.[33]

In Judaism, the same rationality also allowed rulings *lifnim mishurat hadin,* or "beyond the letter of the law." It comes from the recognition that one can sometimes strictly apply the religious law, only to come up with absurd or unethical results. One can even be "a scoundrel with Torah license," as the Sephardic rabbi Nachmanides (d. 1270) famously noted.[34]

An interesting detail is that *lifnim mishurat hadin* is defended in Jewish sources with reference to a Biblical command: "Do what is right and good."[35] The implication is that "right and good" are commanded by the scripture, but not necessarily defined by it, pointing to "an ethic independent of Halakha."[36] Remarkably, the Mu'tazilites had made the exact same argument by referring to a key Qur'anic verse that Muslims hear at every Friday sermon: "God commands justice, virtue."[37] If justice was merely what God commands, the Mu'tazilites argued, then the verse would turn into tautology: "God commands what He commands."[38] Yet, due to the rejection of Mu'tazilite theology, precisely that became a dominant view in Islamic exegesis.[39]

Now, these conceptual differences between the legal theories of Islam and Judaism are interesting. What is even more interesting is how they played out in history.

A LONG DIVERGENCE

Islamic law, as noted above, was initially more flexible and advanced, even to the level of attracting Jews to appeal to Sharia courts. But this very problem was noted in the geonic period of Judaism, that is, the late sixth to mid-eleventh centuries, where rabbis sought solutions with "several innovatory halakhic rulings."[40] One of them was a new takkanah, or enactment, that gave the "rebellious wife" the right to obtain a divorce immediately, instead of waiting for the extensive time required by prior Jewish law.[41]

At this time, Islamic law was also quite advanced in commerce. A key reason was that many Muslims, including jurists, were engaged in trade, the very profession of the Prophet, whose market-friendly teachings helped foster a vibrant and creative merchant capitalism.[42] Consequently, Muslim jurists created new financial tools, which were soon emulated by Jews. One of them was *qirad*—later called *commenda* in Europe—which was the form of agreement to establish a limited company with a few partners. Jews soon adopted it, calling it *qirad al-goyim,* or "mutual loan according to non-Jews," implying Muslims.[43] Another Muslim invention was *suftaja,* which literally means "order of payment." These were signed papers that acted as traveler's checks, allowing merchants to journey long distances without the fear of their money being seized. In the words of a contemporary rabbi,

> The suftaja was a financial leap forward, and in a world where this option existed for Muslim businesspeople, Jewish ones would need to make use of it too, or lose any ability to compete in the market.[44]

For Jews, the problem was that their religious law banned *suftaja* (also called *diokni*), because it looked like a loan bearing a form of tacit interest, and interest itself was strictly forbidden. Yet still, a rational reconsideration of the matter led to a *responsum—* legal opinion, akin to Islamic fatwa—that read:

> Our laws, strictly speaking, do not permit the sending of suftaja, since our Sages said, "It is forbidden to send money by diokni." . . . However, since we have seen that people use it, we have begun to sanction it, so that transactions among people should not be voided. So, we have agreed to sanction it in accordance with the traders' law, no more and no less.[45]

Going back to the issue of women's rights, a major development in Judaism took place around the year 1000, when Rabbi Gershom of Germany issued a takkanah that banned polygamy. A man who married more than one wife, the enactment ruled, could face the punishment of *herem,* or excommunication. Supported by other rabbis, this historic enactment practically ended polygamy among Ashkenazi Jews. Moreover, another takkanah by the same Rabbi Gershom annulled the Talmudic law that gave a man the right to divorce his wife without her consent. Women's consent, from then onward, would be required for divorce.[46] In comparison, in Islam, besides some secular laws issued by modern Muslim-majority states, no such religious ban on polygamy or men's unilateral right to divorce has yet taken place.

Also, in inheritance rights, where Islamic law used to be more favorable to women than Jewish law, the changes in the latter turned the tables. "Modern times and customs," as noted in a comparative study, "have seen a reversal of the advantage that Islamic women had over Jewish women."[47] This was partly thanks to secular legislation but also,

> even for orthodox Jews who remain faithful to the restrictions of the Book of Numbers rather than to secular law, the unfairness to women that is inherent in these Biblical restrictions has been recognized in modern times, and mechanisms for mitigating this inequality have been devised.[48]

Gideon Libson, pointing to such examples, argues that compared with Islamic law, Jewish law has proven to be "more dynamic," enabling halakhists "to cope more easily with changing realities."[49] He also roots this legal difference in their theological postulates:

> In effect . . . Islamic law always remained "in heaven," the sole task of the jurist being to reveal it, with no freedom to exercise discretion in laying down the law. In Jewish law, by contrast, the recognized sources grant halakhists extensive authority to develop legal creativity, on the basis of the biblical verse, "It is not in heaven."[50]

The last phrase above, that the divine law "is not in heaven," is from the Bible. Here, we hear Moses saying, "Now what I am commanding you today is not too difficult for you or beyond your reach. . . . [It] is very near you; it is in your mouth and in your heart."[51]

It has been often referred to in the Jewish tradition to support the validity of the human factor in the continuous interpretation of the Halakha. Such Biblical—in other words, pre-Islamic—basis for rationality in Jewish law reminds that it would be wrong to attribute it to the impact of Islamic rationalism. Yet, in Islamic rationalism, articulated by the Mu'tazilites, the Jewish tradition seems to have found a theology that fits its most pragmatic inclinations.

In which, for contemporary Muslims, there may be an interesting irony to ponder, as well as a calling to rediscover the riches of their own religious tradition. That includes Mu'tazilite theology, especially its rational ethics, which has been needlessly rejected in the Sunni tradition for too long.[52] That also includes rationalist approaches within the Sunni tradition itself. Among them is the Maturidi school of theology, which has parallels to Mu'tazilite ethics, and which has lately been gaining the attention it deserves.[53] Also among them are the rationalist methods of the early jurists, such as *istihsan,* that allowed legal verdicts based on human considerations of "reasonableness, fairness, common sense and benefit."[54] Hashim Kamali, a contemporary scholar of Islamic law, even sees its revival as the key to a better future. "A clear and well-defined role for *istihsan,*" he argues, "would hopefully mark a new opening in the evolutionary process of Islamic law."[55]

Meanwhile, in Judaism, there are scholars who believe that its rational tools have not been used enough—especially on the still challenging issue of women's rights. Among them is Naomi Graetz, who has pushed back against "domestic abuse in Jewish communities in Israel and the Diaspora."[56] As a solution, she calls for a new takkanah, that would declare wife-beating a *hilul hashem* (disgrace of God's name) and make women "equal in all matters of personal status."[57] Reading such works by Jewish feminists reminds us of Islamic feminists—scholars such as Amina Wadud or Asma Barlas—while affirming that both traditions have similar problems as well as similar tools for creating solutions.

MAQASID AL-SHARIA AND TA'AMEI HA-MITZVOT

The connection between divine law and human reason has another dimension that also begs attention. It is about the rationality not *besides* the law, but *beneath* the law. In other words, it is about discerning the rationality that God exercised in decreeing His commandments.

In Islam, this idea was first introduced by the Mu'tazilites, with their theory of *aslah,* or "the best," which held that God always acts or commands with a wise purpose. He especially aims for mankind's best interests that are "discoverable by reason, independently of revelation."[58] Conversely, most of the more orthodox theologians, the Ash'arites, believed that divine commandments "have been established by God at His own discretion and without a basis or purpose accessible to human reason."[59] That is why they were cautious in specifying the *'illa,* or "cause," behind God's commandments, worrying that this would take away from God's authority to legislate according to his unbounded will.[60]

Yet still, the Ash'arite theology, and the Sunni jurisprudence it largely underpinned, got more sophisticated over time. Most jurists realized that discerning *'illa,* or cause, behind God's commands, was necessary to draw any "analogy," which was the only way to make Islamic law speak to new facts and situations. Moreover, "late Ash'arites," beginning with al-Juwayni (d. 1085) and his student al-Ghazali (d. 1111), began reintroducing rationalist approaches and concepts to both theology and jurisprudence. That is how they commenced the concept of *maqasid al-sharia,* or "objectives of Sharia," which al-Ghazali designated as the protection of five values: life, religion, progeny, property, and the intellect. God had banned wine, for example, to protect the human intellect from intoxication. Two centuries later, al-Shatibi (d. 1388), a scholar in Muslim Spain, wrote the most comprehensive book on this theory of "objectives," which, despite being forgotten for centuries, has been rediscovered in the modern era, especially by Muslim scholars who are seeking authentic grounds for legal reform.[61]

Now, what is interesting is that a similarly rationalist approach to law, and a similar tension with a more dogmatic orthodoxy, has also appeared in Judaism—and with the unmistakable influence of Islam.

Surely, even before Islam, back in Hellenistic times, some Jewish scholars tried to show the wisdom behind divine laws, referring to rational values that even the pagans could understand. But this ancient effort to explain "reasons for commandments," or ta'amei ha-mitzvot, had a rebirth under Saadia Gaon, thanks to his engagement with Mu'tazilite theology, as well as Greek philosophy, which also was transmitted by Muslims. As we read in Encyclopaedia Judaica:

> Saadia Gaon was the first Jewish thinker to divide the commandments into those obligatory because they are required by reason and those given through revelation. In making this distinction he followed the parallel teachings of the Mu'tazilite kalam but also added a Platonic account. According to the Mu'tazilite exposition, the rational laws are divided into three kinds: gratitude, reverence, and social conduct; and from these three categories he derived many special laws.[62]

So, according to Saadia Gaon, God had issued most of His commandments not of His unfathomable will but for reasons that are intelligible by all human begins. "Thou shalt not kill" was commanded, obviously, to protect human life. Reason could not only understand the wisdom behind such "rational commandments," but reason could issue these laws "even if they had not been written."[63] On the other hand, there were also "laws of revelation," on "matters regarding which reason passes no judgment," on things such as how ordinary days differ from festival ones. It was only these specific commandments about religious rituals where Jews had to rely on revelation alone.[64]

The Islamic, particularly Mu'tazilite, origins of this new rationality in Judaism can't be missed. It is even evident in the very terms Saadia Gaon used for "rational" and "revelational," which were directly taken from the Arabic: *aqliyyat* and *sam'iyyat*.[65]

Then, some two and a half centuries after Saadia, there came the great Moses Maimonides. He not only embraced Saadia's "reasons for commandments" but took them to the next level. For Maimonides, *all* divine laws were rational, including religious commandments. The latter's reasons may not have been readily obvious, but they could still be discovered thanks to careful examination: of not just the commandments themselves—and this is quite important—but also their historical context, which we can learn from secular sources. For example, Maimonides argued that commandments about animal sacrifice, which may seem devoid of any rational justification, were in fact ordered to root out idolatrous practices of ancient pagan nations, which Maimonides described with references to *Nabatean Agriculture,* a book by Ibn Wahshiyya, a tenth-century Iraqi polymath.[66]

A fascinating detail in Maimonides's writing is that while arguing that all religious commandments have a "cause," he uses the Arabic term *'illa,* which is of course the very term used in the Islamic legal tradition for specifying the cause behind a religious ruling.[67]

Does all this mean that Saadia and Maimonides believed in what philosophers call "natural law"—moral laws accessible to all humans by their reason and conscience? Scholars differ on the answer. According to Tamar Rudavsky, their writings at least reflect an "intuitive sense of what is right and wrong," which can be called "natural law sentiments." In other words,

Maimonides is suggesting that there exists a rational, autonomous nature of what is right: these actions have been commanded because they are intrinsically good and right (justly balanced), and can be ascertained independently of halakha.[68]

Which can be also said for both the early Mu'tazilite theology in Islam and at least some articulations of the later *maqasid al-sharia* theory.[69]

Back in Judaism, the "natural law sentiments" of Saadia and Maimonides were certainly not the only way to look at divine law. Maimonides himself notes the dogmatic resistance to *ta'amei ha-mitzvot* in *The Guide for the Perplexed*. "There are persons who find it difficult to give a reason for any of the commandments," he writes. Instead, these people prefer to "assume that the commandments and prohibitions have no rational basis whatever."[70] Jacob ben Asher, a fourteenth-century rabbi, put the argument boldly when he wrote: "We do not need to ask the reason for the commandments, for it is the King's [God's] decree that is obligatory even if we do not know the reason."[71] Against this line of reasoning, Maimonides relied on the Biblical assertion that even non-Israelite nations would appreciate the wisdom of divine commandments, saying, "Surely this great community is a wise and understanding people."[72] Laws that are irrational would not achieve such recognition by people who don't believe in them in the first place.[73]

Today, anti-rational views are still influential in Judaism, especially within "Hasidic legal thought," as Shneur Zalman of Liadi (1745–1812), the founder of the Chabad Hasidic movement, put boldly: "Jewish laws are to be obeyed because God commanded them, not because they are rationally justified."[74] In Islam, the same view is shared by Salafis and other strictly textualist Sunni and Shiite schools.

However, it is remarkable that both Islam and Judaism have rationalist traditions that study the ethical intentions behind divine law. It is even more remarkable that they are historically connected. So, it may be interesting today for Muslim and Jewish scholars of law to study these two traditions together. Joint conferences on *maqasid al-sharia* and *ta'amei ha-mitzvot* could be a thought-provoking enterprise.

Moreover, what we have covered in this chapter so far is only a part of this intertwined history of Islamic and Jewish thought. The rationalistic approach in early Islam included not only theology, which is an articulation of religious faith and law, but also philosophy, which is an investigation on secular grounds. The latter discipline's journey from Islam to Judaism is another fascinating episode in the medieval "symbiosis" between the two faiths, which we will also briefly see.

ATHENS, JERUSALEM, AND MEDINA

Philosophy, or "love of wisdom," was the gift of ancient Greek thinkers to humanity. It referred to the systematized study of diverse aspects of human knowledge, from metaphysics to physics, from astronomy to medicine, from politics to ethics. It was based on the observation of nature and theorizing about it with the rational methods of systematic questioning and logical reasoning.

In contrast, all major Abrahamic religions—Judaism, Christianity, and Islam—were born out of a different source of wisdom: not philosophy, which is built from the bottom up by human minds, but revelation, which is revealed from above by God. Did this mean that followers of these religions had no need for philosophy? Or, quite to the contrary, were they to engage in philosophy to be both wiser in their beliefs and also to discover the very world that God created? In other words, did "Athens," as the saying goes, have anything to offer to "Jerusalem"—and "Medina" as well?

In Islam, this question proved pertinent in the early Abbasid Empire, which we already mentioned as the birthplace of Islamic rationalism. A part of this cultural flourishing was theology, as spearheaded by the Mu'tazilites, but there was an even more audacious trend that began when some Muslim scholars and rulers discovered the riches of Greek philosophy, which was long lost in Europe but was preserved in the East, especially among Christians. The result was the Graeco-Arabic translation movement, during which all known works of Aristotle, Plato, Hippocrates, Galen, Dioscorides, and Ptolemy were translated from either the original Greek sources or their Syriac and Persian translations into Arabic. In the words of a modern expert, Dimitri Gutas, it was a world-changing event that "demonstrated for the first time in history that scientific and philosophical thought are international, not bound to a specific language or culture."[75]

This intellectual input into the Islamic civilization soon gave rise to Islam's own *falasifa,* or "philosophers." Among them were al-Kindi (Alkindus), al-Farabi (Alfaribus), and Ibn Sina (Avicenna), who lived in the Islamic East, followed by Ibn Bajja (Avempace), Ibn Tufayl (Aben Tofail), and Ibn Rushd (Averroes), who lived in the Islamic West, that is, Muslim Spain. They all have Latinized names because they became quite famous and influential in early modern Europe. Especially Ibn Rushd, as the greatest "commentator" on Aristotle, had a huge impact on the European mind, initiating a philosophical awakening that would pave the way to the Renaissance and even the Enlightenment.

This Muslim impact on Christian Europe is widely known, but there was a similarly important influence on the Jewish tradition. "Medieval Jewish philosophy," notes *Encyclopaedia Judaica,* "began in the early tenth century as part of a general cultural revival in the Islamic East, and continued in Muslim countries— North Africa, Spain, and Egypt—for some 300 years."[76] A pioneer of this medieval Jewish philosophy, Isaac Israeli (ca. 955), a scholar from Muslim Spain, was strongly influenced by his Muslim predecessor, al-Kindi.[77] Similarly, Ibn Gabirol (d. 1058), another Jewish philosopher from the peninsula, used the methodology of *Ikhwan al-Safa,* or Brethren of Purity, a secret society of medieval Muslim philosophers, who produced the world's first known encyclopedia.[78]

Then came Moses Maimonides, who wrote his philosophical magnum opus, *The Guide for the Perplexed,* originally in Arabic as *Dalalat al-Ha'irin.* In this book, the influence of Muslim philosophers, especially al-Farabi, can be easily traced. Moreover, in a letter to Samuel ibn Tibbon, the translator of the *Guide* into Hebrew, Maimonides himself explicitly sings the praises of his Muslim predecessors:

> The works of Aristotle are the roots and foundations of all works on the sciences. But they cannot be understood except with the help of commentaries, those of Alexander of Aphrodisias, those of Themistius, and those of Averroes. . . . As for works on logic, one should only study the writings of Abu Nasr al-Farabi. All his writings are faultlessly excellent. One ought to study and understand them. For he is a great man. Though the work of Avicenna may give rise to objections and are not as [good] as those of Abu Nasr al-Farabi, Abu Bakr al-Sa'igh [ibn Bajja] was also a great philosopher, and all his writings are of a high standard.[79]

In many ways, Maimonides's philosophical views were similar to those of his fellow Córdoban Ibn Rushd. Both were strong Aristotelians who defended the legitimacy of philosophical knowledge, and the reality of an intelligible world with its natural laws. Their theories of the intellect were "identical," and they took the same position with regard to the relation of faith and knowledge.[80]

No wonder, then, that besides Maimonides himself, Ibn Rushd also became a beacon of medieval Jewish philosophy. He even proved "next to Maimonides, the most important influence."[81] Soon after Ibn Rushd's passing, Jewish scholars in Spain, France, and Italy translated almost all his books into Hebrew, and even wrote supercommentaries on them. The result was an intellectual movement today called "Jewish Averroism." It played a major role in the "medieval Jewish enlightenment," which was a precursor to the Jewish Enlightenment of the eighteenth century that we will soon see.[82] Among the notables of this movement was Moses of Narbonne, who translated into Hebrew *Hayy ibn Yaqzan,* the philosophical novel by Ibn Rushd's mentor, Ibn Tufayl. Pico della Mirandola, the key philosopher of the Renaissance, would be fascinated by this book, which had a big impact on the early Enlightenment as well through Latin, English, and Dutch translations, as I related in my earlier book *Reopening Muslim Minds.*[83]

That is why the *Jewish Encyclopedia* praises Ibn Rushd, saying, "Jewish literature . . . is indebted to him, directly and indirectly, for many valuable contributions."[84] Yet we should add that contribution is mutual: thanks to the Jewish tradition, today we know much more about Ibn Rushd than we would otherwise. Because while more than a dozen of Ibn Rushd's original Arabic works have been lost, their translations, mostly in Hebrew and a few in Latin, have survived.[85] Thanks to these ancient translations, we now have a more complete access to the legacy of the greatest Islamic philosopher of all time.

But why would the works of a Muslim thinker, who wrote only in Arabic, survive more safely in Hebrew? Does this tell us something bigger, deeper?

PHILOSOPHY'S FATE IN ISLAM

The question above takes us to a larger question: the fate of philosophy in the medieval Islamic world.

This has been a long and heated debate, especially since Ernest Renan's controversial 1852 book, *Averroès et l'Averroïsme,* or *Averroës and Averroism.* Here the French Orientalist argued that the philosophical revival in the early Islamic civilization was fundamentally alien to the religion and "the Arab mind," which ultimately suffocated it. In other words, "Islamic philosophy" was made possible not thanks to Islam but rather in spite of it. This thesis initiated a long-lasting "Orientalist" narrative, which has been countered by many critics, both at the academic and popular levels.

Much of this debate focused on the impact of al-Ghazali (d. 1111), perhaps the greatest theologian of orthodox Sunni Islam whom we mentioned before, whose landmark book, *Incoherence of the Philosophers,* was key to this story. Here, al-Ghazali had in fact appreciated the neutral aspects of philosophy—such as logic, mathematics, or astronomy—but also condemned "the philosophers" for accepting metaphysical Greek ideas, such as the eternity of the world. This could have been a valid criticism, but al-Ghazali went as far as accusing these Muslim thinkers unfairly of *zandaqa,* or clandestine apostasy, which came with a license to execute them.[86] A few generations after al-Ghazali, Ibn Rushd would respond to him with a smartly titled rejoinder, *Incoherence of the Incoherence,* but it would be al-Ghazali who set the tone for the Islamic world.

That is all why Orientalists like Renan accused al-Ghazali for "killing philosophy" among Muslims, while others accused this very critique as shallow and biased, noting that al-Ghazali instead helped incorporate some Greek disciplines, especially logic, into Sunni theology and jurisprudence. There is certainly some truth in this defense of the great Sunni theologian, which is today the dominant tone in many academic circles.[87] But this defense seems to miss the big difference between "Islamizing" aspects of philosophy and engaging with it as a separate, yet legitimate, search for truth.[88] The first approach helps "argue for one pre-determined thesis," while the latter approach allows for "open-ended rational investigation of all reality."[89] Moreover, regardless of the nuances of his criticisms, with his harsh verdict, al-Ghazali ultimately gave a bad reputation to "the philosophers," and also expanded the scope of thought crimes in Islam.[90]

Nevertheless, the real question here is not what al-Ghazali

did to philosophy in Islam, but what happened to philosophy in Islam? Getting an answer from the prominent American Muslim scholar Shaykh Hamza Yusuf may help, as he is not a critic of al-Ghazali but rather a follower of the mainstream Sunni tradition that al-Ghazali represents. Yet still, Yusuf does concede that philosophy—or "Athena"—"died" in Islam after the early golden age, while flourishing in Christian Europe:

> As Athena receded in the background for Muslims, and the last great Greek adherent, Ibn Rushd, found his books attacked, the Europeans, through Spain, had a great Greek awakening to their Semitic religion through the Muslim intellectual legacy that was spreading among them. Europe reunited with Athena through the Muslim learning that seeped into Europe, and a great "rebirth" occurred—literally, the "Renaissance." In the Muslim world, however, Athena became increasingly anathematized. . . . With the exception of the Shia tradition and small pockets of Sunni metaphysical studies, Greek thought all but died in the Muslim world.[91]

This "divorce between Athena and Medina," Yusuf adds, "explains much of what went wrong with Muslim civilization." While "Muslims developed greater emphasis on the religious sciences," secular sciences began to recede. Logic "lost its edge," whereas arithmetic, geometry, and astronomy "languished and eventually disappeared from religious training."[92] Some wise men, such as the Ottoman polymath Katip Çelebi (1609–1657), had realized the problem early on, but it would not become clear to most Muslims until colonial armies appeared at their door with newer technologies, better weapons, and modern institutions.[93]

But why did this "divorce between Athena and Medina" really take place? Besides racist essentialism, or the fixation on al-Ghazali, there are structural explanations offered by the historian George Makdisi (1920–2002). One is the lack of corporations in Islamic law, as "artificial persons endowed with legal capacity," which kept Muslim intuitions "static" compared with European ones. The other is the encroachment of the rulers on the religious scholars.[94] More recently, the political scientist Ahmet Kuru also demonstrated the same structural impediments. Accordingly, despite the remarkable diversity of thought in the early centuries of Islam, an alliance between political rulers and conservative clergy emerged after the eleventh century—"the ulama-state alliance"—which curbed intellectual dynamism, including philosophical thought.[95]

Such analyses can help compare the Islamic world with Christendom. But what about Judaism? What could be its structural pros and cons?

PHILOSOPHY'S FATE IN JUDAISM

As we have seen, the Jewish engagement with Greek philosophy was largely thanks to the golden age of Islam. This "brilliant period of Mahometan ascendancy," as the British philosopher Alfred North Whitehead (1861–1947) once noted, birthed a "joint association of Mahometan and Jewish activity in the promotion of civilization," which ultimately enlightened Christendom. "Thomas Aquinas received Aristotle from it, Roger Bacon received the foundations of modern science from it."[96]

Yet still, just like in Islam, philosophy faced a religious reaction in Judaism. An early dissenter was Judah Halevi (d. 1141), a compatriot of Maimonides who preceded him by a generation. "Let not Greek wisdom tempt you, for it bears flowers only and no fruit," he wrote, adding: "Why should I search for bypaths, and complicated ones at that, and leave the main road?"[97] His stance has been compared to that of al-Ghazali, whose book, *Incoherence of the Philosophers,* seems to have influenced him.[98] In the next several centuries, Maimonides kept receiving reactions from his more dogmatic coreligionists, initiating what is known in Jewish history as the Maimonidean controversy. At a low point, in the thirteenth century, a Talmudist named Solomon ben Abraham even instigated the Dominican monks in the South of France to burn *The Guide for the Perplexed*. "You burn your heretics," he said to the Christians, "persecute ours also."[99] "The majority of the Jews of Provence," he added with regret, "are perverted by the heretical writings of Maimuni."[100]

However, such dogmatic reactions against Jewish philosophy could not eradicate it. In the words of a modern scholar of philosophy, Oliver Leaman, while "philosophy in the Sunni world of Islam did not really recover from the pressures it felt from such thinkers as al-Ghazali," the Jewish story proved to be different:

> In Judaism, there were also pressures against the pursuit of philosophy, and Maimonides was often challenged by Jews who thought that he overemphasized the significance of reason.... Yet philosophy did become part of the official curriculum of most of the Jewish legal and commentatorial schools: In the view of most of the Jewish authoritative thinkers, it was too useful a way of proceeding not to be employed and combined with more traditional sources of knowledge.[101]

So, what could be the reason beneath these different trajectories? I believe there is again a structural explanation that is all too obvious: Jews did not have a state of their own that could define the true faith and eradicate its heresies. (Hence, the favor of book burning was asked of the ruling Christians.) Rabbis were far from being free-speech advocates, and they did issue various bans on the *minim,* or the heretics, through the centuries. However, "The absence of a universal authority made it possible for certain communities to overlook the ban," and this "effectively enlarged the range of permissible theological ideas."[102] The same permissibility seems to have allowed philosophy to endure as well.

In other words, having their own powerful religious states may, ultimately, not have been a blessing for Muslims. Conversely, being a powerless minority, despite all the discrimination and persecution that came with it, may have been a blessing for Jews, allowing them to preserve traditions that they would use successfully in the modern world.

Today, I would urge my coreligionists, Muslims, to reflect on these trajectories and their consequences. In Islam, the most troubling legacy of our imperial past is still haunting us: the laws, and the urges, to suppress perceived "apostates," "blasphemers," or "heretics."[103] They cause endless sectarian tension and persecution, while curbing critical and innovative thought. In Judaism, however, a religion long accustomed to living without state power, divisions are less bitter and ideas are freer. Jews are not going after their own *minim* and *kofrim,* or "heretics" and "infidels," which may be one of the keys to their remarkable success in the modern world— instead of some mythical conspiratorial power.

In fact, the Jewish success in the modern world begs for more attention from us Muslims, as its very genesis is connected to Islam's past and present, in intricate ways that are noticed by only a few. Hence we will now turn our attention to that genesis, the Jewish Enlightenment, while also discovering what it means today for both Islam and the West.

THE JEWISH HASKALAH AND
THE ISLAMIC ENLIGHTENMENT

*Can a religion centered on fidelity to ancient and divinely
revealed commandments be connected in any meaningful
way to modern sociopolitical theory?
In the light of Mendelssohn, the answer is "yes."*

—H. C. Hillier, scholar of theology and philosophy[1]

SO FAR IN THIS BOOK, WE HAVE FOCUSED ON THE STORY OF JEWS
in the Muslim world. We have seen that it was often more amia-
ble than in Christendom, as the latter had a long history of religious antisemitism that made Jewish life precarious for centuries.
"While the Hebrew and the Moslem lived together congenially and
explored the realms of science hand in hand," as Maurice Harris
contrasted a century ago, in Europe, Jews remained a "helpless minority in a bigoted environment." There were brighter spots, too,
but often theirs was "a life of sufferance with its details of legal
restrictions," as well as "humiliations of badge and ghetto."[2]

One consequence of this hostile environment was self-isolation
by the Central and Eastern European Jews, or the Ashkenazim.
Unlike Jews of Spain, or the Sephardim, most of whom lived in
the freer lands of Islam and were strongly influenced by Arabic
culture and Greek philosophy, European Jews closed themselves

to outside influence. Especially in the post-Reformation period, when Europe was swept by religious fanaticism and sectarian violence, Ashkenazi Jewry "increasingly isolated itself in a world of Talmudic casuistry and mysticism."[3]

However, toward the end of the seventeenth century, in the same Europe, something new would appear under the sun that would radically transform the Jewish condition as well.

This novelty was the Enlightenment, or the intellectual and philosophical movement that influenced European societies—first in Holland and England, then in France and Germany—with new ideas of science, reason, philosophy, and, most important of all, religious tolerance. The latter was partly a fruit of hard-learned lessons of the Protestant Reformation, which had initiated the most intolerant period in Christian history, where Catholics and Protestants persecuted and slaughtered each other for almost two centuries.[4] Finally exhausted from this religious zealotry, some Christians began to seek a way forward. Pioneering thinkers among them, such as the English philosopher John Locke (1632–1704), the Irish writer John Toland (1670–1722), and the French author Pierre Bayle (1647–1706), argued that the solution was in explicitly tolerating all differences of belief.[5] For this end, states had to give up asserting religious truths and suppressing heresies, while just protecting the "commonwealth," or the well-being of all, transcending group boundaries. Also, Christians had to realize that there were universal ethical truths recognizable by all people—namely natural law—so even "heretics" and "infidels" could be morally upright individuals.

This toleration idea was initially focused on ending conflicts among Christians themselves, as evident in Locke's writings, but it would soon extend to all groups, including Jews. Toland made this argument emphatically, to the shock of many, in his 1714 pamphlet: *Reasons for Naturalizing the Jews in Great Britain and Ireland on the Same Foot with All Other Nations.*[6]

However, not every Enlightenment thinker would prove as ecumenical as Toland, as their universalism was curtailed by their political concerns or cultural prejudices. For some, it was especially hard to be too liberal toward Jews, as the historian Michael A. Meyer explains in *The Origins of the Modern Jew*:

> As the eighteenth century wore on, it became more and more apparent that the concepts of a universal human nature, universal natural law, and universal rationality made the exclusion of the Jew a gross anomaly. But it was one thing to draw the conclusion abstractly and another to apply it. For most of the writers of the eighteenth century, particularly on the Continent, the flesh-and-blood Jew with his beard, strange garments, and wholly irrational ceremonial law seemed somewhat less than a human being.[7]

Many Christians at the time also believed that Jews were "intolerant sectarians who looked down on gentiles and hated them," without realizing that they themselves had greatly contributed to the Jews' suspicion of the gentile world.[8]

Moreover, many Christians at the time also were suspicious about the very nature of the Jewish religion. Among them was one of the towering figures of the whole Enlightenment project: the German philosopher Immanuel Kant (1724–1804). In his view, Christianity was the perfect religion to match Enlightenment values, thanks to its "idealized, spiritualized ethical teachings based on pure love."[9] In contrast, Judaism failed to create ethical human beings because it demanded "only external obedience to statutes and laws."[10] The core problem, Kant added, was that Judaism was "originally established . . . [as] a collection of merely statutory laws supporting a political state."[11] He even went as far as to denigrate Judaism as a "political organization which is only masquerading as religion."[12]

Now, in case you have not already noticed, these eighteenth-century European concerns about Judaism sound quite similar to contemporary Western concerns about Islam. Today, it is the latter religion that is distrusted by an Enlightenment humanism—real or ostensible—which does not have a high opinion of the humanist potential of this unfamiliar religion. Today, it is Islam that is seen as hopelessly legalistic and coercive. Today, it is Islam that is denigrated as a "political organization which is only masquerading as religion." This accusation is indeed repeated almost verbatim: "Islam is not even a religion," a Republican lawmaker from Oklahoma claimed in 2014. "It is a political system that uses a deity to advance its agenda of global conquest."[13]

That is why the Jewish response to this eighteenth-century challenge is also quite relevant to Islam today. And that is why we will take a closer look at the brightest Jewish mind of the time who rose to the challenge.

LOCKE, MENDELSSOHN, AND RELIGIOUS FREEDOM

Moses Mendelssohn was born in 1729 to a poor Jewish family in Dessau, Prussia, at a time when Jews did not yet have equal rights with Christians. He was the son of a Torah scribe, and he studied under a local rabbi, gaining mastery of the Jewish tradition. But after moving to Berlin at the age of fourteen, following his rabbi, he also did something that was not expected of Jews at the time: study ancient and modern European languages and literatures, as well as mathematics, logic, and philosophy. He perused the works of Enlightenment thinkers such as John Locke, Gottfried Wilhelm Leibniz, and Christian Wolff. His own writings soon brought him fame as "the German Socrates," while many Christians were surprised to hear that there could really be such a "philosophically minded" Jew. After winning the Prussian Academy of Arts literary prize in 1763, the king of Prussia exempted him from the legal disabilities to which Jews were subjected. Now he was a rare *Schutzjude,* or "protected Jew."

Yet Mendelssohn was not only interested in advancing his

career. He also wanted to uplift his people. Hence, one of his life-long struggles was to establish equal rights and religious freedom for everyone, including Jews. In fact, he proved to be "the first Jew to argue publicly in favor of the right to liberty of conscience and the separation of church and state."[14] If these liberal ideas had been fully accepted by Christians, then Europe would have become a safer place for all, including the much-persecuted descendants of Israel.

However, there was a question that Mendelssohn soon had to face: Was Judaism itself compatible with these liberal ideas? Quite to the contrary, wasn't Judaism born with a theocratic state that used ample means of coercion? The questions were unavoidable because the Laws of Moses clearly included harsh religious decrees. The Jew who violated the Sabbath should be killed: "The man shall surely be put to death; all the congregation shall stone him."[15] Those who "blasphemeth the name of the Lord" should also be killed.[16] Those who said, "Let us go and serve other gods," must also be "surely" executed.[17]

These Biblical laws, which unmistakably call for religious coercion, had to be addressed by anyone who believed in this scripture while also advocating for religious freedom. But how?

One answer, a specifically Christian one, had come from John Locke. In his landmark book *A Letter Concerning Toleration*, after arguing that "the magistrate," or the state, should tolerate every creed including even an "idolatrous church," Locke added:

> But it may be urged farther that, by the law of Moses, idolaters were to be rooted out. True, indeed, by the law of Moses; but that is not obligatory to us Christians. Nobody pretends that everything generally enjoined by the law of Moses ought to be practiced by Christians. . . . "Hear, O Israel," sufficiently restrains the obligations of the law of Moses only to that people. And this consideration alone is answer enough unto those that

urge the authority of the law of Moses for the inflicting of capital punishment upon idolaters.[18]

So, Christians had an easy way out: the law of Moses was just
not binding on them. Jesus Christ had relieved them from most
of the Old Testament rules, including these. The latter were only
relevant to the specific people addressed in the call "Hear, O
Israel."

But what about the children of Israel themselves? Were they
not bound by the law of Moses?

A practical answer to this theoretical question was posed by
the tragic history of Israel itself: after losing their sovereignty to
imperial Rome in the first century of the Common Era, Jews simply lost the political power to implement most punitive decrees
of the law of Moses. There was no Jewish state, so there was no
authority to root out idolaters or blasphemers.

However, giving up religious coercion in practice did not
amount to giving it up in theory as well. The contemporary historian Allan Arkush explains how traditional Judaism remained conceptually at odds with liberalism, at least in theory, for centuries:

> Traditional Judaism is inherently theocratic. Indeed, the term
> theocracy itself stems from the pen of a Jewish writer, the his-
> torian Josephus, who used it to describe the regime prevailing
> in ancient Israel, where, in his words, "all sovereignty and all
> authority were in the hands of God." From the days of Jose-
> phus to modern times, the Jews lacked a state of their own, and
> their theocracy was, therefore, more theoretical than real. It
> existed mostly in blueprints—the most elaborate of which are
> found in Maimonides' legal compilation, the Mishneh Torah.
> Nevertheless, throughout the ages when the Jews did not live
> in a polity governed in accordance with what they took to be
> God's laws, they never ceased to pray for its reestablishment.[19]

Moreover, even in the absence of a theocratic Jewish state, Jewish communities did preserve some religious coercion enforced by rabbinic authority. Accordingly, in the communal space granted to them by Christian or Muslim rulers, rabbis could punish the members of their congregation for religious offenses. They could issue a *herem,* which is a kind of severe excommunication that amounted to "civil death."[20] It included expulsion from the synagogue, permanent or temporary banishment from town, and public denunciations and reprimands.[21]

Therefore, even in the diaspora, "Jewish religion was not voluntary," as the late Israeli philosopher Yirmiyahu Yovel once put it. "It contained an element of coercion." It remained as "a semi-theocratic government of the kind which Mendelssohn opposed."[22] So, how could Mendelssohn really oppose such religious coercion without betraying religion itself?

This question was not only implicitly obvious. It was also explicitly raised by some Christians of the time. Among them was a Prussian theologian named August Friedrich Cranz, who published an anonymous pamphlet titled *The Search for Light and Right: An Epistle to Moses Mendelssohn.* Freedom was a prerequisite for true religion, Cranz argued, because "religion without conviction is not possible at all; and every forced religious act is no longer such."[23] On this, he was in full agreement with Mendelssohn. But therein lay the problem, according to Cranz, because the same Mendelssohn was also loyal to Judaism, while an "armed ecclesiastical law still remains the firmest groundwork of the Jewish polity."[24] Therefore, Cranz publicly challenged Mendelssohn, asking:

> The whole ecclesiastical system of Moses was not a mere instruction in, and a guide to, duties, but there was at the same time, the most rigid church-discipline attached to it. The arm of the church was weaponed with the sword of malediction. . . .

Then, good Mr. Mendelssohn, how can you profess attachment
to the religion of your forefathers, while you are shaking its fab-
ric, by oppugning the ecclesiastical code established by Moses
in consequence of divine revelation?[25]

Now, in case you haven't noticed, this also is similar to questions posed in the contemporary West to liberal-minded Muslims: If you really believe in freedom, how can you remain a
Muslim, as your religion was born and raised with jihad and conquest and a religious law that rooted out idolaters, apostates, and
blasphemers?

Therefore, Mendelssohn's answer is not just historically important but also contemporarily relevant.

HISTORICIZING THEOCRACY

In fact, about a century before Mendelssohn, another Jew had
answered Cranz's question, but in a scandalously heretical way.
This was Baruch Spinoza (1632–1677), the famous philosopher
of Amsterdam who, like Mendelssohn, was raised with a Talmudic education but went on to become a secular thinker who
called into question much of the legal foundation of Judaism.
In his 1670 book, *Theological-Political Treatise,* he admitted that
Mosaic law was indeed the coercive law of an ancient Jewish
theocracy—only to argue that since the theocracy was gone, all
its laws should be gone as well. Since Judaism was born with a
state, he thought, the end of the state made Judaism itself defunct.

This argument was a challenge to the very foundations of the
Jewish religion. No wonder Spinoza was condemned by the very
religious law he wanted to abolish. For his "monstrous deeds" and
"abominable heresies," he was issued the harshest writ of *herem*
ever pronounced by the Sephardic community of Amsterdam.[26]

Mendelssohn, however, was no Spinoza. He was a pious Jew

who believed in his religion and observed its practices. So, he was destined not to be a heretic, but a reformer.

His reform, especially on the thorny issue of religious freedom and coercion, came in the magnum opus Mendelssohn published in 1783: *Jerusalem, or on Religious Power and Judaism*. It was mainly a response to Cranz. Against him, and other suspicious Christians of the time, Mendelssohn painstakingly argued that Judaism, in fact, could be separated from "religious power" and instead be a volitional religion.

To build his argument, Mendelssohn began with accepting what is obvious. Under Moses, Jews were ruled by a theocracy:

> In this original constitution, state and religion were not conjoined, but one; not connected, but identical. Man's relation to society and his relation to God coincided and could never come into conflict. God, the Creator and Preserver of the world, was at the same time the King and Regent of this nation. . . . Under this constitution these crimes [such as blasphemy] could and, indeed, had to be punished civilly, not as erroneous opinion, not as unbelief, but as misdeeds, as sacrilegious crimes aimed at abolishing or weakening the authority of the lawgiver and thereby undermining the state itself.[27]

Yet this "Mosaic constitution" did not last long. "Already in the days of the prophet Samuel," Mendelssohn explained, "the edifice developed a fissure which widened more and more until the parts broke asunder completely."[28] This was a reference to the moment when Jews asked Prophet Samuel to have "a king to lead us . . . like all the other nations."[29] So, even at a time of Jewish sovereignty—and that is a crucial nuance—the "Mosaic constitution" had begun to collapse. Then came the Roman occupation, which ended Jewish sovereignty itself. Mendelssohn explained how these historical developments put a definitive end to the Mosaic constitution:

As the rabbis expressly state, with the destruction of the Temple, all corporal and capital punishments and, indeed, even monetary fines, insofar as they are only national, have ceased to be legal. Perfectly in accordance with my principles, and inexplicable without them! The civil bonds of the nation were dissolved; religious offenses were no longer crimes against the state; and the religion, as religion, knows of no punishment, no other penalty than the one the remorseful sinner voluntarily imposes on himself. It knows of no coercion, uses only the staff [called] gentleness, and affects only mind and heart.[30]

At this point, one may wonder whether Mendelssohn saw this historical progression—loss of the Jewish state—as something good for the Jews. No, he did not make that argument. But he did infer a religious lesson from mundane workings of human history. The lesson was that "the Mosaic constitution . . . existed only once," and it was not something repeatable. At least Jews didn't need to long for its revival. "It has disappeared," Mendelssohn wrote, "and only the Omniscient knows among what people and in what century something similar will again be seen."[31]

With such points, Mendelssohn opposed Christian critics of Judaism, such as Cranz, who saw it as inherently theocratic. But he also opposed Spinoza, who saw the end of Jewish theocracy as the end of Jewish religion as well. In the words of Alexander Altmann, one of Mendelssohn's modern-day students,

In Mendelssohn's view, then, the split between state and religion, which had been sealed by the destruction of the Temple, did not by any means signify the end of the covenant between God and the Jewish people. The Law had remained as valid as before. Transgressions were no longer crimes against the state (which had become defunct) and were therefore no longer punishable as such. . . . Once the union of state and religion had been dissolved, Judaism had become a mere religion and that all coercive power had been renounced.[32]

So, Judaism, as a religion, would live forever, without any need for "religious power." Parts of Mosaic law that were connected to power were obsolete, but "those of its parts which apply to the individual" remained valid, and they were to be observed piously.[33]

To strengthen his case, Mendelssohn referred to an authority, which was an unusual one for a Jew. This was "the founder of the Christian religion," who had given good counsel to his first-century fellow Jews: "Render unto Caesar that which is Caesar's and unto God what is God's."[34] Embracing this advice by Jesus of Nazareth, Mendelssohn wrote:

> And even today, no wiser advice than this can be given to the House of Jacob. Adapt yourselves to the morals and the constitution of the land to which you have been removed; but hold fast to the religion of your fathers too.[35]

Today, scholars have different opinions about how successful Mendelssohn was in building his theological argument for a coercion-free Judaism. But his historical success is evident, as Allan Arkush, the translator of *Jerusalem* and an expert on its author's thought, observes:

> Mendelssohn had succeeded in providing a rationale for the dissolution of what we might call Judaism's coercive, collectivist dimension. He had transformed the Jewish religion into something purely voluntary. Mendelssohn was the first Jewish thinker to declare it to be entirely up to the individual Jew, and not his rabbi or his communal leaders, to determine whether he would fulfill his duty to live in accordance with its demands. He thus showed, for the first time, how one could render the Jewish religion basically compatible with liberalism.[36]

This compatibility between Judaism and liberalism would be quite incomplete, however, if it relied on only the historical development of the Jewish religion. There was also a need to justify liberalism, which itself wasn't based on Judaism. It was instead based on human reason, to which Mendelssohn granted significant epistemic authority. And this part of his reasoning also deserves our attention.

FROM MOSES TO MOSES

An important and defining aspect of Moses Mendelssohn was his deep interest in a great medieval Jewish thinker we have repeatedly met in this book: Moses Maimonides, whose philosophical masterpiece, *The Guide for the Perplexed,* was an eye-opener for the young Mendelssohn. He would even later joke that his famously crooked posture, which in truth came out of an illness in his childhood, was caused by many hours spent studying the works of his medieval namesake. He did not always agree with Maimonides, but he was certainly fascinated with his "synthesis of Judaism with secular knowledge."[37]

That is how medieval Jewish philosophy, which had its roots in the Muslim *falasifa,* as we have seen, had a revival in the writings of Mendelssohn. Among his borrowings, which he reiterates in *Jerusalem,* was the medieval adage of Judeo-Islamic philosophers: "Truth cannot be in conflict with truth." One "truth" here was divine revelation, which was specific to certain peoples such as Jews and Muslims. The other "truth" were things that are known by human reason, which included ethical values that Mendelssohn explicitly called "natural law."[38] These were "laws of wisdom and goodness, and the things which can serve as means of attaining felicity." They included the ideal of justice as well as "rights, duties, and contracts."[39]

Now, here is the key point: since revelation was time-bound and specific, whereas the requirements of reason were rather universal, it was the latter that came first. That is why Mendels-sohn, to the surprise of a Christian critic, spoke of "eternal truths which *religion should teach* [emphasis added]."[40] This was, no-tably, the opposite of dogmatic religious thought: that whatever religion teaches, those are the eternal truths.

These "eternal truths" were taught by none other than God. "Not by sounds or written characters," however, "but through creation itself and its internal relations, which are legible and comprehensible to all men."[41] Judaism, therefore, just like other religions, acted as "reminders of universal truths of reason."[42] Against those who insisted otherwise—that there is no truth be-yond a particular religion—Mendelssohn argued as follows:

> Those who hold this view detract from the omnipotence or the goodness of God. . . . He was, in their opinion, good enough to reveal to men those truths on which their felicity depends, but not omnipotent, or not good enough to grant them the powers to discover these truths themselves. Moreover, by this assertion one makes the necessity of a supernatural revelation more universal than revelation itself. If, therefore, mankind must be corrupt and miserable without revelation, why has the far greater part of mankind lived without true revelation from time immemorial? Why must the two Indies wait un-til it pleases the Europeans to send them a few comforters to bring them a message without which they can, according to this opinion, live neither virtuously nor happily?[43]

In other words, God's own goodness and greatness necessi-tated universal truths that are accessible by reason. And therefore, any God-given religion, including Judaism, could simply not clash with the requirements of reason.[44]

While inheriting this rationalist frame of mind from Maimonides—as well as Joseph Albo (d. 1444), who was the first Jewish thinker to use the term "natural law"—Mendelssohn took it to a new level: he emphasized a value that earlier generations did not speak about: "liberty of conscience," which he defined as mankind's "noblest treasure." It was a crucial part of "man's natural liberty, which makes up a great portion of his felicity."[45]

Therefore, no true religion could violate liberty of conscience. Instead, a true religion would work only by appealing to free conscience. In Mendelssohn's words:

> True, divine religion arrogates to itself no power over opinions and judgments. . . . It knows only the power to win over by arguments, to persuade and create felicity by persuasion. True, divine religion need employ neither arms nor fingers by which to take hold of believers. It is all mind and heart.[46]

Conversely, religious coercion would not even be helpful to true religion, because it would not lead to genuine piety. Mendelssohn put it exquisitely:

> Religious actions without religious thoughts are mere puppetry, not service of God. They themselves must therefore proceed from the spirit and can neither be purchased by reward nor compelled by punishment.[47]

From this premise, Mendelssohn went on to argue for separating religion from the state because it was in the very nature of the state to dictate laws and enforce their application, which was fundamentally different from the way religion operates:

> The state gives orders and coerces, religion teaches and persuades. The state prescribes laws, religion commandments. The state has physical power and uses it when necessary; the power of religion is love and beneficence. . . . The state will therefore be content, if need be, with mechanical deeds, with works without spirit, with conformity of action without con-

formity in thought. Even the man who does not believe in laws must obey them, once they have received official sanction . . . not so with religion! It knows no act without conviction, no work without spirit, no conformity indeed without conformity in the mind.[48]

To advance this argument, Mendelssohn also utilized a concept that we have seen before: *ta'amei ha-mitzvot,* or "reasons for commandments." This was a contribution of Saadia Gaon and Moses Maimonides, with some roots in the rationalist theology of the Muslim Mu'tazilites. Mendelssohn embraced the concept, only to give it a new meaning, as the contemporary scholar Michah Gottlieb explains in *Faith and Freedom: Moses Mendelssohn's Theological-Political Thought*:

Following Maimonides, Mendelssohn maintains that the ritual laws always had a second, religious purpose involving maintaining proper metaphysical and moral beliefs by opposing idolatry. For Mendelssohn, however, this religious purpose was not based on coercion but rather on the free acceptance of halakha and of the universal metaphysical truths to which it directs one's contemplation since there is no value in religious rituals qua religious acts being practiced without conviction.[49]

With such reasoning and rethinking of his religious tradition, Mendelssohn not only made Judaism compatible with liberalism but also advanced the latter philosophy, especially with regard to religious freedom, "further than even Locke did."[50] He boldly advocated tolerance for all, including "pagans, Jews, Moslems, and adherents of natural religion."[51] The very ending of his book *Jerusalem* puts his plea to freedom poetically:

Let everyone be permitted to speak as he thinks, to invoke God after his own manner or that of his fathers, and to seek eternal salvation where he thinks he may find it, as long as he does not disturb public felicity and acts honestly toward the civil laws, toward you and his fellow citizens. Let no one in your states be a searcher of hearts and a judge of thoughts; let no one assume a right that the Omniscient has reserved to himself alone![52]

A "RELIGIOUS ENLIGHTENMENT"

Three years after writing those words, in 1786, Mendelssohn passed away. His writings had not yet helped emancipate the German Jews, but they did initiate a tectonic shift toward that end.

On the one hand, Mendelssohn became one of the pillars of what the historian David Sorkin calls "the religious Enlightenment," which, unlike the secular Enlightenment, didn't clash with religion but rather harmonized it with "reasonableness . . . toleration and natural law."[53] This intellectual movement also built the foundations of a political liberalism that didn't oppose religion but rather grew "within" it.[54]

One the other hand, Mendelssohn initiated a new era among his own people. It is called "the Jewish Enlightenment," or the Haskalah. The term came from the Hebrew word *sekhel,* which means "reason" or "intellect." It implied that Jews should embrace universal rationality by studying all the secular sciences and joining the modern culture of European societies. It also implied that Jews should look back at their religious tradition with less dogmatism and more reason, to be able to introduce reforms.

The Haskalah, which began in the 1770s and continued for more than a century, transformed much of European Jewry. Those who embraced its ideals, the *maskilim,* fully integrated into European society, delving into secular culture, arts and sciences, and philosophy. They mastered gentile languages such as German and French, joined modern schools, and opened new ones where Jewish students could study not just the Torah and

Talmud but also arithmetic, geography, history, and the natural sciences. Jewish girls and women, who received only minimal religious training before, began to study music and modern languages, secular novels, poetry, or plays. Arranged marriages, which Mendelssohn had criticized, became less common.[55] At first, more conversative Jews—who later would be called the Orthodox—were resistant to the Haskalah, but over time most of them accepted many parts of it. Hence, today they are called modern Orthodox. Conversely, those who categorically rejected the Haskalah became known as the ultra-Orthodox.

Ultimately, even with varying degrees, Jewish communities joined the modern liberal world—unless they were targeted by the vitriolic forces of antisemitism. While some Jews went fully secular, those who remained practicing did so thanks not to coercion but volition. In other words, the transformation that Mendelssohn had hoped to fully establish in Judaism—giving up coercive power in the name of religion—was largely accomplished. Jews embraced freedom, and Jewish law became "less about commands imposed from the outside than about an internal desire to follow in God's path."[56]

Meanwhile, Jews increasingly emphasized the meaning of their chosenness in the way that Mendelssohn had defined: "not as innate superiority, but as responsibility to promote the perfection of society as a whole."[57] Joining the gentile world was also a basis to contributing to it.

For our story, what is perhaps most interesting is that this modern Jewish Enlightenment, the Haskalah, had its conceptual roots in the medieval Jewish Enlightenment, which itself had roots in the medieval Islamic Enlightenment.[58] Which also means that Islam, in its own repository, has a rich heritage that may lead to an Islamic Enlightenment similar to the Haskalah.

So, could there be such a modern Islamic Enlightenment?

IS ISLAM A "RELIGION, NOT A STATE"?

An Islamic Enlightenment has in fact been in the air since the nineteenth century, when some Muslim statesmen, scholars, and intellectuals began to absorb modern values and institutions that they had observed and admired in the West. These included modern science and medicine, public education with new secular disciplines, more active participation of women in public life, democratic institutions such as the popular vote and political representation, and liberal values such as freedom of speech and religion. However, this very trend has provoked its own reaction—the forces of "counter-Enlightenment," which assert a religious orthodoxy that is, to varying degrees, at odds with these modern values and institutions.[59] Today, the tension, if not the conflict, between these forces is still present in all four corners of the Muslim world.

An important figure in the late nineteenth-century Islamic Enlightenment—also called *Nahda,* or Awakening—was the Egyptian religious scholar Muhammad Abduh (1849–1905). "Like Mendelssohn," as Oliver Leaman puts it comparatively, "he argued for the compatibility of religion with modernity, and for the superiority of his own religion's rational credentials."[60] Abduh was proud of the foundations of Islam, but critical of some aspects of its traditions. His writings would inspire the intellectual trend often called Islamic modernism.

Islamic modernism has impacted the Muslim world in irreversible ways, as seen in the widespread appreciation of modern science and technology, which often did not face major reactions from traditionalists. However, there has remained a bone of contention, which is also the key issue Mendelssohn had addressed in *Jerusalem*: "religious power." The modern world envisions secular states under which individuals are free to believe in religions and practice them, or not, based on their choices. Traditional Islamic doctrine, however, envisions an Islamic state that uses various means of coercion to "establish" and "protect" the true religion. These means include death penalties for apostates and blasphemers. They include "morality police," or *hisba,* who enforce Islamic practices such as prayers or veiling, and punish sins such as drinking alcohol or having illicit sex. Traditional Islamic doctrine also decrees a hierarchical legal order where Muslims have more rights than non-Muslims, and men have more rights than women.

The details of these coercive verdicts can be debated, as they endlessly are. However, there is an underlying kernel that is also the very same question that Mendelssohn had to address: the foundational story of the religion. Traditional Islamic sources narrate that the Prophet Muhammad established a religious state in Medina and expanded its borders with military conquests. They also report that it was he who commanded the punishment of apostates and blasphemers, or who commissioned the first *hisba* police. The same sources also narrate that Muhammad's legitimate successors, the caliphs, continued the mission with new military conquests, while eradicating renegades and false prophets (with the Ridda Wars of Caliph Abu Bakr), and instituting Muslim legal supremacy over non-Muslims (with the "pact" of Caliph Umar, which we have seen). Moreover, until the modern era, it has been the near consensus among Muslims that this early Islamic state led by the Prophet and his caliphs was normative—that it presented a model to be emulated at every age.

So, with this foundational story, how can Muslims accept the norms of religious freedom as they are defined in the modern liberal world?

A significant answer to this question came not from Muhammad Abduh himself but from one of his students: Ali Abdel Raziq (1888–1966), a jurist who graduated from Egypt's prestigious Al-Azhar University and who also studied modern law at Oxford. In his 1925 book, *Al-Islam Wa Usul Al-Hukm,* or *Islam and the Foundations of Governance,* he offered a revolutionary thesis about Islam and the state. Unlike the traditional view that considered them as twins, Abdel Raziq argued that they were separate and could well be separated.

A big part of Raziq's argument was about the institution of the caliphate, which was abolished just a year earlier by the newly founded Turkish Republic. This revolutionary decision was driven in part by the staunchly secularist agenda of Mustafa Kemal Atatürk, but it also had a reformist Islamic argument behind it, as articulated by the Turkish theologian Mehmed Seyyid Bey (1873–1925). In a long address to the Turkish Parliament, Seyyid Bey had argued that neither the Qur'an nor the sayings of the Prophet actually commanded the establishment of a caliphate, meaning this is "not one of the fundamental religious issues." The caliphate was rather an institution Muslims established within the sphere of "human thought," which could be changed by other considerations of human thought. Seyyid Bey also quoted a saying by Muhammad that reads, "The caliphate after me will last 30 years and then it will be a tyrannical kingdom." So, even if there was some righteous caliphate right after the Prophet, it was long gone. In the modern world, Muslims should rather be ruled by *hakimiyet-i milliye*, or popular sovereignty.[61]

Writing a year after Seyyid Bey, Abdel Raziq mirrored some of these arguments. Yet he went even further and revisited why the Prophet Muhammad had established a religious state in Medina. Unlike the traditional view, which perceived this prophetic state as timelessly normative, he saw it as "conducted merely for the protection of the community and for its immediate material welfare in the dangerous tribal world of seventh-century Arabia."[62] It was, in other words, incidental. The real mission of Muhammad was to convey a religious teaching to the world. No wonder the Qur'an defined him as *muballigh*, or "transmitter of a message." A Qur'anic verse even proclaimed: "The Messenger's duty is *only* to deliver the message clearly."[63]

In other words, like Moses Mendelssohn, Abdel Raziq historicized the theocratic experience that is at the foundational story of his religion: it was an exceptional episode that does not have to be repeated at every age.

Moreover, going further than Mendelssohn, Abdel Raziq argued that even the foundational theocratic experience was free of religious coercion. This argument was supported by Qur'anic verses to which the traditional Islamic doctrine did not pay much attention—and even considered as "abrogated" by belligerent verses—but Abdel Raziq now found definitive. As explained by the contemporary scholar Souad T. Ali:

> Abd al-Raziq explains that the call for religion is exclusively a call for God that is based on peaceful persuasion and heart-winning methods. Force and coercion are not appropriate for a call aimed at guiding the hearts and purifying the beliefs. The prophet, he maintains, followed the same line of messengers before him who did not have any history of forcing people into belief by the sword or invading a nation in order to convince them to believe in his religion. The prophet was inspired by what the Qur'an taught him: "Let there be no coercion in religion"; and "Call on people to go on your God's path by wisdom, good advice, and argue with them with the best method."[64]

The combined result of the three arguments—that the Prophet did not resort to religious coercion, he established a state only incidentally, and the caliphate was a historical institution—was to reject the traditional view that Islam is both *din wa dawla*, or "religion and state." Instead, Abdel Raziq emphatically argued, Islam is "a religion, not a state; a message, not a government."[65]

But if Islam was not a government, how would Muslims form governments? Just like Mendelssohn, Abdel Raziq found the answer in a divine gift that is accessible to not just Muslims but all human beings: reason. He wrote:

There is not a single principle of the faith that forbids Muslims to co-operate with other nations in the total enterprise of
the social and political sciences. . . . Nothing stops them from
building their state and their system of government on the basis of past constructions of human reason, of systems whose
sturdiness have stood the test of time, which the experience of
nations has shown to be effective.[66]

Therefore, Muslims could freely embrace political systems
that have proven to advance human welfare—systems such as
liberal democracy. No wonder Ali Abdel Raziq himself was a
member of the Liberal Constitutionalist Party (Hizb al-Ahrar
al-Dusturiyyun), a political movement that championed a freer
Egypt, until it was banned in 1952 after the military coup led
by Gamal Abdel Nasser—who, regrettably, initiated a pattern of
dictatorship that has continued to date.

In other words, just like Mendelssohn, Abdel Raziq was both
a religious reformer and a political liberal. And just like Mendelssohn, his ideas did not change the world overnight but initiated a new way of thinking. Since his time, the idea that Islam
is "a religion, not a state" has been embraced by many other
Muslim modernists. Among them is the contemporary scholar
Abdullahi Ahmed An-Na'im, who thinks that a secular state
that respects religious freedom is not just compatible with Islam
but even better for it because it allows Muslims to practice the
religion as they sincerely believe in it.[67] Another contemporary
scholar, Ebrahim Moosa, calls on fellow Muslims to question the
"imperial Islamic political theology" and instead develop a new
theology that upholds "the rights of the individual."[68]

What such reformist voices in Islam are really calling for is to
redefine the Islamic Sharia in the same fashion that Moses Mendelssohn redefined the Jewish Halakha: a set of religious commandments to be voluntarily *practiced*—and not a set of public
laws to be coercively *enforced*.

AN EPHEMERAL PROJECT?

Mendelssohn has been compared to some other Muslim reformers of the modern era as well. One of them is Syed Ahmad Khan (1817–1898), the Indian Muslim reformer, philosopher, and educationist in British India. Like Mendelssohn, he called on his fellow Muslims to embrace secular sciences that many conservatives then viewed with suspicion, established modern schools for the "uplift and reform of the Muslim," while also striving for advancing the rights of Muslims. And like Mendelssohn, Khan tried to reconcile Islam with freedom of conscience.[69]

Such parallels between the Jewish Enlightenment and the nascent Islamic Enlightenment have also been noted by Oliver Leaman, who is well versed in both religious traditions. Yet Leaman also stresses the gap between the two trajectories. "The Jewish Enlightenment really came to dominate Jewish culture, and continues to do so today," he observes. In contrast, Islamic Enlightenment "had a far weaker grip on the polity." It remained "more elitist and so ephemeral."[70]

Why is this the case? Why has the Islamic Enlightenment not yet flourished?

One answer to this question is given by strict Muslim traditionalists: there is no need for such a transformation in the first place, because the Islamic tradition is perfect as it is. (And the measure of its perfection is itself. So there is circular reasoning here, but so be it.)

Another answer comes from Western critics of Islam who argue that Islam is troublingly exceptional—that, unlike the two other Abrahamic religions, it is unbreakably wedded to political power. (The same argument was also made for Judaism, as we have seen. So there may be a lack of perspective here, but so be it.)

A third answer, which I find more plausible, is that the Islamic Enlightenment was born in an unhelpful context. Many of its ideas came from the West, which also happened to be home of the colonial powers that had attacked and subjugated Muslim lands over the past two centuries. No wonder the zenith of this colonial intrusion, World War I, was also the very trigger for Islam's "counter-Enlightenment."[71] In contrast, Jews faced the Enlightenment within the West itself, and as a promise of freedom and equality for themselves. Malicious forces in the same West, especially Germany, later crushed their hopes, but it was still fulfilled in liberal democracies such as the United States, proving that Jews were not wrong to throw their lot with liberalism.

If this answer is true, then the "end of history" may not yet have come for Islam, because while colonialism left behind a dark legacy, it is now largely passé. Moreover, Muslims have tried various forms of postcolonial illiberalism—Arab socialism, xenophobic nationalism, and authoritarian Islamism—none of which have worked well, leaving the door still open to liberal ideas.

Meanwhile, within the West itself, there is a new Muslim experience that is quite similar to the Jewish one. Muslims, as minorities in largely Christian or post-Christian societies, are finding themselves appreciative of the freedom and equality that come with liberalism, while being asked whether they really fit in. In return, they are finding solutions in patterns that Jews established centuries ago: to grant *dina d'malkhuta dina,* or "the law of the land is the law," and to practice religion as individual believers and voluntary communities. In the United Kingdom, some Muslims have even established Sharia courts, which clearly follow the example of the Halakhic courts called *beth din.*[72] Meanwhile, Jews and Muslims are coming together in the same West to protect their similar religious practices— such as dress codes, circumcision, ritual slaughter, and halal or kosher demands—from similar threats: Islamophobia, antisemitism, and illiberal secularism. They are, together, showing that what believers need from the state is not religion, but freedom of religion.

Furthermore, some Western Muslims are even coming close to a significant phase in Jewish religious history in which Mendelssohn did not participate, but for which he opened the way.[73]

REFORM JUDAISM, REFORM ISLAM?

Mendelssohn, as we have seen, was an intellectual heir to the rationalist theology that came into medieval Judaism from Islam. An important concept in this theological heritage was *ta'amei ha-mitzvot,* or "reasons for commandments." It pointed not only to *what* God commands but also *why* He commands. However, just like the parallel concept of *maqasid al-sharia,* or "intentions of the law," in traditional Islam, the Jewish study of "reasons for commandments" was mainly about *justifying* religious commandments, not *reformulating* them. If Jews knew the divine wisdom behind the Halakha, they would observe it more properly. They would also be more able to defend it against critics. Yet they would still observe the commandments as they were decreed.

Beginning with Mendelssohn, however, there emerged a new Jewish approach to *ta'amei ha-mitzvot.* "The meaning of the Jewish commandments," as the contemporary scholar Arden Eby puts it, began to switch from "ends in themselves" to "means to attain the spirit of the law." And this "fundamental reorientation" soon gave rise to two radical questions: whether "other means might do the job better than the traditional one," and whether "we are empowered to opt for those newer means."[74]

Many Jews said no to these questions, preserving the Halakha mainly as it is. They would be known as the Orthodox, mainly to distinguish them from those who said yes, who went on to create an unprecedented religious movement known as Reform Judaism.

Reform Judaism began in the early nineteenth century in Germany, and later flourished in the United States. Its pioneers, such as Israel Jacobson (1768–1828), Rabbi Abraham Geiger (1810–1874),

and Rabbi Isaac Mayer Wise (1819–1900), radically broke away
from some traditional Jewish practices. They stopped wearing special religious outfits, made kosher laws less strict, added vernacular
languages to synagogue services, and even ended the separation of
men and women at synagogues, which used to be standard Jewish practice. Reformists reminded that Judaism had changed over
the centuries as society changed. But while change in the past was
"subconscious and organic," the radical novelties of the modern
world now called for "deliberate" change.[75]

A key emphasis in Reform Judaism was that not every commandment of the past is supposed to be implemented today just
for its own sake. For the real value is not in the commandment
but in the underlying ethics. The Declaration of Principles by the
1885 Pittsburgh Platform, a key document in the history of the
Reform movement, put this vision boldly, stating:

> We recognize in the Mosaic legislation a system of training the
> Jewish people for its mission during its national life in Pales-
> tine, and today we accept as binding only its moral laws, and
> maintain only such ceremonies as elevate and sanctify our
> lives.[76]

The same document also declared a Jewish dedication to "justice and righteousness," and duty to "work tirelessly for the rights
of the downtrodden."[77] In this moral struggle, Judaism was in alliance with two of its "daughter religions," as well as the rest of
humanity:

> Christianity and Islam, being daughter religions of Judaism,
> we appreciate their providential mission, to aid in the spread-
> ing of monotheistic and moral truth. . . . We extend the hand
> of fellowship to all who cooperate with us in the establishment
> of the reign of truth and righteousness among men.[78]

A notable aspect of Reform Judaism was the empowerment of women. The early Reform movement in Europe had called for gender equality, and abolished laws and customs that gave women fewer rights than men. This drive went further in America, where women also began taking leadership roles in the religious community. In 1972, the Reform movement ordained the first female American rabbi, Sally Jane Priesand, who would be followed by many others.

The Reform movement has reshaped Judaism in the past two hundred years. Some in the movement realized that its modernizing drive went too far, for there is really something precious about religious customs and traditions even without rationalizing them—a point with which I personally agree. That is why they broke away and followed a more modest reform path, which ultimately became known as Conservative Judaism. Meanwhile, even the Reform movement itself corrected its early zeal for change. This was evident in the Columbus Platform of 1937, which called for "the preservation of the Sabbath, festivals and Holy Days, the retention and development of such customs, symbols and ceremonies as possess inspirational value."

Meanwhile, many Orthodox Jews saw both the Reform and Conservative movements as heretical deviations from the one true Judaism that they represented. The wiser among them, however, realized that these movements kept many modernized Jews, who would otherwise totally drift away, still in the religion.

For our story, the Judeo-Islamic tradition, Reform Judaism presents a road that Islam has not yet taken—but may well begin to take sometime in the twenty-first century.

The building blocks for such a Reform Islam are present. The medieval concept of the *maqasid al-sharia*, Islam's "reasons for commandments," has been revived, so that it has become the cutting-edge theme among Muslim scholars with a reformist outlook. Some of them are even beginning to see it as a basis to switch from "ends in themselves" to means to attain the spirit of the law. Moreover, a distinction made by Reform Jews between Biblical and Talmudic laws—*de-oraita*, "from the Torah," versus *de-rabbanan*, "from the rabbis"—is also present in modern Islam, as many Muslims now differentiate between the Qur'an and the post-Qur'anic traditions, questioning the latter more freely. Meanwhile, the intuitive adoption of modern values, such as gender equality, is leading to small-scale efforts for reform, such as avant-garde mosques with female imams.[79] And perceptive scholars can see the parallels between such Muslim reformists of today and the Reform rabbis of the nineteenth century, such as Abraham Geiger.[80]

Surely, these sporadic efforts for reform in Islam have not yet led to a full-fledged "liberal schism" in the religion, as pointed out by the historian Timur Kuran in his discussion about the "delayed" freedoms in Islam.[81] One big reason is that the defenders of the Islamic orthodoxy often wield enough power to suffocate any reformist effort. However, thanks to the freedom offered by Western democracies as well as the virtual world of the internet, more and more Muslims are being exposed to new ideas about religion, as well as new values about the human condition. Moreover, it is also becoming clear that if there is not much to offer in the name of Islam except an illiberal orthodoxy, more and more Muslims will simply drift away from the faith. Reform, in other words, may be the only way to "save" them.

So, the emergence of a Reform Islam, akin to Reform Judaism, is a possibility in the future. It will not appeal to all Muslims, not even most of them, but it will to some of them.

Meanwhile, the imperative shift that is needed for all Muslims, including the most orthodox, is the transformation that John Locke advocated in Christianity and Moses Mendelssohn advocated in Judaism: giving up coercive power in the name of religion, so that all believers can practice their faith in the way they sincerely believe. That was the most valuable contribution of the Christian Enlightenment as well as the Jewish Haskalah. It is also the biggest shift that needs to mature in Islam today.

Finally, there is another accomplishment of the European Enlightenment that is also relevant to contemporary Muslims: studying a religion other than one's own, objectively and eruditely, and on its own terms. But for that discussion, which will take us into some controversial territory, we will need to open a new chapter.

THE GOOD ORIENTALISTS

*Jews were among the finest scholars and greatest admirers
of Islam in Europe. Their work set an agenda for scholarship.*

—Susannah Heschel, professor of Jewish studies[1]

IN THE MUSLIM WORLD TODAY, ESPECIALLY AMONG THE EDU-
cated circles, few words are dirtier than "Orientalism." It is seen
as the systemic mischaracterization of Islam and Muslim societies by Western academics, journalists, or artists, often to le-
gitimize supremacy and aggression. While the term originally
simply meant the Western study of Eastern cultures, especially
in the eighteenth and nineteenth centuries, it acquired this negative connotation in the late twentieth century. Orientalists, in
this view, were intellectual pawns of Western colonialism, who
created and popularized negative stereotypes about Muslims only
to subjugate them—culturally, politically, and militarily.

No one has been more influential in building this latter-day
meaning of Orientalism than the late, great Edward Said (1935–
2003), a prominent Palestinian American academic who taught
at Columbia University, and a public intellectual who deeply impacted Western discourses. His 1978 book, *Orientalism,* considered one of the most influential scholarly books of the twentieth
century, exposed how indeed many European writers or artists had

projected stereotyped images about the "Orient"—lazy, fanatic, superstitious, barbaric, and sexist—and how these narratives were connected to colonial policies. By showing a mirror to Western prejudices, in my humble view, Said undoubtedly brought forth a necessary revolution in both academic and popular thinking. He also left behind a crucial awareness—that power can manipulate knowledge—that can be applied to any society, any civilization.

Yet exposing Western biases against the Islamic East is one thing; seeing nothing else in the West except bias is another. On the latter point, Said has been criticized, as his critiques against the Orientalists were found too sweeping. So today, "while often acknowledging Said's insights," many historians reject his "description of a monolithic Europe" in favor of a "more pluralistic and multicultural model."[2]

For our story, the Judeo-Islamic tradition, there is also an interesting gap in Said's work that merits attention. In *Orientalism*, he focused on the academic studies and popular narratives in Britain and France, which happened to be the two main colonial powers that invaded Muslim lands from the early nineteenth century onward. That colonial enterprise, Said argued, was precisely why Britain and France were "the pioneer nations in the Orient and Oriental studies," whose positions were later taken over by the United States.[3]

However, there is another country in which Orientalist studies flourished throughout the nineteenth century: Germany. In fact, German Orientalists were "the pacesetting European scholars in virtually every field of oriental studies between about 1830 and 1930."[4] Nevertheless, as Suzanne L. Marchand notes in *German Orientalism in the Age of Empire*, "Said famously, and self-consciously, left the Germans out of his analysis."[5] That is why some suggested that the title of Said's book should have been not *Orientalism*, but *French, British, and American Orientalism*—because Germany, and some other European nations, were clearly left out.[6]

Said himself, to his credit, admitted this gap. In the introduction of his seminal book, he wrote:

> There is a possibly misleading aspect to my study, where, aside from an occasional reference, I do not exhaustively discuss the German developments. . . . I particularly regret not taking more account of the great scientific prestige that accrued to German scholarship by the middle of the nineteenth century.[7]

Now, when we fill that gap, and take a closer look into this important phenomenon of German Orientalism, we see two facts that are quite interesting.

First, the birth of German Orientalism cannot be tied to any colonial project because Germany, which became a unified country only in the 1870s, turned into a colonial power only in the 1880s. So, it makes no sense to tie the rise of German Orientalism in the 1830s to colonialism, as Said himself actually noted. "At no time in German scholarship during the first two thirds of the 19th century," he wrote, "could a close partnership have developed between orientalists and a protracted, sustained national interest in the orient."[8]

Second, there is something curious about the very people who created German Orientalism: most of them were Jews. Beginning in the 1830s, "German Jews began flocking to the study of Arabic and Islam," and "played an altogether disproportionate role" in the development of Islamic studies.[9]

Why could that be the case?

Well, because Jews themselves were "Orientals"![10] At least, that is how they were perceived in nineteenth-century Europe, where Christian prejudices against the two kindred religions—Judaism and Islam—were still strong. Worse, the old religious biases were exacerbated by a new secular bigotry: racism against Semitic people, especially Jews and Arabs. The contemporary scholar Susannah Heschel explains how this context led to a Jewish study of

Islam with motives radically different from what many ascribe to Orientalism today: as Jews were denigrated as "Orientals in Europe," both religiously and racially, they came to "identify with Islam."[11] Therefore,

> Jewish scholars in Europe founded the field of Islamic Studies and created an image of Islam as derived from Judaism and sharing its key principles of monotheism, religious law, tolerance, openness to science, and rejection of anthropomorphism. Uniting Islam with Judaism was an effort to undermine the denigrations of European Orientalism as well as polemicize against Christian hegemony in the West.[12]

Another contemporary scholar, Michael L. Miller, observes, "Jews played a central role in the development of Islamic studies in nineteenth-century Europe, particularly in Germany, France, and Hungary." And their backgrounds made them "favorably inclined toward Islam":

> In their youth, many of these scholars had received a traditional Jewish education, and their knowledge of Semitic languages (Hebrew and Aramaic) and rabbinic literature not only made Arabic and Islam more approachable but also enabled them to notice similarities between Judaism and Islam that were not as apparent to Christian orientalists like de Sacy, Umbreit, Fleischer, and Nöldeke. Jewish orientalists tended to be more favorably inclined toward Islam than their Christian counterparts, which often gave their research a less polemical—and more respectful—character.[13]

One of the contributions of these nineteenth-century Jewish Orientalists was the rediscovery of medieval Muslim Spain as a beacon of religious tolerance. They even painted an "exaggerated picture of a 'golden age' of Jewish-Muslim harmony," while hinting that Christians should imitate this heritage of tolerance in Islam.[14] They also wanted to show the Christians "the intellectual and artistic heights to which Jews could attain if given freedom."[15] All in all, their view of Islam, far from the Islamophobia that is sometimes connected to Orientalism today, reflected a significant "Islamophilia."[16]

We will now take a look at the stories of a few of these prominent Jewish Orientalists, whose views on Islam deserve to be remembered, as they offer a much-forgotten yet fairly important chapter in the Judeo-Islamic tradition.

GEIGER, WEIL, GRAETZ, AND OTHERS

The first of these Jewish Orientalists was someone we met before as one of the founders of Reform Judaism: Abraham Geiger. Born to a traditional Jewish family in Frankfurt and educated in universities in Heidelberg and Bonn, he became a pioneer of *Wissenschaft des Judentums,* or "Science of Judaism," which involved the study of Jewish literature and culture using the tools of modern secular scholarship.

Yet the Science of Judaism wasn't limited to Judaism itself. It extended to its "daughter religions." Geiger was especially interested in Islam, as reflected in his intense study of Arabic and the Qur'an under the distinguished Orientalist Georg Freytag. As a Jew, Geiger found many themes and passages in the Qur'an remarkably familiar. This led him to conclude that this Arabic scripture was largely derived from the Talmud, Midrash, and other rabbinic literature, to carry "the Jewish message of monotheism to the pagan world." He put forth this argument in an 1832 work that earned him both an academic prize and everlasting fame: *Was hat Mohammed aus dem Judenthume Aufgenommen?*, or *What Did Mohammed Take from Judaism?*

Here, I should note that the very notion of the Prophet of Islam "taking" anything from Judaism—or Christianity—would be unacceptable to most Muslims, since according to Islam, Muhammad took everything he preached from divine revelation. Therefore, parallels between the Qur'an and preexisting traditions do not indicate any earthly "learning" or "borrowing." Instead, they show only that God kept revealing the same truths to different messengers, over and over.

However, this view is based on faith, which Muslims can't reasonably expect from non-Muslims. But the latter can still be fair to the Prophet of Islam, granting his sincerity and idealism, or be unfair to him, depicting him as a charlatan. Geiger's work was important, for it presented the former approach at a time and milieu where the latter was the dominant view:

> While the Enlightenment saw the beginnings of a more positive representation of Islam and its founder, many scholars continued to dismiss Muhammad as a hypocrite and deceiver, as Voltaire had done, or they concurred with Herder, who called the prophet "fanatic," while still others agreed with the great nineteenth-century Semiticist, Theodor Nöldeke, who diagnosed him as "hysterical." Geiger declared such opinions to be the product of "outright bias and misunderstanding of the human heart" (einseitigkeit und ganzlicher Verkennung des menschlichen Herzens). By contrast, Geiger saw Muhammad as "genuine enthusiast (wirklicher Schwarmer) who was himself convinced of his divine mission, and to whom the union of all religions appeared necessary for the welfare of mankind."[17]

Geiger also praised the Islamic civilization, in part for its tolerance of Jews. Judaism, in his view, had "developed its own fullest potential in closest union with Arab civilization."[18] This was especially true of Muslim Spain, which was "a high point in Jewish history" and proof that medieval Islam, unlike medieval Christendom, was "open to science and scholarly inquiry."[19]

Geiger opened the way for Gustav Weil (1808–1899), the son

of a rabbi, who studied Islam not just in Heidelberg and Paris but also for five years among Muslims in Algiers, Cairo, and Istanbul. After his return to Germany, Weil wrote the first-ever Western biography of the Prophet Muhammad that was "free from prejudice and polemic, based on a profound yet critical knowledge of the Arabic sources, and informed by a sympathetic understanding of Muslim belief and piety."[20] In another book, *Geschichte der Islamitischen Volker,* or *A History of the Islamic Peoples,* Weil praised Muhammad's character with remarkable words. "Mohamed set a shining example to his people," he wrote, adding:

> His character was pure and stainless. His house, his dress, his food; they were characterised by a rare simplicity. So unpretentious was he that he would receive from his companions no special mark of reverence, nor would he accept any service from his slave which he could do himself. Often and often indeed was he seen in the market purchasing provisions; often and often was he seen mending his clothes in his room, or milking a goat in his courtyard. He was accessible to all, and at all times. He visited the sick and was full of sympathy for all, and whenever politics was not in the way he was generous and forbearing to a degree. Unlimited was his benevolence and generosity, and so was his anxious care for the welfare of the community. Despite innumerable presents which from all quarters unceasingly poured in for him; despite rich booty which streamed in, he left very little behind, and even that he regarded as State property.[21]

Weil, in line with Geiger, also applied his insights from Reform Judaism to Islam. In his view, "the Muslim religion" would have more "improvement and spiritualization" when its believers "differentiate the elements of their Koran which come from specific circumstances from those that are eternally true and are not subject to change."[22]

Another towering scholar from the same era was Heinrich Graetz (1817–1891), who is considered the greatest Jewish historian of the nineteenth century. His eleven-volume *Geschichte der Juden,* or *History of the Jews,* published between 1853 and 1876, included many positive remarks about Islam, one of which you can find in the very beginning of this book. Graetz had some critical remarks on Islam as well, yet he defined almost every premodern encounter between Jews and Muslims as "a story of liberation for Jews."[23] He noted the negative encounters, too, but only to grant, "the dominion of Islam furthered the elevation of Judaism from its deepest degradation."[24]

"MOORISH" SYNAGOGUES AND BURNED BOOKS

These Islamophilic views by Jewish scholars also had an impact on Jewish culture, first in Germany and then elsewhere, with visible results in architecture. The historian Martin Kramer, who also wrote about the "pro-Islamic Jews" of the time, explains its remarkable scope:

> As the nineteenth century progressed, German-speaking Jews actively sought to be associated with the legacy of Islam, and to bask in its reflected glory. The tangible evidence . . . may be seen in mid-nineteenth-century urban synagogue architecture in the "Moorish" style. Minarets and domes rose above the skylines of Leipzig, Frankfurt, Berlin, and Cologne. The style spread eastward to Budapest and St. Petersburg, southward to Florence, and westward to New York, Philadelphia, and Cincinnati. In some of these synagogues, opined one contemporary Jewish critic, "the crescent alone is wanting at the summit."[25]

These "mosque-like synagogues erected by Jewish communities in the nineteenth century," Kramer adds, "prepared Europe to accept the real mosques which Muslim communities erected across the continent in the twentieth."[26]

European Jewish sympathy for Islam was also expressed in literature. A very early example was the famous poet and essayist Heinrich Heine (1797–1856), whose 1823 play, *Almansor,* told the story of the Catholic "reconquest" of Spain and the destruction of Islam during the Spanish Inquisition. Clearly intended to enlighten Christian audiences about the horrors of religious persecution, the play displays "a profound empathy for the Muslims themselves."[27] In one passage, where the eponymous hero, Almansor, converses with the servant Hassan, the latter says something that would prove all too prophetic:

> Almansor: We heard that Ximenes the Terrible in Granada, in the middle of the market-place—my tongue refuses to say it!— cast the Koran into the flames of a burning pyre!
> Hassan: That was only a prelude; where they burn books they will, in the end, burn human beings too.[28]

Today, many people are familiar with these words of wisdom: where they burn books, they will eventually burn human beings too. Yet not all may be aware that it was written by a Jewish author, in solidarity with Muslims, and in the context of the burning of a copy of the Qur'an.

The oppressors who burned first books then people would reappear in Germany, and dominate it, in the 1930s. These were the Nazis, who purged Jews from academia, a tragic persecution that also "decimated" the field of Islamic studies, which even included the very first studies on the Jewish Mu'tazila that we met earlier.[29] Yet still the Judeo-Islamic spirit survived. As observed by Susannah Heschel, many Jewish books published in Germany during the Third Reich, especially around the eight-hundredth anniversary of Maimonides's birth in 1935, "emphasize[d] approvingly Islam's rejection of anthropomorphism, as if symbolically repudiating the deification of Hitler."[30]

During the unspeakable evil that followed, the Holocaust, some of the Jewish Orientalists perished, but others were able to flee and to continue their study of Islam elsewhere. Among them, Franz Rosenthal (1914–2003), who left his native Berlin soon after Kristallnacht, ended up at Yale University, and made major contributions to the Western understanding of Islam, which included the first English translation of *Muqaddimah,* or *Prolegomenon,* the masterpiece by the medieval Muslim scholar Ibn Khaldun. Another was Shelomo Dov Goitein, whom you have met repeatedly in this book, with his insights about the medieval "symbiosis" between Islam and Judaism. One of the Jewish Orientalists even ultimately chose Islam. This was the Austro-Hungarian journalist Leopold Weiss (1900–1992), the grandson of a rabbi, who converted to Islam at the age of twenty-six, took the name Muhammad Asad, and became one of the most prominent Muslim intellectuals and Qur'anic commentators of the past century.

IGNAZ GOLDZIHER, HADITH, AND BLIND SPOTS

At the beginning of the twentieth century, the Ottoman historian Ahmet Refik went on a tour of Europe. On his return to Istanbul, his friends asked him what was the most remarkable thing he had seen on his travels. "The University of Budapest," he replied, "where I found a Jewish professor expounding the Qur'an to a class of Christian pupils."[31] That Jewish professor was Ignaz Goldziher (1850–1921), who deserves special attention in our hall of fame of the good Orientalists.

Goldziher was Hungarian, not German, but he inherited the German Orientalists' fascination with Islam, only to advance it much further, so that today he is considered the very founder of modern Islamic studies in Europe. He was educated in Budapest, Berlin, Leipzig, and Leiden, and then, with the support of the Hungarian government, he journeyed through Syria, Palestine, and Egypt. In Cairo, he attended lectures at the famous Al-Azhar University, where he even joined a Friday prayer. "I rubbed my forehead against the floor of the mosque," he noted in his journal. "Never in my life was I more devout, more truly devout, than on that exalted Friday."[32] He also wrote:

> In those weeks, I truly entered into the spirit of Islam to such an extent that ultimately I became inwardly convinced that I myself was a Muslim, and judiciously discovered that this was the only religion which, even in its doctrinal and official formulation, can satisfy philosophic minds. My ideal was to elevate Judaism to a similar rational level.[33]

Goldziher's will to "elevate" Judaism was reflective of his sympathies for Reform Judaism. He was an admirer of Abraham Geiger, the very founder of the movement, whose ideas Goldziher tried to advance in Hungary. Therefore, he always remained a pious Jew, but ceased to observe religious practices that he considered "dead." He also criticized the "religious fossilization" he observed among his Orthodox coreligionists.[34] Goldziher, in other words, was a reformist Jew, and his view of Islam was an expression of his rational religious outlook.

Yet precisely for that reason, Goldziher noticed a certain problem in Islam.[35] This was the vast literature of hadith, or sayings, which are reports about the words and deeds of the Prophet Muhammad. While this rich corpus constitutes the second textual source of Islam after the Qur'an, there is a big difference between the two: the Qur'an was largely written and fully memorized during the time of the Prophet, and it was canonized soon after his death, at most two decades later, under the third caliph, Uthman ibn Affan. Therefore, Muslims have never disputed the authentic-

ity of the Qur'anic text. (Western scholarship and surviving manuscripts also largely testify to its "early" composition.) However,
hadith were canonized much later, almost two centuries after
the Prophet, before which they circulated mainly as oral reports,
passing on from ear to ear, generation to generation, while getting
mixed with hearsay and forgeries. The movement that compiled
and canonized them—the *ahl al-hadith,* or "people of hadith"—
claimed to have sorted out all the *sahih,* or "authentic ones," by
establishing *isnad,* or "chain of transmission," for each report.
Yet their rivals—the *ahl al-ray,* or "people of reason"—remained
doubtful of their methods, with "skepticism" or even "wholesale
rejection" of hadith.[36] Nevertheless, the people of hadith dominated Sunni Islam, and put a lid on a more complex tradition.

Goldziher's historical contribution was to help reopen this
lid. As the first non-Muslim scholar to ever examine the hadith
corpus carefully, he found good reasons to doubt the authenticity of many of the so-called authentic reports: they contained
various anachronisms, as well as suspiciously partisan takes on
the political or theological disputes that took place many decades after Muhammad. So, they could well be later inventions
"projected back into the time of the Prophet."[37] The chains of
transmission themselves could be forged or imagined. Hadith,
therefore, taught us more about the history of the early Muslim
community, in which these reports emerged, than the actual
teachings of the Prophet.

Goldziher's hadith criticism would later be advanced, and re-
fined, by other Western scholars of Islam such as Joseph Schacht
and G. H. A. Juynboll.[38] Among Muslims, in the meantime,
Goldziher's work helped popularize a new way of thinking, which
had been marginalized for a millennium: taking the Qur'an as
the primary source of Islam, while judging the hadith corpus, including its ethical content, in the light of the Qur'an and universal human reason.[39] The implication was a major reform in Islam,
as hadith are the main source of the Sharia, and also the basis of

its most controversial elements. A short list would include death penalties for apostasy and blasphemy, stoning of adulterers, demeaning of women as "deficient in intelligence and religion," child marriage, obedience to tyrannical rulers, sectarianism, and a ban on music and "images."

No wonder, then, that today, questioning the hadith corpus is the hallmark of almost any Islamic movement that is called "reformist," "modernist," or "liberal." Despite many nuances, they all argue that the "Qur'an must be returned to its rightful place as the supreme arbiter of the authenticity of hadith."[40] In return, defenders of Islamic orthodoxy denounce the "hadith rejectors," often also by conspiracy theories about how the enemies of Islam are trying to subvert the religion by insinuating doubts about its impeccable tradition. And Goldziher often looms large in these conspiracy theories for all the easy reasons: he was an Orientalist as well as a Jew. So, what else do Muslims need to know to decipher his real agenda?

That is why, today, "Goldziher's image in the Islamic world is so bad, whereas the view which he himself had of Islam was overall so positive."[41] But this negative image is largely unfair. First, just like the Jewish Orientalists before him, Goldziher had no sympathy for European colonialism. Quite to the contrary, he "supported the movement of Islamic revival and sympathized with resistance to Western imperialism."[42] No wonder he formed a friendship with Jamal al-Din al-Afghani (1838–1897), the most vocal anti-imperialist Muslim intellectual of the time. Meanwhile, a textbook written by Goldziher was used by the Austro-Hungarian government in Bosnia—the only connection he may have with colonial rule over Muslims—but in it he "did not corrupt his tone or language to incorporate political messages."[43]

Second, Goldziher's Jewishness did not imply any "Jewish conspiracy" against Islam but only sympathy for it, if not solidarity with it. The latter was evident in his stance against the French scholar Ernest Renan, whom we met before, who represented the kind of prejudiced Orientalism that people have in mind today. The "Semitic mind" is primitive, Renan argued, demeaning both Jews and Muslims, both of which supposedly lacked the scientific and philosophical sophistication of the "Aryan mind." Against him, Goldziher was on the same side with al-Afghani and the Ottoman Islamic liberal Namık Kemal (1840–1888), all of whom wrote rejoinders to Renan. In fact, it would be a "lifelong preoccupation" for Goldziher to repudiate "both Renan's stance on the Hebrews and Judaism and his stance on the Arabs and Islam."[44]

Fortunately, today, there are some fair Muslim views on Goldziher as well. In his 2019 book, *Goldziher ve Hadis*, the Turkish theologian Hüseyin Akgün shows that Goldziher was "against the attacks and exploitations" on the Muslim world and "quite positive" toward Islam. While Goldziher's skepticism of hadith went too far, Akgün thinks, some of his arguments are valid and still worthy of consideration.[45] Another Turkish theologian, Hayri Kırbaşoğlu, a professor of hadith studies himself, is even more cordial in his monograph, *Understanding Goldziher*. Goldziher was a friend of Islam and Muslims, Kırbaşoğlu says, and his analyses and criticisms "are important because they show us our blind spots."[46]

Which brings us full circle from Edward Said's bad Orientalism to the legacy of the good Orientalists. Said's key contribution was to awaken the Western tradition to its own blind spots. Power can manipulate knowledge, he warned, demonstrating how the power of Western imperialism did precisely that. Yet Western imperialism is not the only power story in world history. Islam had its own imperialism, from the very beginning, with many virtues for its time, as we have seen in this book, as well as undeniable flaws. To assume that this power—and other mundane forces such as religious, sectarian, or patriarchal supremacism—didn't leave a mark on the Islamic tradition would be naïve. It would be a blind spot, on which light should be shed. And the good Orientalists, both in the past and present, whether they be Jewish or gentile, deserve appreciation for doing precisely that.

A CASE FOR GOOD OCCIDENTALISTS

Before closing this chapter, we have one more stone to turn over. Any discussion on Orientalism would be incomplete without considering its mirror image, which is Occidentalism.

The term has been defined as "a distorted and stereotyped image of Western society, which can be held by people inside and outside the West."[47] In this sense, it is a counterpart to Edward Said's Orientalism. As various scholars have shown, and I have observed personally, it is unmistakable in the contemporary Muslim world, especially among Islamists, who often caricaturize the West as an immoral, soulless, degenerate civilization that values nothing but greed, lust, and profanity.[48]

So, there seems to be some balance in Orientalism and Occidentalism, in the sense of each generating negative stereotypes of the other side. But what about the better sense of the word? Do Muslims have "good Occidentalists," so to speak, who study Western civilization, including its religious traditions, not with any apologetic intent but to really understand and to contribute?

Historically, Muslims were actually quite advanced at studying other traditions. The medieval polymaths al-Biruni (d. 1050) and al-Shahrastani (d. 1153) examined the religious culture of India with remarkable accuracy and objectivity. Their works have been hailed as pioneering in the comparative study of religions. Franz Rosenthal even wrote, "The comparative study of religions has been rightly acclaimed as one of the great contributions of Muslim civilization to mankind's intellectual progress."[49]

Today, however, those great contributions are long gone. There are certainly some Muslim academics who study other religions with the scholarly standards of our time, and a few of them have been quoted in this book. However, the Muslim study of the other is nowhere near the study of Islam by others. In any academic field of Islamic studies, you can come across many non-Muslim experts who are as erudite as their Muslim counterparts. But it is hard to find a similar Muslim contribution to the academic study of Christianity, Judaism, or other religions.[50]

One of the contemporary representatives of the good Orientalist tradition we have been examining, Lenn Goodman, a Jewish American philosopher who published extensively about medieval Islamic thought, points to this fact in a work on religious pluralism. "I have devoted fifty years now to the study of Islam," says Goodman, adding:

> In particular, I have tracked the philosophers, scientists, and humanists of Islam and their struggles to give definition and critical credibility to the Islamic legacy. In chronicling some of their finest works, my hope in part has been that non-Muslims will see a more open, thoughtful, tolerant face than Islamic militants, extremists, and irredentists have shown. I have also hoped that greater access to their own tradition's riches will inspire and empower committed Muslims to build on the achievements of some of the world's greatest minds and souls, contributing to the mosaic of humane and humanistic civilizations. But that is not a goal to be won by wishful thinking or mere stipulations. Much work needs to be done.[51]

The disappointing gap, Goodman adds, is that "religious authorities of mainstream Islam do not promote the treatment of other religions or even secular individuals in their own societies— let alone heretics, misbelievers, or converts to other religions—with the honor and respect" needed for a pluralist world.[52] Similarly,

> we do not see extensive study of Buddhism, Hinduism, Confucianism, Taoism, Christianity, or Judaism among Muslim scholars today, let alone a desire to situate those traditions (and the myriad varieties of belief and practice adopted by their followers) in the same intellectual and moral world as their own.[53]

So, perhaps it is time for more Muslims to recall the good Orientalists, not only to be fair to their heritage but also to take an example from their intellectual curiosity and openness. The world will become a better place only when religions, cultures, and civilizations try to understand each other, sincerely and truthfully, instead of depicting each other as hopelessly inferior, corrupt, or nefarious. And to nurture such understanding, we need only more Orientalism and Occidentalism—just of the better kind.

THE OTTOMAN HAVEN

*This country [Turkey] is like a broad and expansive sea
which our Lord has opened with the rod of His mercy, as
Moses did for you in the Exodus from Egypt. . . .*
*Here the gates of Liberty are always wide open for you
that you may fully practice your Judaism.*

—Samuel Usque, *The Consolation for the
Tribulations of Israel,* 1553[1]

ON THE NIGHT OF MARCH 3, 1924, THE LAST CALIPH OF ISLAM
who walked on this earth, Abdülmecid II, embarked on a journey that he had never anticipated. On the very morning of that
day, the parliament of the newly established Turkish Republic,
under the leadership of arch-secularist Mustafa Kemal Atatürk,
passed a law that abolished the very institution of the caliphate.
With the same decree, all members of the Ottoman dynasty, which
had ruled Turkey since the fourteenth century, were expelled from
the country. The law had given them fifteen days to leave, but in
practice, Abdülmecid Efendi, as he is honorifically called, was ordered to depart immediately.

So, the last caliph, with his close family members and a few
aides, had to leave his home, the majestic Dolmabahçe Palace in
Istanbul, in a big rush. They were given special Turkish passports

that were valid only for leaving the country. Besides a bit of cash, which would not last long, they were also given tickets on the famous Orient Express, which would take them to Switzerland.

Istanbul had its own train station, but the government wanted to avoid any public spectacle. So, the caliph and his entourage were driven to the next train station, in Çatalca, a town some thirty-five miles west of Istanbul. It was a rainy night and the cars got stuck in mud, while the gendarmes worked hard to clear the way. We learn all these details from one of the passengers on that historic trip: the caliph's private secretary, Salih Keramet Nigâr, who published his memoirs forty years later in a touching book, *Son Halife Abdülmecid*, or *The Last Caliph Abdülmecid*.[2]

Finally, Nigâr writes, after a long and dark night, the convoy arrived at the train station, which would be their last stop before their permanent expulsion. Trains were not frequent in those days, so the caliph and his family had to wait for quite a while. Luckily, at a time when public sympathy for them could be politically risky, the manager of the station proved to be an exceptionally gracious man. He welcomed the royal family to his own apartment and served them by his own hands and those of his children "with sincere respect and love."[3]

Now, there was something notable about this train station manager: he was a Jew. We learn this again from Nigâr, who also quotes this unnamed official on why he and his family were so kind to the last caliph:

> The Ottoman dynasty is the protector of Turkey's Jews. When our ancestors were expelled from Spain, when they looked for a country who could shelter them, they [Ottomans] saved them from destruction. Under the shade of their state, [Jews] found safety of life, honor and property, the freedom of religion and language. It is our conscientious duty to help them in their dark days, as much as we can.[4]

"These words brought tears to our eyes," Nigâr adds. Apparently, the last caliph and his family were moved to see this gratitude from an Ottoman Jew, when their fellow Turks were banishing them from what had been their homeland for over six hundred years.

The members of the Ottoman family would not be allowed to return to Turkey until the 1970s. The last caliph would sustain himself in France until his passing in 1944, and his charming daughter Dürrüşehvar would become a princess in the Muslim kingdom of Hyderabad in central India, but many of the exiled Ottomans had very difficult lives in an unknown world, living in despair and dying in poverty. Still, many kept the hope that they would return one day. They also kept praying for the nation that seemed to have forgotten them.

Their contributions to humanity, however, should not be forgotten. The Ottoman dynasty created one of the world's largest and most enduring empires, and established a level of religious freedom that, for its time, was remarkable. And thanks to its pluralism, it presented a safe haven to many endangered Jews, writing an important chapter in the Judeo-Islamic tradition that we will now look into.

"THE BEST PLACE IN THE WORLD FOR JEWS"

"Ottoman" is the English word for *Osmanlı,* which means "the sons of Osman." It comes from the founder of the dynasty, Osman I (r. 1299–1324), whose own name comes from the third caliph of Islam. He was a prince (*bey*) of a small Turkish Muslim principality in western Anatolia, right on the border of the decaying Byzantine Empire. At that time, Osman's dominion was just one of the various petty kingdoms in a chaotic Anatolia, and nobody could guess that one of them would ultimately conquer them all and even become a world empire. But that was the destiny ahead.

The first big leap would be the conquest of Bursa, a city separated from Istanbul by the small Marmara Sea, which was then a stronghold of Byzantium. The campaign was initiated by Osman himself, but it was completed by Osman's son and successor, Sultan Orhan (r. 1323–1362). The latter also made Bursa the Ottoman capital for the next four decades, during which the city witnessed remarkable urban growth with new hospitals, schools, and a growing population. It also became a haven for Jews, as *Encyclopaedia Judaica* notes:

> The conquest was a blessing for the Jews after the experience of servitude under Byzantium, which had decreed harsh laws upon them. The Jews were permitted by the sultan, who issued a firman (royal order), to build a synagogue (Ez Hayyim). They were also allowed to engage in business in the country without hindrance and to purchase houses and land in the towns and villages.[5]

As Ottoman conquests advanced, more Jews entered under Ottoman rule, often seeing it as a blessing in comparison to the less tolerant Christian kingdoms of the time. Even Ashkenazi communities expelled from Hungary in 1376, from France in 1394, and from Sicily, Bavaria, and Venetian-ruled Salonika, ended up in Ottoman lands.[6] One of those immigrants gratefully noted that the Ottoman state was the only place around the Mediterranean where the Jews' "weary feet could find rest."[7]

In 1453, under the young Sultan Mehmed II, the Ottomans had their greatest conquest ever by seizing Constantinople, the very heart of the Byzantine Empire, which simply ceased to exist with this historic takeover. After the initial destruction, the visionary sultan wanted to rebuild the city, now called Istanbul, as a diverse cosmopolis. While he offered his blessings to the Greek Orthodox Ecumenical Patriarchate, he also established the institution of *Haham Başı,* or Chief Rabbi, which would hold broad powers to legislate and enforce the laws among Jews across the Ottoman Empire and even sit on the Sultan's *divan*, or imperial council. This pluralist structure would be known as the millet system. *Millet*, meaning nation, designated autonomous self-governing religious communities. Muslims were the *millet-i hakime*, or "ruling nation," while Greeks, Armenians, and Jews were *dhimmi*, or protected nations.

Sultan Mehmed II also transferred some Muslim, Christian, and Jewish populations, especially merchants and craftsmen, from various parts of the empire to his new capital. These were called *sürgün*, or exiles, but there were also Jews who were *kendi gelen*, or "those who came of their own free will," arriving from Spain, Portugal, Germany, and other European lands.[8] The reason for the attraction was obvious. "After 1453, Istanbul was unquestionably the best place in the world for Jews to live," the historian Alan Mikhail notes. "Nowhere were Jews as prosperous and free as they were in Istanbul."[9]

One of the newcomers to the Ottoman capital was Rabbi Isaac Zarfati, who was delighted by the freedom he found here, in contrast to the "great torture chamber" he had left behind. Hence, in 1454, he penned his famous letter to the Jewish communities in the Rhineland, Swabia, Moravia, Styria, and Hungary, where he said:

I have heard of the afflictions, more bitter than death, that have befallen our brethren in Germany—of the tyrannical laws, the compulsory baptisms and the banishments, which are of daily occurrence. I am told that when they flee from one place a yet harder fate befalls them in another. . . . Brothers and teachers, friends and acquaintances! I, Isaac Zarfati, though I spring from a French stock, yet I was born in Germany, and sat there at the feet of my esteemed teachers. I proclaim to you that Turkey is a land wherein nothing is lacking, and where, if you will, all shall yet be well with you. The way to the Holy Land lies open to you through Turkey. Is it not better for you to live under Muslims than under Christians? Here every man may dwell at peace under his own vine and fig tree.[10]

"O Israel," Zarfati added a call to his brethren in Europe, "Arise! And leave this accursed land forever!"[11]

Naturally, many Jews remained in that "accursed land," but some would soon be forced to leave en masse. These were the Jews of Spain, whose centuries-long life in the peninsula tragically ended with the end of Muslim rule, when the Catholic *Reconquista* captured the last stronghold of Al-Andalus, Granada, in January 1492. Just two months later, the victorious power couple King Ferdinand and Queen Isabella issued the infamous Alhambra Decree, which declared that, unless they converted to Christianity, all Jews would be driven out of their kingdom. By the end of July 1492, almost the entire Jewish community, some two hundred thousand people, were expelled from Spain. Reports show that tens of thousands died trying to reach safety. In some cases, Spanish ship captains charged Jewish passengers exorbitant sums, only to throw them overboard in the middle of the ocean. Some were savagely slaughtered by bandits who were eager to find treasures in their stomachs.[12] Meanwhile, the Muslims of Spain, or the *moriscos* as Christians called them, were initially allowed to stay, but they would face the same fate as the Jews in a long expulsion process that would be completed in 1614.[13]

The Jewish survivors of the 1492 expulsion headed to various destinations, including Amsterdam, Italian city-states, North Africa, and Egypt. Yet, in the words of a rabbi at that time, "The most fortunate of the expelled Jews succeeded in escaping to Turkey."[14] They were welcomed by Sultan Bayezid II, the son of Mehmed II and a pious Muslim, who even actively courted Spanish Jews, going so far as to send ships to the Iberian coastline, led by Admiral Kemal Reis, to bring them to Istanbul. The sultan also ordered all his provincial governors to welcome and protect any Jewish refugee.[15] Consequently, Sephardic communities were established in Ottoman western cities such as Istanbul, Sarajevo, Salonika, and Edirne, and even eastern ones such as Jerusalem, Safed, and Damascus. By the sixteenth century, the Ottoman Empire had become home to the largest Jewish community in the world.[16]

Jerusalem deserves special attention here. Before the Ottoman conquest in 1517 under the son of Bayezid II, Selim I ("The Grim"), it was ruled by Muslim Mamluks, who were not too friendly to the Jews, as we have seen. So, with no surprise, many Jews joined the Ottoman army when it was about to conquer Jerusalem.[17] Selim's successor, Suleyman the Magnificent, who made the Ottomans a true world power, invested great effort and funds to rebuild Jerusalem, constructing the city walls that exist today. Meanwhile, his positive attitude toward Jews persuaded many European Jews to settle in the holy city. Soon after the Ottoman conquest, Jews also received formal permission to pray at the Wailing Wall, and "it seems that the Turkish authorities even built a place of prayer for the Jewish worshippers."[18] Until the end of the Ottoman era, Jews would always be free to pray at this sacred site, as was also documented by various photographs from the late nineteenth and early twentieth centuries.

On the other hand, during Ottoman times, Jews, like all non-Muslims, were banned from entering the Temple Mount, or al-Aqsa. Yet this was due not merely to Ottoman law but also a prohibition in Jewish law that local rabbis vehemently upheld. Nevertheless, a Jew who spent the whole night on the Temple Mount in 1833 wasn't heavily punished, because, as the Muslim ruler of the time put it, "the Jew is also circumcised, and is thus somewhat akin to a Muslim."[19] Moreover, after the Treaty of Paris, which ended the Crimean War of 1856, during which Ottomans allied with the British and French against Russia, the Ottomans would open the Temple Mount for visitors of all faiths, keeping it exclusive to Muslims only on Fridays.[20]

IMMIGRANTS WITH BLESSINGS

While welcoming Sephardic Jews, Sultan Bayezid II made a re-
mark that should be noted by xenophobic nativists everywhere,
past and present. "How can you call Ferdinand of Aragon a wise
king," the sultan asked, "the same Ferdinand who impoverished
his own land and enriched ours?"[21]

This insight was right on point, because the Sephardic Jews
came to the Ottoman Empire with new skills, as well as "a big
cultural heritage, and crates filled with books."[22] A year after
their arrival in Istanbul, in 1493, they established the very first
printing press the Middle East had ever seen.[23] They would be
followed by Armenians in 1567, then by the Greeks in 1627. (The
empire's ruling Muslims, however, with a staggering delay of 236
years, would establish their first printing press only in 1726. The
main rationale was keeping the jobs of scribes, through what
we would today call "economic protectionism," with the usual
consequence of underdevelopment.[24]) Yet still, books printed by
the Jewish press helped establish big libraries, both in Istanbul
and Salonika, which included not only the Torah, Talmud, and
other Jewish texts but also "translations of books by Islamic
scholars."[25]

A little-known contribution of Ottoman Jews to the empire
took place at the time of Taqi ad-Din (1521–1585), an Arab Muslim polymath from Egypt brought to Istanbul in 1574 by Sultan
Murad III in order to establish the first Ottoman observatory.
While calculating the course of a solar eclipse, Taqi ad-Din got
help from a "David the mathematician" in Salonika, who was a
Sephardic Jew. Soon, David was transferred to Istanbul to join
the team at the observatory. "He knew both astronomy and philosophy," wrote a later historian. "He also was well versed in the
books of the Muslims, so that Islamic scholars and jurists would
come to him for consultations."[26]

Unfortunately, though, the Istanbul observatory would survive for only a few years. In 1580, after a plague that hit the capital and a fatwa from the top cleric against the dangers of "watching the stars," the sultan ordered the observatory to be destroyed, together with all its instruments and the collections within it, marking a sad turn in Islamic civilization against the intellectual curiosity and scientific progress that had enlightened its earlier centuries.

Nevertheless, Sephardic Jews added what they could to an increasingly stagnant empire. The Turkish historian Ekmeleddin İhsanoğlu notes that thanks to the immigrants from Spain— mostly Jewish, but Muslim as well—"Ottoman scholars came into contact with new sources, which were different from those they were familiar with."[27] A document from the late fifteenth century even shows that some Jews in Istanbul educated some Muslims, among others, on "the books written by Greek philosophers."[28]

As the Ottoman state turned into a superpower in the sixteenth century, Jews proved to be a vital component as "the leading doctors, tax and customs officials, financiers, traders and manufacturers."[29] While the ruling Muslims began to look down on any job other than state, military, and religious posts, as we read in the journal *European Judaism*:

> The Jews provided the Ottoman Empire with the nucleus of a new middle class, one that was free from political ambition and on which the Turks could rely for a degree of loyalty not expected from their other subject peoples. To the Turks, the Jews were the most productive and stable minority in their domains. They valued them for their loyalty as well as for the personal contacts, skills and languages brought with them from their countries of origin.[30]

This Muslim and Jewish symbiosis in the Ottoman Empire has fascinating relics that have survived to date, one of which is the famous Sarajevo *Haggadah*: a beautifully illuminated manuscript that depicts scenes from the Bible, from Genesis through the death of Moses. It was created in Barcelona in 1350, when Jews could still live in Spain, but with the expulsion of 1492 it traveled with Jewish exiles to Italy, to somehow end up in Sarajevo, which was then an Ottoman city with a predominantly Muslim population.

Since then, those Bosnian Muslims, Bosniaks, protected the *Haggadah* as if it were one of their own sacred books. During World War II, when the Nazis and their allies were seeking all those of Jewish heritage to destroy them, the Bosnian Muslim scholar Derviš Korkut risked his life to smuggle the *Haggadah* out of Sarajevo, to be hidden in a remote mosque in the safer mountains. Then, during the early 1990s, when Bosnian Muslims suffered their own genocide at the hands of Serbian ultranationalists, the Sarajevo *Haggadah* was protected by Muslim librarians who hid the manuscript in a bank vault. Today, it is proudly displayed in the National Museum of Bosnia and Herzegovina as a precious artifact that survived first the Inquisition, then the Holocaust, and then the Bosnian genocide.[31]

BLOOD LIBELS AND MUSLIM PROTECTORS

By the seventeenth century, Ottoman military might and economic power entered a long decline, at least in comparison to the unprecedented scientific, industrial, and political developments in Europe. In this overall decay, the Ottoman Jewish communities were negatively affected as well. Moreover, a pseudo-messiah who appeared in İzmir in the 1660s, Sabbatai Zevi, left the broader Jewish community in a "state of despair," with a more insular worldview in which the earlier cosmopolitanism waned.[32] (Sabbatai Zevi's false conversion to Islam, an act followed by his sect, also created a community of the *Dönme,* or crypto Jews, whose influence on Turkish life would be much exaggerated, and exploited, by various conspiracy theorists to this day.[33])

Yet still, Jews kept finding freedom and safety in Ottoman lands, and remained loyal subjects of the empire. And if they were concerned about anything, it was not the ruling nation of the empire, that is, Muslims, but the other "ruled nation," that is, Christians. That is because antisemitism was still virulent among Christians, both within the Ottoman Empire itself as well as the European powers and Russia.

This can be observed in the course of the quintessential antisemitic canard: the blood libel. It is the totally false and absurd accusation that Jews kidnap and murder little Christian boys in order to use their blood to make the unleavened flatbread eaten during Passover. While this libel appeared in medieval Christianity and led to many pogroms against Jews, it was unknown to Muslims. However, as the Ottoman Empire westernized, it also met with the blood libel. "It almost certainly originated among the large Greek-Christian population under Ottoman rule," and its reoccurrences were "usually condemned by the Ottoman authorities."[34]

In the nineteenth century, this old myth had a new revival in the empire. As Bernard Lewis observed, blood libels became "almost commonplace in the Ottoman lands," but not among the Muslims:

> First, the libel almost invariably originated among the Christian population and was often promoted by the Christian, especially the Greek press; second, these accusations were sometimes supported and occasionally even instigated by foreign diplomatic representatives, especially Greek and French; third, Jews were usually able to count on the goodwill of the Ottoman authorities and on their help, where they were capable of providing it.[35]

The most dramatic example of this libel was the infamous Damascus Affair of 1840. It began in February of that year when a Franciscan friar and his Muslim servant disappeared in Damascus, which was then an Ottoman city with an Egyptian governor and an influential French consulate. The friars soon began circulating the news that the Jews had murdered both men in order to use their blood for Passover. The French consul, Count de Ratti-Menton, allied himself with the accusers, and supervised the investigation. Jewish leaders were arrested and brutally interrogated. Two of them died under torture, others "confessed" out of agony. Then, the authorities seized sixty-three Jewish children to extort the hiding place of the victims' blood from their mothers. Meanwhile, another blood libel case appeared in Rhodes, a Mediterranean island then ruled by Ottomans. The island's Greek Orthodox community blamed Jews for murdering a Christian boy, and convinced the Muslim governor, who went on to arrest and torture several Jews.

These horrors caused shock in the European press, alarming Western Jews. Soon, a delegation led by the British philanthropist Sir Moses Montefiore convinced the Egyptian ruler Muhammad Ali, who then had achieved control over Damascus, to free the Jewish prisoners. They were indeed released at the end of August, but without being officially acquitted. The real relief came in November, when Ottoman control of Damascus was restored, and Sir Montefiore went to Istanbul to seek help from Ottoman sultan Abdülmecid I. The sultan, who also held the title of the caliph of Islam, welcomed the delegation, heard their case, and issued a *firman,* or edict, that declared, in Montefiore's own translation:

> An ancient prejudice prevailed against the Jews. The ignorant believed that the Jews were accustomed to sacrifice a human being to make use of his blood at their feast of Passover. In consequence of this opinion, the Jews of Damascus and Rhodes, who are subjects of our Empire, have been persecuted by other nations. The calumnies which have been uttered against the

Jews, and the vexations to which they have been subjected, have at last reached our Imperial Throne. . . .

The religious books of the Hebrews have been examined by learned men . . . [and] it is found that the Jews are strongly prohibited, not only from using human blood, but even that of animals. It therefore follows that the charges made against them and their religion are nothing but pure calumny. For this reason, and for the love we bear to our subjects, we cannot permit the Jewish nation, whose innocence of the crime alleged against them is evident, to be vexed and tormented upon accusations which have not the least foundation in truth. . . .

The Jewish nation shall be protected and defended. To accomplish this object, we have given the most positive orders that the Jewish nation, dwelling in all parts of our empire, shall be perfectly protected, as well as all other subjects of the sublime Porte [Ottoman government], and that no person shall molest them in any manner whatever, except for a just cause, neither in the free exercise of their religion, nor in that which concerns their safety and tranquillity.[36]

Thanks to this edict, the blood libel incidents waned and the legal charges were dropped. The Jews who had survived imprisonment were freed. In Damascus, a Muslim was instead arrested as the true killer of the Franciscan friar and his servant. To further spread the good message, Sir Montefiore got the sultan's edict, along with a letter by London rabbis against the ritual-murder myth, translated into Greek, Arabic, and Hebrew and distributed them widely.[37] For him, it was "the Magna Carta for the Jews in the Turkish dominions."[38]

Today, a copy of this imperial edict is proudly displayed on a wall of the small Jewish museum in Istanbul.[39] It is a testimony to the fact that the "Jewish nation" had indeed found protection in the Ottoman Empire. Yet it is also a source of disappointment.

Because while Christianity largely got rid of its antisemitic myths in the twentieth century, the same tropes began gaining traction in the lands of Islam. So, the blood libel spread in the Arab world, appearing in popular books, magazines, TV series, and even public statements by rulers.[40] Those who promote it should have known that, in Islam, it was a *bid'a*—a novelty of the bad kind—and it was Muslims themselves who used to protect Jews from it.

A FAREWELL TO DHIMMI STATUS

The nineteenth century was the "longest century" of the Ottoman Empire, as a Turkish historian metaphorically called it, referring to the complexity of this turbulent era.[41] On the one hand, the Ottomans gradually lost large territories to encroaching powers such as Russia, and rising nationalisms like that of Greece, Serbia, and Bulgaria. On the other hand, they tried to modernize their state to catch up with the European superpowers. They also tried to liberalize their system in order to win the hearts and minds of their diverse peoples, many of which were now being tempted by the new currents of nationalism.

This reform effort, which had precursory steps, took its boldest form with the *Tanzimat,* or Reorganization Edict of 1839, which initiated a whole new era in the empire, putting it on track to become a constitutional monarchy with equal rights for all citizens. Its chief architect was the prominent diplomat Mustafa Reşit Paşa, who had served as the Ottoman ambassador to France and Great Britain, where he developed an affinity for liberal ideas. Its promulgator was Sultan Abdülmecid I, the reformist sultan who also issued the edict against blood libels.

In other words, in the middle of the nineteenth century, the Islamic civilization took an unprecedented step: replacing the *dhimmi* status given to Jews and Christians, which made them "protected" yet second-class citizens, with the modern principle of equal citizenship with equal rights and responsibilities. This was evident in the *Tanzimat,* which affirmed the "inviolability of life, property, and honor" of all Ottomans, "equally applicable to all Muslims and to the peoples of the millets."[42] The shift was made more explicit with an additional proclamation in 1856, the *Islahat,* which guaranteed "equality" in taxes, burdens, duties, and rights.[43] The zenith would be the Ottoman Constitution of 1876, which declared, "All subjects of the empire are called Ottomans, without distinction whatever faith they profess." It also added: "All Ottomans are equal in the eyes of the law. They have the same rights, and owe the same duties towards their country, without prejudice to religion."[44]

How did Ottoman Jews and Christians see this new legal equality under the Ottoman dome? The answer is complicated. On the one hand, the 1856 edict was "a day of rejoicing" for non-Muslims, for they had finally gained equality with Muslims.[45] However, among heads of millets, there was some discomfort, as they could lose their control over their communities. Moreover, some of the Greek Orthodox had a baffling concern, which we learn from the Ottoman statesman and scholar Ahmed Cevdet Paşa:

> In former times, in the Ottoman state, the communities were ranked, with the Muslims first, then the Greeks, then the Armenians, then the Jews, now all of them were put on the same level. Some Greeks objected to this, saying: "The government has put us together with the Jews. We were content with the supremacy of Islam."[46]

This interesting anecdote reminds us that, in the nineteenth century, antisemitic biases were still pervasive among Christians. It also shows that defining the communal gap in the late Ottoman Empire as between "Muslims" and "non-Muslims," as it is often done, is inaccurate.

The real communal gap in the late Ottoman Empire, which unfortunately escalated into violent conflict, was rather between

Muslims and Christians. The latter included Greeks, Serbs, Bulgarians, Montenegrins, and Armenians, among whom nationalist movements arose, one after another, all of which aimed at carving out new nation-states from the decaying empire through armed rebellions. In return, the Ottomans—both the state and its ruling Muslim "nation"—reacted violently. The result was a series of tragic revolts, suppressions, persecutions, expulsions, and massacres that marked the last three decades of the Ottoman Empire, putting a dark ending to a brighter story. The worst episode came in 1915, when over a million Armenians perished due to mass deportation and mass killings, in what the survivors have commemorated as *Medz Yeghern,* or Great Catastrophe. Today, I believe, it is time for the heirs of the Ottoman Empire, the Turks, to recognize this tragedy by showing empathy, expressing remorse, and offering an apology to the descendants of the victims.

OTTOMAN JEWISH EXCEPTIONALISM

It is also quite remarkable, though, that the Turkish wrath during this tumultuous era never turned against the Jews. There has been no Ottoman policy against the Jews—except limiting the number of Jewish immigrants to Palestine while welcoming them elsewhere—and there has been no intercommunal violence between Turks and Jews, no pogroms against the latter.[47]

The explanation for that exceptional state of affairs is obvious: Jews remained loyal to the Ottoman state until its very end. The Ottoman Turks faced a Serbian revolt, a Greek revolt, an Armenian revolt—they even faced a limited Arab revolt, in the Hijaz, during World War I—but they never faced a Jewish revolt.

That is because no nationalist movement emerged among Ottoman Jews to claim a part of the empire for themselves.[48] In fact, in the words of the Turkish historian Ortaylı, as late as 1908, "Turks and Jews were two groups within the Empire which were among the least exposed to nationalism."[49] No wonder an Ottoman politician of the time defined Jews as the "most reliable element."[50]

None of this proves a totally amicable relationship between Ottoman Turks and Jews. Throughout the centuries, the ruling "nation" of the empire had developed certain religious and cultural prejudices against Jews, as well as Christians, as is common in human history. Moreover, in the final decades of the empire, a new antisemitic literature appeared, most visibly in the writings of the nationalist journalist Ebüziyya Tevfik. Notably, though, this was largely an import from Europe, even copied "almost verbatim from the anti-Semitic literature in French."[51] Moreover, it did not have much impact on the Ottoman elite.[52]

For Jews, it made ample sense to be a "reliable element" of the empire, for this was the best home they had found in centuries. Also, when they looked at the forces that threatened the Ottomans, they had good reasons to be alarmed. The Eastern Christians who revolted against the Ottomans were all backed by notoriously antisemitic Czarist Russia, the very inventor of *The Protocols of the Elders of Zion*. No wonder the anti-Ottoman revolts in the Balkans often proved to be antisemitic, as the historian Stanford J. Shaw once observed:

The invading armies of Russia and Austria as well as the revolting nationalists and, later, successfully established independent Christian states, committed systematic genocide against Jews and Muslims throughout the nineteenth century. . . . In 1807, the Serbs who were revolting against the Janissary garrison of Belgrade (dahu) expelled all the Jews and Turks. . . . The Serbian press was virulently anti-Semitic, accusing Jews of robbing the peasants and debauching them with drink, as well as of being Ottoman agents because of their continued support of Ottoman rule. . . . During the height of the Greek revolution in 1821, five thousand Jews were massacred in the Morea along with most of the Muslim population. Greek nationalists went from town to town on the mainland and from island to island in the Aegean, exterminating all the Jews and Muslims they could find, many along the roads as they desperately fled to safety in what was left of the Ottoman Empire.[53]

No wonder that, at the height of the Ottoman-Russian war of 1876–1878, prayers were held in Istanbul's Ahrida Synagogue for the victory of Ottoman armies, as reported in *The Illustrated London News*.[54] In the next big conflict, the Balkan Wars, Turks and Jews again found themselves on the same side, as *The New York Times* reported in 1913. The Greek nationalists, the paper explained, were threatening the Jewish community in Çeşme, a beach town on Turkey's Mediterranean coast, with accusations of "ritual murder," which was only "a pretext for punishing them for being friendly with the Turks."[55]

Today, these stories are worth remembering not to put the Balkan peoples in the spotlight but to recall how, just a century ago, the relations between Jews, Christians, and Muslims looked remarkably different from how they are perceived in the West today. And this was true not just around the Ottoman territories but within Europe as well.

THE PRO-OTTOMAN JEWISH LOBBY

In Great Britain, the superpower of the time, two different views of the Ottoman Empire, and Muslims broadly, competed throughout the latter half of the nineteenth century. On the one side there were "Turcophiles," who believed that, in the words of Prime Minister Lord Palmerston, "the integrity and independence of the Ottoman Empire are necessary to the maintenance of the tranquility, the liberty, and the balance of power in the rest of Europe."[56] This camp also supported the Ottomans against their deadliest enemies, the Russians. On the other side, there were "Turcophobes," who "rejected the Turks as infidels, barbarians, and aliens in Europe and saw no reason to obstruct the Russians in the work of removing them."[57]

These opposing views had complex roots, but there is an interesting element that is relevant to our story: Jews in England, as well as virtually everywhere, were staunchly in the Turcophile camp. This was observed by Thomas P. O'Connor, a member of the British Parliament, who wrote the following about the Russo-Turkish war of 1877:

One of the most remarkable phenomena in the course of the war between Russia and Turkey was the extraordinary unanimity with which the Jews of every part of the world took the side of the Sultan against the Czar. People living within the same frontiers, speaking the same language, professing the same creed, with exactly the same interests, have held the most opposite views upon this Russo-Turkish question. . . . But here are the Jews, dispersed over every part of the globe, speaking different tongues, divided in nearly every sympathy—separated, in fact, by everything that can separate man, except the one point of race—all united in their feelings on this great contest![58]

Then O'Connor asked why Jews were so united in their support for the Ottoman sultan. The obvious answer was that Turks had some toleration of their subjects, "while the Russian Government is known to be even still one of the most determined oppressors of the Jewish race."[59] But there was the even deeper history of the Judeo-Islamic tradition that we have examined in this book, and O'Connor was also aware:

For many ages—more in the past than in the present, of course—there has been among large sections of the Jews the strongest sympathy with the Mohammedan peoples. . . . This alliance has been most close on many occasions. In the time

of the Crusaders, the Jews were the friends who aided the Mohammedans in keeping back the tide of Christian invasion,
which was floating against the East, and in Spain the Jews
were the constant friends and allies of the Moorish against
the Christian inhabitants of the country. The alliance must
have been very close in the past indeed to have left such deep
traces behind.[60]

These comments carried a certain dose of ire against the
Jews for being so pro-Muslim, for their own reasons, and trying
to steer British foreign policy accordingly. The immediate target
of this particular criticism was the conservative British prime
minister at the time, from 1874 to 1880, Benjamin Disraeli. He
was born in 1804 to a British Jewish family of Italian origin,
but his father had converted the family to Anglicanism when
Benjamin was twelve. Yet his Jewish roots never disappeared,
as obviously evident from his surname. To this day, he is recognized, officially, as "Britain's first, and so far only, Jewish Prime
Minister."[61]

Now, the problem with this exceptional Jewish prime minister, according to his critics, especially from the opposition Liberal
Party, was that he was exceptionally pro-Ottoman. Thomas P.
O'Connor was making this point when he wrote, annoyedly, that
Disraeli "is a kinsman of the Turk, and that, as a Jew, he feels bound
to make common cause with the Turk against the Christian."[62] The
"Christian" here was the Russian Empire, against which Disraeli
really favored the Ottomans. The English historian Edward Augustus Freeman, who despised Disraeli in private as "a dirty Jew," was
also annoyed with his pro-Ottoman policy, behind which he saw a
Jewish conspiracy, as he put in his 1877 book, *The Ottoman Power
in Europe*:

> The time has come to speak out plainly. No well-disposed per-
> son would reproach another either with his nationality or his

religion, unless that nationality or that religion leads to some direct mischief. No one wishes to place the Jew, whether Jew by birth or by religion, under any disability as compared with the European Christian. But it will not do to have the policy of England, the welfare of Europe, sacrificed to Hebrew sentiment. The danger is no imaginary one.[63]

The "danger," according to Freeman, was that Benjamin Disraeli was "the active friend of the Turk." Moreover, Freeman observed, "the most fiercely Turkish part of the press is largely in Jewish hands."[64] So, there must have been an effective Judeo-Islamic conspiracy:

The alliance runs through all Europe. Throughout the East, the Turk and the Jew are leagued against the Christian. We cannot have the policy of Europe dealt with in the like sort. . . . We cannot sacrifice our people, the people of Aryan and Christian Europe, to the most genuine belief in an Asian mystery.[65]

Bernard Lewis, who uncovered this much-forgotten story of "the pro-Islamic Jews" of nineteenth-century Europe, explained that there was no real conspiracy. Defending the Ottoman Empire against Russia was a reasonable policy from the perspective of British interests, and no wonder it was also favored by some prominent British Christians. Nevertheless, added Lewis:

Beneath the distortions and slanders of Disraeli's political enemies, there was an important element of truth. Disraeli was an admirer of Islam, of the Persians and Turks as well as the Arabs, and in his youth had even thought of joining the Turkish army as a volunteer. Moreover, his pro-Turkish sentiments were connected with his vestigial Jewishness and are typical of a good deal of Jewish opinion at the time. O'Connor, despite his malicious exaggerations, was not far wrong in speaking of the Jews in nineteenth-century Europe as a pro-Turkish, and more generally pro-Muslim, element.[66]

Disraeli's admiration for Islam was indeed all too evident in his writings. He wrote how Spanish Jews, under the persecution of Visigoths, "looked to their sympathizing brethren of the Crescent," who indeed came to their help. Thanks to those Muslims, he also wrote, "a fair and unrivalled civilization arose which preserved for Europe arts and letters when Christendom was plunged in darkness." "During these halcyon centuries," according to Disraeli, in fact it was "difficult to distinguish the followers of Moses from the votary of Mahomet."[67]

"THE MOSLEM IS SO LIBERAL . . ."

While Great Britain was the center of the alliance between "the followers of Moses" and "the votary of Muhammad," Americans also had a sense of it in a most unexpected place: the Chicago's World Fair of 1893, which was organized to celebrate the four hundredth anniversary of Christopher Columbus's arrival in the New World back in 1492. It was a major world event participated in by various nations, including the Ottomans. The latter, under the auspices of the sultan-caliph Abdülhamid II, built a pavilion in the fair called Turkish Village. It included great tents, a bazaar, a theater, and a pretty big mosque, which was "one of the earliest mosques built by a caliph on the lands where Islam is not widespread."[68]

However, besides curious Christian visitors, there were few Muslims in Chicago at the time who could use this place of worship for worship. Yet there was another religious community that came as a part of the Ottoman delegation and filled that role. "About four-fifths of the inhabitants of the Turkish village on the Midway Plaisance at the Chicago Exposition were Jews," as the journalist Isidor Lewi reported in the *New-York Tribune*. "Merchants, clerks, actors, servants, musicians, and even the dancing girls, were of the Mosaic faith, though their looks and garb would lead one to believe them Mohammedans."[69] Moreover, when the sacred day of Yom Kippur came, these Jews saw the Ottoman mosque as the ideal place of worship, and the latter had no qualms in welcoming them. As we learn in the same report from Lewi,

> the Turkish mosque was so arranged that it could be used as a Jewish house of worship also. . . . It was in this gorgeously equipped and dimly lighted mosque that the oriental Jews assembled on Tuesday evening, September 19, 1893, and read the Kol Nidra service [for Yom Kippur]. A screen of carved wood was placed across one corner of the mosque, and behind this the women, robed in white, with faces partially concealed behind white veils, worshipped. . . . Above all rose the chant of these strangely habited men and women: "Hear, O Israel! The Lord our God, the Lord is one."[70]

This Jewish service in a mosque was truly remarkable, which led Lewi to conclude: "The Moslem is liberal enough to allow religious services other than his own to take place in his houses of worship." It was a lesson in religious tolerance, he added, that "the Western people would do well to ponder."[71]

THE ZIONIST CONSPIRACY THAT NEVER WAS

The most remarkable thing about the Jewish-Ottoman friendship is that it is almost completely forgotten today, especially among Muslims. Quite to the contrary, many among the latter instead believe that Jews conspired against this last great Islamic empire and helped bring about its destruction in World War I.

This story, which is quite popular in the Islamist literature across the Muslim world and even in Turkey itself, appearing even in state-sponsored TV dramas, goes something like this:

since the Ottomans controlled Palestine, the Zionist movement, which emerged in the late nineteenth century with the aim of establishing a Jewish State in Palestine, wanted to either coopt or defeat the empire. The very founder of the movement, Theodor Herzl, met with Ottoman sultan Abdülhamid II in Istanbul in 1901 to convince him to "sell" Palestine to Jews. When the sultan boldly refused Herzl's proposal, the plot began. The Committee of Union and Progress, also known as the Young Turks, a secular political movement orchestrated by none other than Jews and freemasons, organized against Abdülhamid II, and finally toppled him in 1909. The Young Turks' championship of *Hürriyet,* or liberty, meaning the constitutional regime, was merely a pretext to sabotage the empire. No wonder the Ottomans fell into ruins in World War I, and Zionists got their hands on Palestine, soon to establish the State of Israel.[72]

The historical truth, however, is much less conspiratorial. First, the Zionist movement in Europe was indeed disillusioned with Abdülhamid's refusal to allow more Jewish settlement in Palestine, but there is no evidence that this led to a plot against the sultan or the empire itself. The Zionists lobbied European and Ottoman governments for their cause, but they did not know which would be most helpful to them. They also "knew nothing of the secret negotiations between Britain and France," which led to the Sykes-Picot Agreement of 1916 that designed the post-Ottoman Middle East.[73]

Second, there were a few prominent Jews among the Young Turks—most notably the Salonikan lawyer Emmanuel Carasso, and the economist Javid Bey, a member of the *Dönme*—but their genuine motivation was "Ottoman patriotism."[74] With the same spirit, many Ottoman Jews were either indifferent or even opposed to Zionism, as they believed, "We are Ottomans and nothing else."[75] Other Ottoman Jews were sympathetic to Zionism, but mainly as "a cultural form of nationalism . . . which did not clash with their loyalty to the Ottoman state."[76] No wonder, then, that despite such political nuances, Ottoman Jews remained loyal to the empire to the end and supported it actively before and during World War I.[77]

Third, the Young Turks were no Zionist agents, as they were eager to fiercely protect all Ottoman territories, including Palestine.[78] This became evident soon after they captured power, as *The New York Times* reported in a story dated July 26, 1909. "Young Turks Oppose a Zionist State," the headline read, quoting the novelist Herman Bernstein, who had recently returned from Turkey. "There is even less hope of establishing a Jewish State in Palestine or Mesopotamia," he observed, "under the Young Turks than under Abdul Hamid."[79] In 1917, in his last hopes to halt the British advance on Ottoman Palestine, the Young Turk general Jemal Pasha—also notoriously harsh on Arab nationalists—even deported the Jewish population of Jaffa, for he saw "Jewish colonization . . . as injurious to Ottoman interests."[80]

The deeper truth is that depicting the Young Turks as Zionist agents was a propaganda item popularized by the British and the French during World War I in order to "discredit the Young Turk regime in the Arab and more generally in the Islamic world."[81] It was echoed by some Ottoman opponents of the Young Turks as well, most notably Derviş Vahdeti, the Islamist politician who led the failed anti-constitutionalist insurrection in 1909, after which he was executed. Notably, as a native of British Cyprus, Vahdeti was educated at a missionary school where "he could have been introduced to British antisemitism."[82]

Yet this propaganda item about the Young Turks had its real impact in the later twentieth century when certain nationalists or Islamists in the Middle East looked for a conspiracy theory to explain the demise of the Ottoman Empire—instead of understanding its complex causes—and the Jewish conspiracy theory came in handy.

In post-Ottoman Turkey itself, this conspiracy theory was popularized by the new Islamist ideologues of the mid-twentieth

century, the most prominent of whom was the famous poet Necip Fazıl Kısakürek (1904–1983), whose passionate poems, pro-
pagandistic books, and provocative tabloid, *Büyük Doğu,* had
a huge impact on Turkey's Islamic circles. Kısakürek was a big
admirer of the Ottoman Empire as the standard-bearer of Islam,
but he himself was quite far from its tolerance and pluralism.
This was most evident in his vicious antisemitism, which would
have been all too surprising to most Ottomans themselves, an
irony noted by the Turkish academics Burhanettin Duran and
Cemil Aydın:

> Appropriating many of his anti-Semitic ideas from Europe,
> Kısakürek depicted Jews as the originator of Marxism and
> capitalism, and held them responsible for the early conflicts
> among Muslims, the decline of the Ottoman Empire, the im-
> itative modernization movement of Turkey and the abolition
> of the caliphate in 1924 soon after the victories of Turkish Na-
> tional Struggle. Given the fact that Ottoman Jews remained
> loyal to the Ottoman Empire and usually sided with Ottoman
> Muslims in relation to Christian nationalisms, for example,
> Kısakürek's assertion about Jewish conspiracy to weaken the
> Ottoman empire had no historical validity. Furthermore, late
> Ottoman era Islamists did not express anti-Semitic views. On
> the contrary, many Islamists of that period saw similarities in
> the destiny of Muslims and Jews as the oppressed other of Eu-
> ropean Christians. Given this background, Kısakürek's new
> Islamist discourse on Jews marks a nationalist break with the
> cosmopolitan Ottoman past as well as the influence of Eu-
> ropean anti-Semitic literature on Republican era intellectual
> life.[83]

A break with the cosmopolitan Ottoman past, and an indul-
gence in European antisemitic bilge, would indeed be a popular
trend among hard-line nationalists and radical Islamists of the

modern-day Middle East. The worst products of Christian antisemitism, from the blood libel to the *Protocols* began to be absorbed by reactionary groups. The latter, ironically, often believed that they were rejecting anything that was "un-Islamic," while in fact swallowing many Western ideas—just of the worst kind.

This is quite evident in conspiracy theories, which are still a dominant theme in nationalist or Islamist thinking in the contemporary Middle East, including in Turkey. The irony is that this kind of thinking—where internal problems are always ascribed to outside forces and their "agents" within—is quite a novelty in the Islamic civilization, as observed by a Jewish historian:

> Linguistic evidence confirms the paucity of conspiracy theories before 1800; remarkably, Middle Eastern languages even lacked a word for "conspiracy." Turkish lacking an indigenous term, the modern language uses the word *komplo*, a transliteration of the French *complot*. To conspire is rendered *komplo kurmak* (to prepare a plot). Until the twentieth century, the Arabic word for conspiracy, *mu'amara*, meant consultation. In Persian, too, *tawti'a* and *dasisa* came to mean conspiracy only in the modern era.[84]

And almost always, Jews were at the heart of all these *komplo, mu'amara,* and *dasisa,* with themes such as "invented Talmud quotations, ritual murder, the hatred of mankind, the Masonic and other conspiracy theories, taking over the world."[85] All these were "essentially alien to Islamic traditions, culture, and modes of thought." So, they were all imported from European antisemitism, just given "an Islamic twist."[86]

In the meantime, Christians, especially in the liberal West, were coming to terms with the centuries-old hatred and persecution of Jews. Admitting the flaws in their tradition and outgrowing them, many Christians also realized their affinity with Jews. The change in Catholic doctrine was nothing short of "revolutionary," as centuries-old teachings about Jews being "cursed by God" were replaced by the liberal spirit of the Second Vatican Council (1962–1965), where the Catholic Church affirmed "the spiritual patrimony common to Christians and Jews," and even declared, "God holds the Jews most dear."[87] Similarly, many Protestant denominations, especially after the Holocaust, published declarations that condemned anti-Jewish hatred, and expressed "regret for past persecutions of the Jews fomented by the churches."[88]

That is how, in the twentieth century, we also began to hear about "Judeo-Christian values" and "the Judeo-Christian tradition." The Judeo-Islamic tradition, meanwhile, began to fade from memory—of Muslims, of Jews, of everyone. Today, it is so forgotten that many would find it surprising, if not incredible.

But is it gone forever, to be buried in history? Or is there a chance for a revival? Even at this darkest hour of brutal conflict?

That is the last question on which I will say a few words.

IN THE DARKEST HOUR

*"From the river to the sea,
both people should be free."*

—My motto, November 2023*

In September 2023, I finished the first draft of this book and submitted it to my editors at St. Martin's Press. I was hoping that it could help build better understanding and sympathy between Jews and Muslims, and, perhaps, even contribute to the prospects of peace in the Middle East.

However, only days later, on October 7, I woke up to terrible news from that very Middle East. On that infamous morning, when many Israelis were observing the annual Simchat Torah holiday as well as the weekly Sabbath, hundreds of armed attackers from the Gaza Strip breached the border with Israel to raid not only nearby military posts but also civilian targets such as

---

* I used this motto in my article in the Spanish newspaper *El Pais* dated November 14, 2023: "From the River to the Sea, Both People Should Be Free." The article concluded: "The only ethical and feasible way is to promise security and dignity to both Israelis and Palestinians. It is a vision that should offer this contested land between 'the river to the sea' to not one of these peoples, but both. 'From the river to the sea,' we should cry, 'all children will be safe, and both people will be free.'"

kibbutzim and a music festival, killing more than a thousand people and taking more than two hundred hostages.

I was shocked by these atrocities and reached out to some Jewish friends, in Israel and the United States, to express my condolences. At the same time, I was concerned about what may follow. So, I opened my account on X, which many of us still recall as Twitter, and wrote:

> I am sad to see the news of innocent civilians killed & terrorized in Israel with surprise attacks by Hamas. I am worried about the innocent civilians in Gaza who may pay a terrible price. This horrific cycle of violence is endless. May God not extinguish our hopes for peace.[1]

Not everyone welcomed these thoughts. Those who rather welcomed the attacks objected to me online, claiming, "settlers are not innocent civilians," reiterating a chilling line that pro-Hamas circles, both religious and secular, have long advocated.[2] Another objector also asked me, "How do you thought [sic] dismantling colonialization would look like?"[3]

Then, in the days, weeks and months that followed, my worries about the innocent civilians in Gaza turned out to be true—and at a horrific level that I could not have imagined. The Israeli military, instead of surgical attacks on Hamas and other militant groups responsible for October 7, launched a ferocious onslaught on the whole Gaza Strip, with "indiscriminate bombing," as even the president of the United States, who supported the campaign, admitted in passing.[4] Whole neighborhoods, mosques, churches, hospitals, cemeteries, schools, and university buildings were destroyed. When I was writing these lines, more than thirty thousand people in Gaza, most of them women and children, were reportedly killed by Israeli attacks.[5] Most of the remaining 2.3 million were left homeless and were at the brink of famine, as children were dying of malnutrition. Even in the relatively calmer West Bank, hundreds of Palestinians were killed by Israeli forces or extremist settlers.[6]

Meanwhile, alarming statements came out from the Israeli side mirroring the ruthless mood I had seen on the other side. A week after October 7, Israeli president Isaac Herzog was on the news declaring, "there are no innocent civilians in Gaza."[7] He later corrected that quote, but the same line was reiterated by certain hawks, both in Israel and the United States.[8] Israeli prime minister Benjamin Netanyahu also revived an ancient reference that we have seen before in this book, in chapter 4, in the words of Pope Urban II who had launched the First Crusade against "Amalek." Netanyahu, too, defined the enemy as "Amalek," leaving many, including myself, shocked, as we do know what the Bible commands for that ancient tribe: "Spare no one, but kill alike men and women, infants and sucklings."[9]

As I was writing this epilogue, in early March 2024, this was the grim reality in the holy land, which kept sending shockwaves around the world. Israelis were mourning their losses on October 7, were still worried about the hostages kept in Gaza, and were feeling fear about the future. Jews around the world were experiencing the pain of their extended family in Israel, even as they saw a rise in antisemitic attacks and tropes in their own countries. Palestinians, and many others who felt for them, including myself, were tormented by the unprecedented destruction and misery inflicted on this already unfree people, with families losing hundreds of loved ones and seeing no signs of relief. Meanwhile, anti-Muslim and anti-Arab bigotries had resurfaced in the West, leading to ugly cases of harassment and brutal hate crimes.

Now, if you have been reading this book from the beginning up to this point, you may wonder how the rather cordial Judeo-Islamic tradition that we have been examining has collapsed into such mutually cruel bloodshed. How did Jews and Muslims, who for centuries lived together, learned from each other, and even saw each other as allies, find themselves in such a bitter enmity that some of them even began to see no innocent civilians on the other side?

AN UNEXPECTED CONFLICT

It is worth asking the question above, because this enmity was really not inevitable. A little more than a century ago, it was even unthinkable. This fact is noted by the historian Alan Dowty in his book *Arabs and Jews in Ottoman Palestine*. "Could a sharp-eyed observer of mid-nineteenth-century Palestine have detected hints of the future struggle between Jews and Arabs over this land?," he asks. The answer is "unlikely." In fact, Dowty adds, "none of the observers at the time foresaw the conflict that was yet to come."[10]

Far from signaling conflict, Ottoman Palestine rather impressed visitors from Europe with its peaceful coexistence. Among them was Rabbi Abraham Gershon (d. 1761) of Kitov, Poland, who migrated to the holy land in the mid-eighteenth century with a few hundred fellow Hasidic Jews. In a 1748 letter from Hebron, he expressed his "astonishment" in seeing that Jews "have virtually no fear of gentiles." "When there is a celebration, such as circumcision or some other occasion, the Muslim elders come, and all rejoice," the rabbi observed. "The local gentiles, even the greatest ones, love the Jews very much."[11]

No wonder the seeds of the conflict were planted not in the holy land, but in the historic hotbeds of antisemitism: Europe and Russia. Their endless persecution of Jews convinced some that the only redemption, in an age of nationalism, was to establish a Jewish nation-state in the nation's ancient homeland:

Palestine. That is how Zionism was born, at the end of the nineteenth century, as a new hope for the Jewish people. For the Arab people who already lived in Palestine for centuries, however, it would be a new threat.

Hence arose the conflict, first slowly and then rapidly. In 1917, Great Britain, the greatest colonial power of the time, took control of Palestine, putting an end to four centuries of Ottoman rule. In the same year, with the historic Balfour Declaration, the British gave a new impetus to Zionism, promising "the establishment in Palestine of a national home for the Jewish people." The growing Jewish settlement, and the Arab reaction to it, led to intercommunal violence under the British mandate. In 1947, the newly founded United Nations proposed a peaceful partition plan, but the Arab rejection led to the First Arab-Israeli War, where Israel not only defended itself but also expanded its UN-designated territory, expelling more than seven hundred thousand Palestinians. While Israelis were celebrating their independence, therefore, the Palestinians were weeping for their *Nakba,* or "catastrophe." With another major Arab-Israeli war in 1967, which erupted as an escalation in an ongoing state of conflict, Israel further expanded by seizing all the remaining Palestinian territories—East Jerusalem, West Bank, and the Gaza Strip—leaving the Palestinians living there in a constant state of occupation and subjugation. Palestinian resistance, expressed peacefully at times, also led to the rise of armed groups, which resorted to terrorist tactics, to which Israel often responded heavily, which created the cycle of violence that ultimately brought us to October 7 and its aftermath—this darkest hour.

Many volumes have been written on this painful history and by people who have much more authority than me to speak about it. For our story, though, I must emphasize a truth: This is not a religious war. It is not a war between Jews and Muslims, let alone Judaism and Islam.† It is rather a political war between two peoples for sovereignty over land—that uniquely precious land "from the river to the sea."[12]

Nevertheless, this political war in the Middle East did create a rift between Jews and Muslims around the world. It also acquired many religious symbols, emotions, and narratives—in part due to the involvement of Jerusalem and other sites holy to both faiths. Consequently, the Judeo-Islamic tradition, which had lasted for centuries, began to fade away. In fact, according to Bernard Lewis, one of the rare scholars who wrote about "the Judeo-Islamic tradition," this "long, rich, and vital chapter in Jewish history" was remarkable, but in the latter half of the twentieth century it had "come to an end."[13]

A TRAGIC ECLIPSE

On the Muslim side, this tragic eclipse was reflected by three wrong turns. One was the expulsion of hundreds of thousands of Jews that used to live in Muslim-majority countries such as Iraq, Syria, Egypt, Yemen, Algeria, Tunisia, and Morocco, most of whom ended up in Israel.[14] The very fact that those Jewish minorities lived and mostly flourished till the mid-twentieth century—as recalled nostalgically today with books such as

---

† There are various indications that the Israeli-Palestinian conflict is not a "religious war." Israel, unlike Islamophobic regimes such as China, does not target the religious freedoms of its Muslim citizens. It even has an Islamic political party—United Arab List, or *Ra'am*—that has joined the Knesset and even a coalition government. On the Palestinian side, there have been various nationalist, socialist, and even Christian parties and figures that stood up against Israel. Hamas has been explicitly Islamist, and its 1998 charter includes various religious themes, but its modified charter in 2017 declares that the group "does not wage a struggle against the Jews because they are Jewish, but wages a struggle against the Zionists who occupy Palestine."

When We Were Arabs—was a testimony to the Judeo-Islamic tradition.[15] But their exodus became a testimony to its passing.

The second wrong turn was to take the reactions against Israeli policies and turn it into hatred against Jews. This happened on a popular level, across the Arab world and even beyond, with new narratives about the perfidy of "the Jews." Ironically, but also tellingly, this new Muslim antisemitism was largely an import from its real home base: Europe. "Most common themes in the Arab antisemitic discourse," as the late scholar Esther Webbman observed, were "derived from classical Christian and Western vocabulary, especially conspiracy theories, the blood libel, Nazi imagery, and Holocaust denial."[16] There was also the infamous Russian hoax, *The Protocols of the Elders of Zion*, which was rightly discredited in the West while finding new audiences "throughout the Arab and Islamic world."[17]

Yet some "Islamic" motifs were also found for this new antisemitism. One was to revamp the ancient conflict in Medina, which we revisited in chapters 2 and 3, as a template for a permanent conflict, as the Egyptian Islamist thinker Sayyid Qutb did in his 1951 essay, "Our Struggle with the Jews." "The Jewish enmity against Islam began in Medina and has continued ceaselessly in the past fourteen centuries," he claimed, in contradiction to the facts we have seen in this book.[18] Many other modern-day Qur'anic commentators began to "absolutize" verses about the conflict with Medinan Jews, turning them "into an ideological weapon."[19] Similarly, Qur'anic verses about God punishing some past Israelites by turning them to "apes and pigs" were turned into a vilification of all Jews, though they were clearly about "a particular group of Jews in a particular time."[20]

Meanwhile, bizarre prophecies attributed to the Prophet Muhammad turned all too popular, one of them telling that Muslims, at the end of times, will set on killing "Jews," who will hide behind "Gharqad trees."[21] It has to be noted, however, that such apocalyptic tales have no basis in the Qur'an, which stresses that neither the Prophet nor any human has knowledge of the unknown.[22]

The third wrong turn, and perhaps the biggest mistake, was to justify terrorism—in the sense of deliberate attacks on civilians—as a legitimate form of Palestinian resistance. This was against Islam's traditional rules of war, rooted in Prophet Muhammad's commandment to his own soldiers: "Do not kill women, children, the old, or the infirm."[23] But some militant groups, and some scholars who support them, created loopholes to justify indiscriminate violence, which was both ethically wrong and strategically unwise.[24]

Meanwhile, on the Jewish side, too, the Arab-Israeli conflict overshadowed the Judeo-Islamic tradition. In the words of Susannah Heschel, who highlighted the pro-Islamic Jewish Orientalists that we met in chapter 8, "Jewish attitudes shifted . . . with the rise of Zionism." The establishment of the State of Israel "created entirely new conditions, political and theological, in Jewish self-understanding and relations with Islam."[25] With the exodus of Jews from Muslim countries and the recurrent Arab-Israeli wars, Jews around the world began to experience Muslims and Islam primarily through the lens of conflict. A new Jewish narrative appeared on "Islamic antisemitism," often cherry-picking the worst teachings or episodes in the Islamic tradition, or by judging its treatment of Jews not by its time but by modern liberal standards. The pro-Nazi mufti of Jerusalem, Hajj Amin al-Husayni (d. 1974), gained notoriety as if he represented all Arabs, eclipsing more noble figures such as the Moroccan King Mohammed V (d. 1961) who protected his country's 250,000 Jews during the Holocaust.[26]

For worse, two decades after its founding, a new radical right emerged in Israel, an ethno-religious chauvinism, which set on building a "Greater Israel," by constantly appropriating Palestinian lands. The leaders of this settler movement explicitly deny that Palestinians, or any non-Jews, deserve to have the same rights with Jews.[27] While their ideology does not speak to the aspirations of many Jews and Israelis, it has gained significant traction in recent years, including within political parties in Israel's governing coalition in the current war. It is a far cry, and a big regression, from the liberal humanism of Moses Mendelssohn and the Jewish Haskalah that we saw in chapter 7.

Perhaps the most popular mistake on the Israeli side was to assume that Palestinians will either accept whatever is imposed on them, or stay silent, or somehow go away—just with enough denial, deterrence, and suppression. This was an "illusion," as Israeli politician Avraham Burg warned back in 2003. "We love the entire land of our forefathers and in some other time we would have wanted to live here alone," he wrote, frankly. "But that will not happen. The Arabs, too, have dreams and needs."[28]

Twenty years later, in this darkest hour, another Israeli voice for peace, Ami Dar, also called on his fellow Jews to understand the Palestinians—and precisely because who they themselves are:

We Jews have many stories about how we never surrendered. So why does anyone think the Palestinians will give up their aspirations? They won't, and the idea that with just enough repression they will, harms all of us. The only thing that ends this is freedom and dignity for all.[29]

THE PATH TO PEACE

Freedom and dignity for all is indeed what we should all aim for. But what is the path to that bright ideal from the darkness of today?

Let me first note two popular views in the West that will *not* take us there—one of them found on the political left, the other one found on the political right.

The first view, the left-wing one, sees the problem as *colonialism*. It assumes that Israel is yet another European colony, the last remaining one, which came and seized the country of non-white natives—and it has to be "decolonized." There is some truth to it, in the sense that Zionist immigration and expansion do have resemblances to "settler colonial" movements in history.[30] However, many other Jews—including the *Mizrahim,* or "Easterners," who were expelled from Arab countries—came to Israel as refugees. Moreover, the French, the British, or the Italian colonizers knew that they were colonizers. They had a homeland, a metropole, to which they would return when they were given enough trouble—as they really did. But Israelis do not see Israel as their colony. They rather see it as their historical homeland, to which they finally returned, and which they will defend to death. When they are threatened, they will fight like hell, as they did after October 7.

The second view, the right-wing one, sees the problem as *terrorism.* It assumes that Israel cannot find peace because all these vile terrorists and their wicked patrons keep attacking it out of mere malice, religious extremism, and antisemitism. There is some truth to it, in the sense that extremism and antisemitism are real problems in the Muslim world today, and radical actors like the Iranian regime can wield them as spoilers to peace in the region. But the real driver behind Hamas and its ilk—or the nationalist or Marxist factions that preceded them, with no less militancy—is the plight of the Palestinian people. Unless Palestinians find freedom and dignity, there will be always young men who will take up arms for that cause—or even just to avenge their own family who may have been killed in the latest round of the brutal "war on terror."

Both of these views seem to miss the true nature of the conflict, which appears obvious to me, as someone with a sense of the Ottoman Empire and its long and bloody aftermath, from the Balkans to the Middle East: it is *nationalism,* the most definitive, and often the most dangerous, political force of our modern times. This is a conflict, in other words, between Jewish and Palestinian nationalisms. The former has been able to establish its nation-state, on the very territory that the latter one also claims. To resolve such conflicts, you can neither disestablish the nation-state, nor extinguish the nationalism that aspires for its own. All you can do is to reconcile them, by curbing their maximalist ambitions, redrawing maps and carving territories, offering both of them a future of their own and a peace that they could live with.

In other words, the much-aspired yet never realized "two-state solution" may still be our best hope. Or a perhaps a confederated version of it—"two states, one homeland"—as a group of Israeli and Palestinian peaceniks were calling for when I was writing these lines.[31]

Of course, it is up to Israelis and Palestinians to decide upon their future. The rest of us can respectfully hope and pray that they can find a path to peace.

However, as a believer in the Judeo-Islamic tradition, I will dare to end with a religious call.

As Jews and Muslims, let's understand that we are not irreconcilable enemies. In this political war that is tearing us apart, there is really no "Amalek," as there are no Meccan polytheists. Rather, on both sides, there are religious zealots and nationalist fanatics, as well as ordinary people who, understandably, only feel the pain on their own side.

But our religious traditions can offer better. From the Torah, Jews can revive that noble instruction: "You shall not wrong a stranger or oppress him, for you were strangers in the land of Egypt."[32] From the Qur'an, Muslim can revive another noble command: "Do not let the hatred of a people lead you to injustice. Be just. That is closer to righteousness."[33]

Even more, both Jews and Muslims can come together in the spirit of that great prophet in whose footsteps we have been walking: Moses. His legacy, as we saw earlier in this book, included two separate liberations. First, in his actual life in ancient Egypt, Moses liberated Jews from oppression. Then, almost two millennia later, the mere story of Moses inspired the first Muslims of Mecca in their own liberation from oppression.

Moses, in other words, is the symbol of liberty for both Jews and Muslims.

So, could he symbolize that again? Could we perhaps see, one day, "Moses Accords," securing freedom and dignity for all Israelis and Palestinians, from the river to the sea?

Let us hope and pray with all our hearts that that day may yet come.

I will do so, even in this darkest hour.

Mustafa Akyol
Washington, D.C.
March 2024

ACKNOWLEDGMENTS

First of all, I would like to thank all my colleagues at the Cato Institute, beginning with Peter Goettler, president and CEO, and Ian Vasquez, vice president for international studies. Since 2018, they have provided me a safe harbor in Washington, D.C., to work on the key issues of Islam in the modern world, at a time when the world I used to know turned increasingly bleak. That gratitude also extends to the generous donors of the Cato Institute, enabling its principled and unwavering defense of human freedom since 1977.

Then I would like to thank my editors at St. Martin's Essentials, Joel Fotinos, and Emily Anderson, in addition to my literary agents, Jeff Gerecke and Diana Finch, for making this book possible.

There are also many friends to whom I am grateful for helping me in my writing and research. First and foremost, Jack Miles has been a precious companion and a wise mentor, who shared many thoughts, suggestions and corrections which made this book much better than what it would otherwise be. I am also grateful to his endearing wife, Kitty Miles, for the wonderful hospitality in California. Then, there are other friends who graciously devoted their time to read my manuscript, at least in part, to make very thoughtful and helpful suggestions. They include

Rabbi Reuven Firestone, Ari Gordon, Steven Grosby, Mirnes Kovac, Ahmet Kuru, Haroon Moghul, Shahid Rahman, Jonathan Jacobs, Martino Diez, Ayman S. Ibrahim, Rumee Ahmed, Celeste Marcus, Louis Fishman, and Afzal Amin. Thanks also to Leon Wieseltier, who generously shared his insights as well as his rich library at the journal *Liberties*, as well as Lenn Goodman, Hayri Kırbaşoğlu, Sadreddin Berk Metin, Hüseyin Akgün, David Sklare, John Barton, and Gabriel Said Reynolds who helped me with my research. Many thanks to Cato Institute interns Faris Pohan and Rifal Imam for their help in editing.

There are also institutions where I have had the privilege to teach, engage, and learn about some of the issues covered in this book. They include the Acton Institute and its Collins Center for Abrahamic Heritage, where I have made friends with many believers from different traditions, with a common belief in human dignity and liberty. Special thanks there go to Kris Mauren, Nathan Mech, and Stephen P. Barrows. I am also thankful to the Islamic Civilization and Societies Program at Boston College, where I have had the chance to teach brilliant students and team up with accomplished academics. They include Kathleen Bailey, David M. DiPasquale, Peter Skerry, and Martha Bayles.

Then there are people closer to my heart. I am forever indebted to my parents, Taha and Tülin Akyol, who have given me all the love and support a son can dream of. The wisdom and integrity of my father, Taha Akyol, a prominent Turkish intellectual, has been my guide for decades, and it will forever remain so. His deep knowledge of Ottoman history also helped me gain some of the perspectives you may see in chapter 9. I am also happy to see my younger brother, Ertuğrul, flourish as an academic in his field, and I expect even greater works from him in the future.

Then there is my nuclear family. My three beloved sons, Levent Taha (nine), Efe Rauf (six), and Danin Murad (three) may not yet go through this book, but I hope they will be drawn to it in the future. May they discover within it that their father tried to do some good in a tragic era marred by enmity and violence. My deepest wish for them, as I expressed in its opening pages, is to inherit a world marked by greater peace, justice, and liberty for all.

Finally, the greatest praise should go to my beloved spouse, Riada Ašimović Akyol. In the tapestry of our shared story, her discerning eye and unmatched emotional intelligence have illuminated my work and our journey alike. Amid joys and blessings, trials and anxieties, she has been a steadfast companion, guiding light, and source of unwavering support. I am committed to supporting her personal growth and flourishing career, while cherishing together each moment of this miracle that we call life.

In closing, I extend my gratitude to God, to whom I owe my very existence, as I believe. He is the God of Abraham, Moses, Jesus, Muhammad, and each one of us, as I also profess. Throughout the discourse of this book, amidst the exploration of various religious arguments, I've remained acutely aware of my huge limitations in contrast to His infinite wisdom. Thus, I conclude with a humble reminder from the Islamic tradition: In this book, I've endeavored to seek the truth as best as I could, yet it is God who knows best.

NOTES

Unless stated otherwise, all quotes from the Qur'an in this book are from M. A. S. Abdel Haleem, *The Qur'an: A New Translation* (Oxford: Oxford World Classics, 2004).

INTRODUCTION

1. S. D. Goitein, *Jews and Arabs* (New York: Dover Publications, 1955), 130. The full quote reads: "Modern Western civilization, like the ancient civilization of the Greeks, is essentially at variance with the religious culture of the Jewish people. Islam, however, is from the very flesh and bone of Judaism. It is, so to say, a recast, an enlargement of the latter, just as Arabic is closely related to Hebrew. Therefore, Judaism could draw freely and copiously from Muslim civilization and, at the same time, preserve its independence and integrity far more completely than it was able to do in the modern world or in the Hellenistic society of Alexandria."

2. Remarks by Hamza Yusuf on the *Jordan B. Peterson Podcast*, May 23, 2022. Hamza Yusuf, "Becoming a Muslim," *Jordan B. Peterson Podcast*, https://www.youtube.com/watch?v=x7ZlXD7COMU.

3. The very term "theocracy" was in fact coined by the first-century Jewish historian Josephus to define the very system established by "our legislator," meaning Moses: "He ordained our government to be what, by a strained expression, may be termed a *theokratia*, by ascribing the authority and power to God." As for Islam, the eminent historian Montgomery Watt defined the Medinan state as a "theocratic polity," only to specify that it is "not very like the Israelite theocracy of the judges. It is closer to the theocracy under Moses." Montgomery Watt, *Muhammad at Medina* (London: Oxford University Press, 1968), 240.

4. Patricia Crone, *God's Rule: Government in Islam* (New York: Columbia University Press, 2004), 15–16.

5. See Mustafa Akyol, *The Islamic Jesus* (New York: St. Martin's Press, 2017), 152–57. Also see the section "A Dispute over Jesus?" in chapter 2.

6. "Jews have always regarded the doctrine of the Trinity," in the words of the *Jewish Encyclopedia,* "as one irreconcilable with the spirit of the Jewish religion and with monotheism." Samuel Krauss, "Trinity," in *Jewish Encyclopedia,* ed. Isidore Singer (New York: Funk & Wagnalls, 1901), 12:261.

7. Galatians 2:15.

8. Qur'an 3:3.

9. The Qur'anic Ten Commandments, although not explicitly called that, are in verses 17:22–38. "They begin with the worship of one God followed by kindness to parents, giving in charity to the poor, and moderation in spending. It prohibits adultery, unjust killing, robbing orphans' property and cheating in trade. These laws correspond to the parts of the Decalogue (Exodus 20:1–21) minus the Sabbath observance." Shabir Akhtar, *Islam as Political Religion* (New York: Routledge, 2011), 205.

10. Ali Tabari, *The Book of Religion and Empire: A Semi-official Defence and Exposition of Islam Written by Order at the Court and with the Assistance of the Caliph Mutawakkil (A.D. 847–861),* trans. Alphonse Mingana (London: University Press, 1922), 1:159.

11. Patricia Crone and Michael Cook, *Hagarism: The Making of the Islamic World* (New York: Cambridge University Press, 1972), 77. The speculative thesis of "Hagarism" that Crone and Cook offered in this book was largely discredited later, but some of their more factual observations are still valid.

12. In his *Guide for the Perplexed,* written originally in Judeo-Arabic (Arabic language with Hebrew letters), "Maimonides uses the term sharia . . . [as] corresponding to the Torah." With an interesting nuance, he also uses *fiqh,* the interpretation of Sharia, to refer to the Halakha. See Leora Batnitzky and Yonatan Y. Brafman, *Jewish Legal Theories: Writings on State, Religion, and Morality* (Waltham, MA: Brandeis University Press, 2018), xxviii.

13. See Aaron W. Hughes, *Shared Identities: Medieval and Modern Imaginings of Judeo-Islam* (New York: Oxford University Press, 2017), 26.

14. The term "creative symbiosis" was promulgated by Shelomo Dov Goitein in the mid-twentieth century and later widely adopted by others to define the nature of the relationship between medieval Jews and Muslims. For a recent discussion of the concept, see Steven M. Wasserstrom, *Between Muslim and Jew: The Problem of Symbiosis Under Early Islam* (Princeton: Princeton University Press, 1995).

CHAPTER 1: THE MOSES OF MECCA

1. A. Guillaume, *The Life of Muhammad: A Translation of ibn Ishaq's Sirat Rasul Allah* (Oxford: Oxford University Press, 1955), 160.

2. Qur'an 92:1–2.
3. Qur'an 28:31.
4. Muhammad al-Bukhari, *Sahih al-Bukhari*, Book 1, Hadith 3.
5. Martin Lings, *Muhammad: His Life Based on the Earliest Sources* (Rochester, VT: Inner Traditions: 2006), 44. The original source is Ibn Ishaq in Guillaume, *The Life of Muhammad*, 107. The story is also narrated in brief in *Sahih al-Bukhari*, 3392.
6. Ibid.
7. There is indeed evidence that the first Muslims perceived their mission "as a venture of Ishmael's children." See Mohsen Goudarzi, "The Ascent of Ishmael: Genealogy, Covenant, and Identity in Early Islam," *Arabica* 66, no. 5 (November 2019): 415–84.
8. Qur'an 36:6.
9. Guillaume, *The Life of Muhammad*, 107.
10. Ahmet Önkal, "Hicret," *İslâm Ansiklopedisi* (İstanbul: TDV, 1998), 17:459.
11. There are no recorded numbers about the population of Mecca at the time of Muhammad and estimates vary. A 2022 study suggested as low as some five hundred people (Majied Robinson, "The Population Size of Muḥammad's Mecca and the Creation of the Quraysh," *Der Islam* 99, issue 1, 2022). However, Islamic sources give the number of the Meccan soldiers in the Battle of Badr as 950, which, with estimated noncombatants, suggests a population of a few thousand people. Nebi Bozkurt, "Nüfus," *İslâm Ansiklopedisi* (İstanbul: TDV, 2007), 33:293–294.
12. Qur'an 46:9.
13. Reuven Firestone, *An Introduction to Islam for Jews* (Philadelphia: Jewish Publication Society, 2010), 153.
14. Another Qur'anic character who does not appear in the Bible is Luqman, but it is not clear whether he is a prophet, or *rasul,* and opinions about that differ in the Islamic tradition. Shuayb is another Qur'anic prophet, who may or may not be Biblical: by some exegetes he is identified as the Biblical Jethro, Moses' father-in-law, but others think he is a different person.
15. The most notable passages about Moses are in the chapters *al-A'raf* (7), *Yunus* or "Jonah" (10), *Ta-Ha* (20), *al-Shu'ara* (26), *al-Naml* (27), *al-Qasas* (28), *Ghafir* (40), *al-Zukhruf* (43), and *al-Nazi'at* (79).
16. "All but seven of the some 309 [Qur'anic verses] concerning Mūsā's mission in Egypt were revealed in the Meccan period." See Michael D. Calabria, "The Foremost of Believers: The Egyptians in the Qur'ān, Islamic Exegesis, and Extra-Canonical Texts" (PhD dissertation, University of Exeter, December 2014), 260.
17. Qur'an 28:4–6.
18. As the Ottoman polymath Katip Çelebi wrote in the seventeenth century: "'Pharaoh' is the title applied to the kings of Egypt. In olden times every Egyptian sovereign was called Pharaoh. The tyrant who reigned in the time of

Moses (the blessing of God be upon our Prophet and upon him), and whom
Muslim historians name Walid, is distinguished from the rest by the ap-
pellation 'the Pharaoh of Moses.' Three, or by another account seven, of the
Pharaohs were tyrants and oppressors, and the last and greatest of these was
the Pharaoh of Moses. His story is current and celebrated and is recorded in
the histories. He is notorious among the Jews for his unjust treatment and
oppression of the Children of Israel. Among the community of Islam too he
has become a byword: if anyone is notorious for cruelty and tyranny and is
to be exposed to blame and censure and regarded as corrupt, they say, 'He is
like Pharaoh.' In all Koran commentaries and histories he is described as a
misguided infidel, and people at large have adopted this view." Katip Çelebi,
Balance of Truth (London: George Allen and Unwin, 1957), 75.

19. Exodus 1:22.
20. Adam Silverstein, "Haman's Transition from the Jahiliyya to Islam," *Jerusa-
    lem Studies in Arabic and Islam* 34 (2008): 292.
21. Ibid.
22. On 28:6, see Seyyed Hossein Nasr et al., eds., *The Study Qur'an* (San Fran-
    cisco: Harper One, 2015), 947; Caner K. Dagli, "On Al-Qasas," ibid.
23. Silverstein, "Haman's Transition from the Jahiliyya to Islam," 303. Silverstein
    also shows that premodern Muslim exegetes didn't see a problem in connect-
    ing the Qur'anic and Biblical Hamans.
24. Ibid.
25. Ibid, 304–5.
26. Qur'an 28:7–9. A version of the same story is also narrated in 20:38–40.
27. Qur'an 28:13.
28. Qur'an 20:11–14.
29. Qur'an 28:31, 32, 34.
30. There is a tendency among some classical exegetes of the Qur'an to equate
    the Biblical Jethro with the Qur'anic Prophet Shu'ayb, especially since the
    latter was "sent to Midian" (7:85; 11:84; 29:36). But others think that these
    two figures couldn't be the same person and the Qur'an suggests no connec-
    tion, which is also what I understand.
31. See Qur'an 28:27 vs. Exodus 2:16.
32. Exodus 9:1.
33. Qur'an 20:47–52.
34. Qur'an 26:29.
35. Jack Miles, *God in the Qur'an* (New York: Knopf, 2019), 155.
36. Qur'an 20:44.
37. Qur'an 26:28.
38. Miles, *God in the Qur'an,* 170.
39. Qur'an 10:78.
40. Qur'an 5:104.

41. Exodus 7:11–12.
42. Exodus 8:19.
43. Qur'an 26:45–50. Versions of the same story are also narrated in 7:111–128 and 20:60–73.
44. Miles, *God in the Qur'an*, 174–75.
45. See Bat-Sheva Garsiel, "The Qur'an's Depiction of Abraham in Light of the Hebrew Bible and Midrash," in *The Convergence of Judaism and Islam*, ed. Michael M. Laskier and Yaacov Lev (Gainesville: University Press of Florida, 2011).
46. John Barton, "The Hebrew Bible in the Muslim Imagination," in *Adaptable for Life: The Message of the Old Testament for Contemporary Readers* (Eugene, OR: Cascade Books, forthcoming). Also see Jon D. Levenson, *Inheriting Abraham: The Legacy of the Patriarch in Judaism, Christianity, and Islam* (Princeton: Princeton University Press, 2012), 144–45. Levenson notes that both Christianity and Islam universalize Abraham's importance for the whole human race, but Christianity does so through Christ fulfilling the covenantal promises made to Abraham through Isaac, and Islam does so by "omitting the Abrahamic covenant altogether," 144.
47. Qur'an 22:78.
48. Exodus 9–11.
49. Some have suggested that the Qur'anic *ṭūfān* could refer to the ninth plague (darkness) or the tenth plague (the death of Egypt's firstborn), but it is hard to know. Meanwhile, another Qur'anic verse states that Moses was given "nine clear signs" (17:101), although these may include not just punishments on Egypt but also the two miracles of Moses: his staff and hand.
50. Qur'an 26:60–66.
51. Qur'an 10:90–92.
52. Ömer Faruk Harman, "Firavun," in *İslâm Ansiklopedisi* (İstanbul: TDV, 1996), 13:118–21.
53. Çelebi, *Balance of Truth*, 78.
54. Qur'an 7:136–7.
55. Mustafa Öztürk, "Ehl-i Kitap Söyleşisi (Bölüm 1: Mekke Dönemi)," Berlin Türk Eğitim Derneği, YouTube, July 24, 2021, https://www.youtube.com/watch?v=phqOtQNcatg.
56. Sayed Abul Hasan Ali Nadwi, *Muhammad, the Last Prophet: A Model for All Time* (Lucknow: India Academy of Islamic Research and Publications, 2008), 94.
57. Qur'an 7:138–40.
58. Qur'an 7:144.
59. Qur'an 7:145.
60. Qur'an 7:150.
61. Ibid.
62. Qur'an 20:88.

63. Qur'an 20:97.
64. "Sâmirî," *İslâm Ansiklopedisi* (İstanbul: TDV, 2009), 36:78–79; Bernard Heller, "al-Sāmirī," in *Encyclopaedia of Islam*, 2nd ed. P. Bearman et. al. (Leiden: Brill, 2012), 8:1046.
65. Maulana Abdul Majid Daryabadi, *Tafsir ul-Qur'an* (Karachi: Darul Ishaat, 1991), 3:113–14. In the original work, Daryabadi gives reference to *Jewish Encyclopedia* and Abdullah Yusuf Ali's translation of the Qur'an.
66. Qur'an 7:152.
67. Qur'an 7:153.
68. Qur'an 7:155.
69. Qur'an 7:156.
70. Exodus 32:28.
71. Miles, *God in the Qur'an*, 191. Miles also observes: "In the story that the biblical narrator tells, Yahweh is far more violent with the Israelites than Allah is in the story that He tells. Moses as well is a far angrier, more impetuous figure in the Bible than in the Qur'an," 197.
72. Qur'an 7:159.
73. *The Study Qur'an*, 462.
74. Ibid. In their commentary, the authors also remind of another verse from the same sura, or chapter, with a similarly nuanced message: "We dispersed them over the earth in separate communities; some are righteous and some less so" (7:168).
75. This reported Medinan insertion into the Meccan chapter *al-A'raf* is, quite notably, 163–170. It is a passage that describes the "disobedience" and "arrogance" of the Israelites, and adds, "We said to them, 'Be like apes! Be outcasts!'" (7:166). It reflects a tone that is harsher than the Meccan verses on Israelites.
76. Guillaume, *Life of Muhammad*, 197.
77. Michael Lecker, "Muhammad," *Encyclopaedia Judaica*, 2nd edition, ed. Fred Skolnik (Detroit: Thomson Gale, 2007), 14:602.
78. Fakhr ad-Din al-Razi, *The Great Exegesis*, commentary on 28:48–55.
79. Qur'an 28:48.
80. In Islamic literature, the incident is called *Isra'* and *Mi'raj*, the former term referring to the journey from Mecca to Jerusalem, the latter referring to the journey to the heavens. In 17:1, the Qur'an briefly refers to the *Isra'*, but not the *Mi'raj*, which only comes from hadith sources. Meanwhile, "the identity of 'the furthest place of prayer' has been disputed, leading to several traditions." Michael Sells, "Ascension," *Encyclopedia of the Qur'an*, ed. Jane Dammen McAuliffe (Leiden: Brill, 2001), 1:177.
81. The most famous of these miracles is the story that a spider built a web at the entrance of the cave in which the Prophet and Abu Bakr hid, making the polytheists think that the cave must be empty. The hadith that relate the

story are widely considered *hasan* or "good," which means not as strongly established as *sahih*, but still sufficiently established as supporting evidence.

82. Qur'an 9:40.
83. Qur'an 2:248. See Reuven Firestone, "Shekhinah," *Encyclopedia of the Qur'an*, 5:589.

CHAPTER 2: WHAT REALLY HAPPENED IN MEDINA (PART I)

1. *Sahih al-Bukhari*, 2411.
2. A. Guillaume, *The Life of Muhammad: A Translation of ibn Ishaq's Sirat Rasul Allah* (Oxford: Oxford University Press, 1955), 241.
3. "Muhayrîk en-Nadrî," *İslâm Ansiklopedisi* (Ankara: TDV, 2020), 32:22.
4. Omid Safi, *Memories of Muhammad* (New York: Harper Collins, 2009), 134.
5. Ibn Sa'd, Kitāb aṭ-Ṭabaqāt, I:501–503; "Muhayrîk en-Nadrî."
6. Whether Jews can fight on the Sabbath has been discussed in the Jewish tradition. During the Maccabean revolt against the Seleucid Empire (167–160 BCE), the rebel priest Mattathias famously ruled that "self-defense on the sabbath was permissible." John P. Meier, *A Marginal Jew: Rethinking the Historical Jesus* (New Haven: Yale University Press, 2009), 33.
7. Muqtedar Khan, "'He Was the Best of the Jews' Said Prophet Muhammad," *American Muslim*, December 1, 2009, http://theamericanmuslim.org/tam.php/features/articles/he_was_the_best_of_the_jews_said_prophet_muhammad. Also see Allen S. Maller, "An Unorthodox Rabbi Allied with Prophet Muhammad," *Times of Israel*, March 11, 2015.
8. Rizwi Faizer, ed., *The Life of Muhammad: Al-Waqidi's Kitab al-Maghazi* (New York: Routledge, 2011), 91.
9. Guillaume, *The Life of Muhammad*, 231.
10. Muhammad Hamidullah, *The First Written Constitution in the World: An Important Document of the Time of the Holy Prophet* (Lahore: Sh. Muhammad Ashraf Publishers, 1968), 12, 15.
11. In the words of Lecker, the so-called Constitution of Medina is "the most significant document that has survived from the time of the Prophet Muhammad," and "although the original document was not preserved and is only known from literary sources, it is widely acknowledged as authentic and as dating back to the time of the Prophet." Michael Lecker, *The "Constitution of Medina": Muhammad's First Legal Document* (Princeton: Darwin Press, 2004), ix.
12. See Ovamir Anjum, "The 'Constitution' of Medina: Translation, Commentary, and Meaning Today," Yaqeen Institute, January 14, 2022. The Qur'an's distinction between "those who believe" and "those who submit" in 49:18 is a helpful guide to these terms.
13. Articles 18 and 27. See Lecker, *The "Constitution of Medina": Muhammad's First Legal Document*, 34, 35.

14. The term "one community" (*umma wahida*) is used earlier in the text, in article 2, to define all participants. Here, Jews are defined as *ummah ma'a al-mu'minīn*, or "one community with the believers," suggesting that Jews and Muslims made a single political community. However, there are also alternative readings of the phrase: "Due perhaps to scribal error or the underdeterminacy of the Arabic script at the time, four variants of this clause are preserved. The standard version is Ibn Isḥāq's: *ummah ma'a al-mu'minīn*: one community with the Believers. Abū 'Ubayd's version: *ummah min al-mu'minīn*: one community from among the Believers. At least two other variants exist. One is: *amanah min al-mu'minīn*: secure from the believers, and finally, a different reading of Ibn Isḥāq: *lil-yahūd banī 'awf dhimmah min al-mu'minīn*: the Jews have the *dhimmah* protection from/by the Believers." (Anjum, "The 'Constitution' of Medina.") Michael Lecker also prefers the third meaning mentioned above: "the Jews of Banu Awf are secure from the believers." (Lecker, *The "Constitution of Medina": Muhammad's First Legal Document*, 35.)

15. Article 28. See Lecker, *The "Constitution of Medina": Muhammad's First Legal Document*, 35.

16. Articles 44, 45, 46, ibid., 37.

17. Ibid., 76. Ibn Ishaq in Guillaume, *The Life of Muhammad*, 48. Also see Uri Rubin, "The 'Constitution of Medina': Some Notes," *Studia Islamica*, no. 62 (1985): 9–10.

18. Scholars like Wellhousen, Watt, and Goto have argued that the text is "a composite form of several documents of various dates." See Lecker, *The "Constitution of Medina": Muhammad's First Legal Document*, 183.

19. Ibid., 76. Ibn Ishaq in Guillaume, *The Life of Muhammad*, 239.

20. Mohammad Jebara, *Muhammad, the World-Changer* (New York: St. Martin's Essentials, 2021), 233.

21. *Sahih al-Bukhari*, 4680.

22. For Shiites, meanwhile, the tenth day of Muharram, or 'Ashura, gained an additional significance as the day of mourning for the tragic murder of the Prophet's grandson, Hussein, at the infamous massacre of Karbala in the year 680.

23. Qur'an 3:68.

24. As Montgomery Watt observes: "Muhammad contemplated a religious and political arrangement which would give a measure of unity but would not demand from the Jews any renunciation of their faith or acceptance of Muhammad as prophet with a message for them. Such an arrangement would be in accordance with the general idea that each prophet was sent to a particular community, and that the community to which he was sent was the Arabs." Watt, *Muhammad at Medina* (London: Oxford University Press, 1968), 201.

25. Qur'an 2:62.

26. Qur'an 2:41.

27. Abdullah ibn Salam was a convert who played prominent roles in the next

few decades of Islam. Some exegetes of the Qur'an even think that verse 13:43 referred mainly to him. "You have not been sent," that verse reads, quoting the "unbelievers" who rejected Muhammad. In return, Muhammad is commanded to say: "God and whosoever possesses knowledge of the Book suffices as a witness between you and me." (Translation from *The Study Qur'an.*)

28. Qur'an 26:197. Chapter 26, *al-Shu'ara,* is considered to be Meccan. But various classical exegetes have thought that this particular verse must be an addition from the Medinan period, as it does not fit the Meccan context, where we know of no Jews who "recognized" the truth of the Qur'an.

29. Qur'an 2:91–92.

30. "Jewish rabbis showed hostility to the apostle in envy, hatred, and malice," Ibn Ishaq writes, "because God had chosen His apostle from the Arabs." Guillaume, *The Life of Muhammad,* 239.

31. Reuven Firestone, "The Problematic of Prophecy," Keynote address at the International Qur'anic Studies Association Conference, Atlanta, November 20, 2015.

32. Guillaume, *The Life of Muhammad,* 266.

33. Qur'an 2:146.

34. Muqatil ibn Sulayman writes this in his commentary on Qur'an 2:146. *Tefsir-i Kebir,* trans. Beşir Eryarsoy (İstanbul: İşaret, 2006), 1:136. Mustafa Öztürk also confirms that, in the history of Qur'anic exegesis, the replacement of the Kaaba with the Prophet Muhammad was a later development, which ultimately became the standard view.

35. Reuven Firestone, *An Introduction to Islam for Jews* (Philadelphia: Jewish Publication Society, 2010), 35.

36. Moshe Gil, *A History of Palestine, 634–1099* (Cambridge: Cambridge University Press, 1992), 62. Gil quotes this text from the Midrash, only to add that some Jews who welcomed Islamic conquests in Palestine and Syria may have seen Prophet Muhammad in this light.

37. Frank Talmage, "Nethanel Ben al-Fayyumi," *Encyclopaedia Judaica,* 15:92.

38. Steven M. Wasserstrom, *Between Muslim and Jew: The Problem of Symbiosis Under Early Islam* (Princeton: Princeton University Press, 1995), 78. Wasserstrom's original source is Goldziher, "Usages Juifs: d'après la littérature religieuse des Musulmans," *Revue des Études Juives* 28 (1894), 75–84.

39. Guillaume, *The Life of Muhammad,* 261. The rabbi reportedly had come from Najran, with a group of Christians, whose visit to Medina is a well-known story. In Ibn Ishaq's words, "When the Christians of Najran came to the apostle the Jewish rabbis came also and they disputed one with the other before the apostle." Ibid., 258.

40. Qur'an 29:46.

41. Rizwi Faizer, *The Life of Muhammad, Al-Waqidi's Kitab al-Maghazi* (New York: Routledge, 2011), 91. The Qur'anic verse quoted in the passage is 3:186.

42. Ali ibn Ahmad al-Wahidi, *Asbab al-Nuzul,* trans. Mokrane Guezzou (Amman: Royal Aal al-Bayt Institute for Islamic Thought, 2008), 137.
43. *Sahih al-Bukhari,* 2411.
44. *Sahih al-Bukhari,* 1312–1313.
45. Imam Muhammad Al-Bukhari, *Al-Adab Al-Mufrad,* comp. Abu Naasir Ibrahim Abdur Rauf (Dakwah Corner Publications, 2014), 105.
46. Qur'an 4:105–106. For the occasion of this verse, see *The Study Qur'an,* 242.
47. Fakhr al-Din al-Razi shares this report in his monumental work, *The Great Exegesis,* in the commentary on verse 4:105, as well as Ibn Kathir in his exegesis. Most exegetes don't mention the name of the falsely accused Jew, but he is named as Zayd ibn Samin by Ibn Abbas, *Tanwir al-Miqbas min Tafsir Ibn 'Abbas,* trans. Mokrane Guezzou (Amman: Royal Aal al-Bayt Institute for Islamic Thought, 2007), 100–101.
48. Qur'an 2:144.
49. Qur'an 2:148. This verse comes soon after the verse that orders the change of *qibla,* confirming "each community has its own direction," so Jews could continue with their own direction, too.
50. Faizer, *The Life of Muhammad: Al-Waqidi's Kitab al-Maghazi,* 92.
51. Mehmet Ali Kapar, "Kâ'b b. Eşref," *İslâm Ansiklopedisi* (TDV: Istanbul, 2001), 24:3–4.
52. For more on this argument, see my book *Reopening Muslim Minds: A Return to Reason, Freedom, and Tolerance* (New York: St. Martin's Press, 2021), 207–10.
53. Guillaume, *The Life of Muhammad,* 363.
54. Faizer, *The Life of Muhammad: Al-Waqidi's Kitab al-Maghazi,* 87–88.
55. Those leaders of Banu Nadir had moved to Khaybar to "prepare for war against Muhammad and to recruit the aid of Arab tribes." Leah Bornstein-Makovetsky, "Khaybar," in Skolnik, *Encyclopaedia Judaica,* 12:107.
56. Ibid.
57. Ibn Kathir, *Tafsir Ibn Kathir,* abridged, ed. Safiur-Rahman Al-Mubarakpuri, et al. (Lebanon: Maktaba Dar-us-Salam, 2003), 30.
58. Ibid.
59. According to the second narration about 2:256, the verse was revealed when a Muslim man in Medina, who had sons who adopted Christianity before the emergence of Islam, wanted to convert those sons again to Islam. See al-Wahidi, *Asbab al-Nuzul,* 24–25.
60. *Al-Azhab,* or "The Parties," is the name of a whole Qur'anic chapter, 33, where a big section (verses 9–27) is about the Battle of the Trench.
61. Martin Lings, *Muhammad: His Life Based on the Earliest Sources* (Rochester, VT: Inner Traditions, 2006), 225–26.
62. Ibid.
63. Guillaume, *The Life of Muhammad,* 464.

64. Muqatil ibn Sulayman, *Tafsir Muqatil,* 33:26.

65. The Biblical passage reads: "When you march up to attack a city . . . [and] if they refuse to make peace and they engage you in battle, lay siege to that city. When the Lord your God delivers it into your hand, put to the sword all the men in it. As for the women, the children, the livestock and everything else in the city, you may take these as plunder for yourselves" (Deuteronomy 20:10–14). Various Muslim writers have pointed to this passage as the source of the punishment on Banu Qurayza. Among them is the Saudi bureaucrat Ahmed Zaki Yamani, who argued, "The rule applied to Bani Qurayza is not Islamic, but an application of Deuteronomy, the enemy's Book." Ahmed Zaki Yamani, "Humanitarian International Law in Islam: A General Outlook," in *Understanding Islamic Law: From Classical to Contemporary,* ed. Hisham M. Ramadan (Oxford: Altamira Press, 2006), 78.

66. Hans Küng, for example, says: "Much of Muhammad's crude power politics, like those of the Hebrew Bible, can be explained in terms of the time, which as yet knew no human rights and was accustomed to brutal methods of waging war without mercy." Küng, *Islam: Past, Present, Future* (Oxford: Oneworld Publications 2007), 111.

67. W. N. Arafat, "New Light on the Story of Banū Qurayza and the Jews of Medina," *Journal of the Royal Asiatic Society of Great Britain and Ireland* no. 2 (1976): 100–107. For a critique of Arafat's article, see M. J. Kister, "The Massacre of the Banu Qurayza: A Re-examination of a Tradition," *Jerusalem Studies in Arabic and Islam* 8 (1986): 61–96.

68. Barakat Ahmad, *Muhammad and the Jews: A Re-examination* (New Delhi: Vikas Publishing House, 1979), 85.

69. See "Did Muhammad (pbuh) Kill 800 Jews of Banu Quraiza? Dr. Shabir Ally," public talk on June 30, 2015, YouTube, https://www.youtube.com/watch?v=OxST_mauX88.

70. Hamza Yusuf, "A New History of the Prophet of Islam," *Renovatio,* March 24, 2021, https://renovatio.zaytuna.edu/article/a-new-history-of-the-prophet-of-islam.

71. Mohamad Jebara, *Muhammad, the World-Changer: An Intimate Portrait* (New York: St. Martin's Press, 2021), 11–12.

72. Fred Donner, *Muhammad and the Believers: At the Origins of Islam* (Cambridge, MA: Harvard University Press, 2010), 73.

73. Tom Holland, *In the Shadow of the Sword: The Birth of Islam and the Rise of the Global Arab Empire* (New York: Doubleday, 2012), 353.

74. Ibid., 477. Holland refers to the Dutch historian Hans Jansen for this view.

75. One example is the story that Muhammad was fatally poisoned by Zaynab bint Al-Harith, a Jewish woman from the Banu Nadir tribe whose family members were reportedly killed by Muslims at the Battle of Khaybar. In Ibrahim's words,

"The poison narrative remains a major source of anti-Jewish detestation in Muslim circles, despite its implausibility. Not only does it depict Muhammad as naïve, coveting a cooked meal by a Jewess after he reportedly killed members of her family . . . but it also invites us to believe that the effect of the poison remained in Muhammad's blood for over four years . . . [during which] Muhammad remained an unstoppable commander-in-chief." Ayman Ibrahim, *Muhammad's Military Expeditions: A Critical Reading in Original Muslim Sources* (forthcoming), chapter 5. My thanks to Ibrahim for granting access to this book before its release date.

76. See Ehsan Roohi, "Muhammad's Disruptive Measures Against the Meccan Trade: A Historiographical Reassessment," *Der Islam* 100, no. 1 (2023): 40–80. Roohi argues that the sira (Prophetic biography) literature may be "portray[ing] things in a much harsher light," for political and sectarian reasons, and that "this leaves us with our (near-)contemporary evidence, primarily the Qur'an, as the main, if not always so promising, avenue for Islamic origins" (74–75).

77. Ibrahim, *Muhammad's Military Expeditions*, chapter 5.

78. Ibid.

79. Qur'an 8:56.

80. Qur'an 8:58.

81. For example, in a highly polemical tone, the Libyan scholar Ali Muhammad Al-Sallabi writes: "Under the terms of the constitution, Jews were guaranteed a free and noble life under the banner of the newly-formed Islamic country. . . . But none of this consoled or pleased the Jews; they did not live up to the terms of the agreement, at first showing envy and minor rebelliousness and eventually attempting to kill the Prophet and support invading armies against their Muslim neighbours. And so in the end, each of the three Jewish tribes of Al-Madeenah was soon punished for its betrayal and treachery." *Noble Life of the Prophet*, trans. Faisal Shafeeq (Houston, TX: Dar-us-Salam Publications, 2017), 2:847.

82. Watt, *Muhammad at Medina*, 216.

83. Ibid., 217.

84. Al-Tabari, *The History of Al-Tabari*, trans. David Waines (Albany: State University of New York Press, 1992), 36:46. Tabari mentions this "Jew from Khaybar" while narrating "The events of the year 255," which corresponds to the Gregorian year 869 CE.

85. Harry Munt, "No Two Religions: Non-Muslims in the Early Islamic Hijaz," *Bulletin of the School of Oriental and African Studies*, no. 2 (2015): 78:261.

86. Ibid.

87. Ibid.

88. Yosef Tobi, *The Jews of Yemen: Studies in Their History and Culture* (Leiden: Brill, 1999), 35.

89. Yohanan Friedmann, *Tolerance and Coercion in Islam* (Cambridge University Press: 2003), 153.

90. Al Wahidi, for example, writes: "Jews acted wrongfully and destroyed the agreement that was between them and the Messenger of God." *Asbab al-Nuzul*, 87.

CHAPTER 3: WHAT REALLY HAPPENED IN MEDINA (PART II)

1. Haroon Moghul, *Two Billion Caliphs: A Vision of Muslim Future* (Boston: Beacon Press, 2022), 150.

2. James Parkes, *A History of Palestine from 135 AD to Modern Times* (London: Victor Gollancz, 1949), 81.

3. Ibid., 82. Also see Michael Avi-Yonah, "Benjamin of Tiberias," *Encyclopaedia Judaica*, 2nd edition, ed. Fred Skolnik (Detroit: Thomson Gale, 2007), 3:362.

4. Jacob Neusner, "Exilarch," ibid., 6:602.

5. A. V. W. Jackson, "Persia," *Jewish Encyclopedia*, ed. Isidore Singer (New York: Funk & Wagnalls, 1901), 9:648.

6. Andrew Sharf, "Byzantine Empire," in Skolnik, *Encyclopaedia Judaica*, 4:326.

7. Ibid.

8. The term "Judaizing monotheism" is from Shelomo Dov Goitein, who finds it a more appropriate definition of the faith of "Himyar kings" than Judaism proper in *The Jewish World: History and Culture of the Jewish People*, ed. Eli Kedourie (New York: Harry N. Abrams, 1979), 179.

9. The "reprisal" comment is from Heinrich Graetz, *The History of the Jews* (Philadelphia: Jewish Publication Society of America, 1891), 3:66.

10. Ibid., 3:64.

11. A. Guillaume, *The Life of Muhammad: A Translation of Ibn Ishaq's Sirat Rasul Allah* (Oxford: Oxford University Press, 1955), 152.

12. See Qur'an 85:4–10. The identity of the "makers of the trench," or *ashab al-uhdud*, has been discussed in the Islamic tradition, with various explanations. But the most cited and "strongest" view is that they were the people of King Dhu Nuwas who persecuted the Christians of Najran. Muhammed Eroğlu, "Ashâbü'l-Uhdûd," *İslâm Ansiklopedisi* (İstanbul: TDV, 1991), 3:471.

13. Qur'an 30:2–4.

14. Mokrane Guezzou, *Asbab al-Nuzul by Ahmad al-Wahidi*, ed. Youser Meni (Amman: Royal Aal al-Bayt Institute for Islamic Thought, 2008), 125.

15. Qur'an 5:82.

16. See G. W. Bowersock, *Crucible of Islam* (Cambridge, MA: Harvard University Press, 2017); Juan Cole, *Muhammad: Prophet of Peace Amid the Clash of Empires* (New York: Bold Type Books, 2018). Also, in *A History of Palestine*, Moshe Gil touched upon the war between Byzantines and Sassanids, noting that Muslims and Jews took opposite sides. He even argued, "One can assume

that [Muhammad's campaign on Khaybar] was in some way connected with the defeat of the Persians, assumed to be the defenders of the Jews." Gil, *A History of Palestine, 634–1099* (Cambridge: Cambridge University Press, 1992), 8.

17. See Michael Lecker, "The Jews of Northern Arabia in Early Islam," in *The Cambridge History of Judaism,* vol. 5, *Jews in the Medieval Islamic World,* ed. Phillip I. Lieberman (Cambridge: Cambridge University Press, 2021), 263. Here Lecker argues that the particular groups mentioned in the Covenant of Medina, including Banu Tha'laba, the tribe of Rabbi Mukhayriq, were Ghassanid in origin and were politically allied with Byzantium. Also see Michael Lecker, "Were the Ghassanids and the Byzantines Behind Muhammad's Hijra?," in *Les Jafnides: Des rois arabes au service de Byzance,* eds. Denis Genequand and Christian Julien Robin (Paris: De Boccard, 2015). Here, Lecker writes: "The Ghassanids—and indirectly their Byzantine overlords—intervened with the Khazraj and their collaborators from the Aws on behalf of Muhammad and convinced them to provide him with a safe haven. . . . And the Byzantine/Ghassanid cause would have been served by the destabilization of Medina and the replacement of the Jews, longtime allies of the Sassanians, with a political entity friendly to Byzantium" (289).

18. The virgin birth of Jesus, as well as his own miracle of speaking at the cradle, is narrated in chapter *Maryam* (19:16–22, 29–33). And in the Meccan chapter *al-Zukhruf,* Jesus is called "an example for the Children of Israel" (43:59).

19. It is notable that the term appears only in Medinan chapters (3, 4, 5, 9), but not Meccan ones. Jesus is also called "word" of God in 3:45 and 4:171, a term whose theological significance is unmistakable from a Christian point of view.

20. Mustafa Akyol, *The Islamic Jesus: How the King of the Jews Became a Prophet of the Muslims* (New York: St. Martin's Press, 2017), chapter 7, "Islamic Christology."

21. Ibid., chapters 2 and 3. Notably, Jewish Christianity was an abominable heresy for both mainstream Christians and mainstream Jews. As Rabbi Reuven Firestone kindly reminded in a private note: "Jewish Christianity . . . was extremely threatening to early rabbinic Jewish communities. They even composed a prayer that is still said to this day in traditional prayer services in the core prayer of the Amidah that calls for God to cure the 'minim,' which is understood by many to refer to Jews who 'look' Jewish but also accept Jesus." The *Jewish Encyclopedia* explains that the term *minim,* or "heretic," was used for various groups, including "the Judæo-Christian," and the latter increasingly became a concern for Judaism, as they "separated themselves from all connection with the Jews and propagated writings which the Rabbis considered more dangerous to the unity of Judaism than those of the pagans." Joseph Jacobs and Isaac Broydé, "Min (p. Minim)," *Jewish Encyclopedia* (1906), 8:595.

22. Qur'an 4:156–57.

23. Montgomery Watt, *Muhammad at Medina* (London: Oxford University Press, 1968), 317. Watt also observes: "We find that stories of Jesus the Messiah (*Isa al-Masih*) are used in the Qur'an as part of the intellectual attack on the Jews. He is represented as having gone to the children of Israel with a message from God confirmed by evidences (*bayyinat*) and having been rejected by many of them. It is significant that the twelve apostles are called the *ansar* or 'helpers' of Jesus, the name applied to the Arabs of Medina who supported Muhammad and opposed the Jews."

24. Peter Schäfer, *Jesus in the Talmud* (Princeton: Princeton University Press, 2007), 74. Also see my book *The Islamic Jesus*, 154.

25. Ian Mevorach, "Qur'an, Crucifixion, and Talmud: A New Reading of Q 4:157–58," *Journal of Religion and Society* 19 (2017): 3. Also see Peter Laffoon, "Polyphony and Symphony: A Rereading of Q 4.157," *Islam and Christian–Muslim Relations* 32, no. 2 (2021).

26. Unpacked Staff, "Muhammad and the Jews," Jewish Unpacked, https://jewishunpacked.com/muhammad-and-the-jews/.

27. Rabbi Allen S. Maller, "Did Some Rabbis Once Think Prophet Muhammad Was Authentic?," *Eurasia Review*, December 17, 2021, https://www.eurasiareview.com/17122021-did-some-rabbis-once-think-prophet-muhammad-was-authentic-oped/.

28. Guillaume, *The Life of Muhammad*, 261.

29. Watt, *Muhammad at Medina*, 219.

30. Salime Leyla Gürkan, "Jews in the Qur'an: An Evaluation of the Naming and the Content," *İlahiyat Studies: A Journal on Islamic and Religious Studies* 7, no. 2 (Summer/Fall 2016): 200.

31. Asaad Alsaleh, "The Concept of Rida in the Qur'an: Popular Misunderstanding and the Westernization of Jews and Christians," in *Islamic Law and Ethics*, ed. David R. Vishanoff (London: IIIT, 2020), 136. Alsaleh observes: "Misinterpretations of this verse have eclipsed and blurred an established opinion that the verse was directed to Prophet Muhammad within a specific historical context, and that its use as a timeless reference overlooks that context."

32. Ibid., 148.

33. Qur'an 5:64. Quoting this verse, the 1998 charter of Hamas claimed, "There is no war going on anywhere, without having their finger in it." The 2017 charter of the militant group, however, omitted some of these categorically antisemitic accusations.

34. Ibid.

35. In his *Grand Exegesis*, Razi addresses the "difficulty" in this verse, 5:64, by noting that "Jews are united in that they have not said such a thing [God's Hand is shackled] and that they don't believe in that." Then he goes on to suggest explanations. Maybe Medinan Jews may have said this as mere polemic against Muslims, or maybe some of them were influenced by "the philosophers" who

may have such beliefs which limit the power of God. Fahruddin Er-Râzi, *Tefsir-i Kebir Mefâtihu'l-Gayb* (Ankara: Akçağ Yayınları, 1992), 9:142.

36. Qur'an 9:30.

37. Mahmoud Ayoub, "Uzayr in the Qur'an and Muslim Tradition," in *Studies in Islamic and Judaic Traditions*, ed. W. M. Brinner and S. D. Ricks (Atlanta: Scholars Press, 1986), 10. In his *al-Tafsir al-Kabir*, in his commentary on 9:30, Fakhr al-Din al-Razi shares the same view, referring to Ubayd ibn Umayr. He also gives other options: perhaps it was a group of Jews who held this view but in Arabic it is common to attribute the acts of some to many; or perhaps some ancient Jews held this view but it was later abandoned.

38. Meir M. Bar-Asher, *Jews and the Qur'an* (Princeton: Princeton University Press, 2021), 45–46.

39. Marc B. Shapiro, "Islam and the Halakhah," *Judaism: A Quarterly Journal of Jewish Life and Thought* 42, no. 3 (Summer 1993): 334–35.

40. Qur'an 3:113–114.

CHAPTER 4: UNDER THE KINGDOMS OF ISHMAEL

1. The quote is from an article adapted from David J. Wasserstein's lecture at the School of Oriental and African Studies in London: "So, what did the Muslims do for the Jews?," *Jewish Chronicle*, November 24, 2016. Decades ago, a similar conclusion was also offered by Shelomo Dov Goitein, who wrote, "Islam saved the Jewish people." Goitein, "On Jewish-Arabic Symbiosis," *Molad* 2 (1949): 261 [Hebrew]; quoted in Susannah Heschel, "Orientalist Triangulations," in *The Muslim Reception of European Orientalism: Reversing the Gaze*, ed. Susannah Heschel and Umar Ryad (London: Routledge, 2018), 167.

2. As Bernard Lewis observed, "There are some parallels between the Muslim doctrine of jihad and the rabbinical Jewish doctrine of *milhemet mitsva* or *milhemet hova*, with the important difference that the Jewish notion is limited to one country whereas the Islamic jihad is worldwide." Bernard Lewis, *The Jews of Islam* (Princeton: Princeton University Press, 1987), 21.

3. I rely on Shoemaker, who estimates that the "early apocalyptic tradition that has been adopted and adapted by this more recent text was originally produced sometime in the middle of the seventh century," which "must have been produced not long after Muhammad's followers arrived in Syro-Palestine, most likely within a decade or so of their conquests." Stephen J. Shoemaker, *A Prophet Has Appeared: The Rise of Islam Through Christian and Jewish Eyes, A Sourcebook* (Oakland: University of California Press, 2021), 138, 142.

4. The translation is taken from ibid., 139.

5. Ibid.

6. Ibid., 141.

7. Nadia Maria El-Cheikh, "Muhammad and Heraclius: A Study in Legitimacy," *Studia Islamica,* no. 89 (1999): 5.
8. See Qur'an 9:5 and 9:29.
9. For a defense of this interpretation, with reference to some classical exegetes, see Asma Afsaruddin, *Jihad: What Everyone Needs to Know* (New York: Oxford University Press, 2022), 29–32.
10. See Eli Barnavi, *A Historical Atlas of the Jewish People,* revised edition (New York: Schocken, 2002), 77.
11. Daniel J. Sahas, "The Face-to-Face Encounter Between Patriarch Sophronius of Jerusalem and the Caliph Umar Ibn al-Khattab: Friends or Foes?," in *The Encounter of Eastern Christianity with Early Islam,* ed. Emmanouela Grypeou, Mark Swanson, and David Thomas (Leiden: Brill, 2006), 38.
12. Ibid.
13. Al-Tabari, *The History of Al-Tabari,* trans. David Waines (Albany: State University of New York Press, 1992), 11:191.
14. Moshe Gil, *A History of Palestine, 634–1099* (Cambridge: Cambridge University Press, 1992), 57.
15. Andrew Sharf, "Byzantine Empire," *Encyclopaedia Judaica,* 2nd edition, ed. Fred Skolnik (Detroit: Thomson Gale, 2007), 4:326.
16. Eliyahu Ashtor, Haïm Z'ew Hirschberg, and Shimon Gibson, "Arab Period," ibid., 11:154.
17. Robert G. Hoyland, *Seeing Islam as Others Saw It: A Survey and Evaluation of Christian, Jewish and Zoroastrian Writings on Early Islam* (Princeton: Darwin Press, 1997), 450.
18. Ashtor, Hirschberg, and Gibson, "Arab Period."
19. The quote "more than five hundred years" is from Gil, *A History of Palestine, 634–1099,* 69.
20. Ibid., 70.
21. Ashtor, Hirschberg, and Gibson, "Arab Period," 156.
22. Ibid.
23. Shoemaker, *A Prophet Has Appeared,* 140.
24. Ashtor, Hirschberg, and Gibson, "Arab Period," 155.
25. F. E. Peters, *Jerusalem: The Holy City in the Eyes of Chroniclers, Visitors, Pilgrims, and Prophets from the Days of Abraham to the Beginnings of Modern Times* (Princeton: Princeton University Press, 1985), 193.
26. Ibid.
27. Gil, *A History of Palestine, 634–1099,* 92.
28. Ibid.
29. See Oded Peri, *Christianity Under Islam in Jerusalem: The Question of the Holy Sites in Early Ottoman Times* (Leiden: Brill, 2001), 52. Also see Maher Y. Abu-Munshar, "In the Shadow of Muslim-Christian Relations: A Critical

Analytical Study to the Narration of the Pact of 'Umar," *Al-Bayan—Journal of Qur'ān and Ḥadīth Studies*, (2021): 19. Abu-Munshar concludes: "The chain of narrators contains untrustworthy narrators. The main defects in the text are: it contains a nameless city; it uses unfamiliar vocabulary to those prevailing at the time of 'Umar such as *zunnār*; prohibition from teaching the Qur'ān; and with whom the treaty was concluded. These defects assert the claim that 'Umar is not the originator of this document" (22).

30. Abu-Munshar, "In the Shadow of Muslim-Christian Relations," 5, 19.
31. Ibid., 6–7.
32. Qur'an 9:29.
33. Robert G. Hoyland, *In God's Path: The Arab Conquests and the Creation of an Islamic Empire* (New York: Oxford University Press, 2015), 198.
34. Ziauddin Ahmad, "The Concept of Jizya in Early Islam," *Islamic Studies* 14, no. 4 (Winter 1975): 294. According to Ahmad, it seemed "certain that the Arabs first knew about this tax from the Persians."
35. Paul L. Heck, "Poll Tax," *Encyclopedia of the Qur'an*, ed. Jane Dammen McAuliffe (Leiden: Brill, 2001), 4:153.
36. Barnavi, *A Historical Atlas of the Jewish People*, 80.
37. Gil, *A History of Palestine, 634–1099*, 57.
38. Stefan Leder, "The Attitude of the Population, Especially the Jews, Towards the Arab-Islamic Conquest of Bilād al-Shām and the Question of Their Role Therein," *Die Welt des Orients* 18 (1987): 67.
39. Ibid.
40. Michael Lecker, "The Jewish Reaction to the Islamic Conquests," in *Dynamics in the History of Religions Between Asia and Europe: Encounters, Notions, and Comparative Perspectives*, ed. Volkhard Krech and Marion Steinicke (Leiden: Brill, 2012), 185. Lecker refers to the books of Qudāma ibn Ja'far and Ibn 'Asākir.
41. Ibid. The comment is from Lecker.
42. Hoyland, *Seeing Islam as Others Saw It*, 528.
43. Ibid.
44. Shoemaker, *A Prophet Has Appeared*, 64.
45. Ibid. According to Sebeos, these mysterious Jews from Edessa who went to "the sons of Ishmael" were not successful at first because of the religious difference between them and Arabs.
46. Ibid.
47. Ibid.
48. Ibid., 68.
49. Gil, *A History of Palestine, 634–1099*, 61.
50. Maurice Henry Harris, *History of the Mediaeval Jews: From the Moslem Conquest of Spain to the Discovery of America* (New York: Bloch, 1921), 25.
51. Ibid., 25–26.

52. Hoyland, *Seeing Islam as Others Saw It,* 528.

53. Ibid.

54. I. M. Casanowicz, "Spain," *Jewish Encyclopedia,* ed. Isidore Singer (New York: Funk & Wagnalls, 1901), 11:485.

55. R. Dykes Shaw, "The Fall of the Visigothic Power in Spain," *English Historical Review* 21, no. 82 (1906): 214.

56. Edward Gibbon, *The History of the Decline and Fall of the Roman Empire* (London: E. Duyckinck, Collins, 1822), 5:294.

57. Eliyahu Ashtor, "Muslim Spain," in Skolnik, *Encyclopaedia Judaica,* 19:68.

58. Salo Wittmayer Baron, *A Social and Religious History of the Jews* (New York: Columbia University Press, 1958), 3:92. Baron added, "We must, of course, discount many legendary accretions, gross exaggerations by later Christian chroniclers," while also noting: "Such active revenge of decimated Spanish Jewry on their Visigothic oppressors need not be doubted."

59. Jane S. Gerber, "The Jews of Muslim Spain," in *Cambridge History of Judaism,* vol. 5, *Jews in the Medieval Islamic World,* ed. Phillip I. Lieberman (Cambridge: Cambridge University Press, 2021), 172.

60. Norman Roth, "The Jews and the Muslim Conquest of Spain," *Jewish Social Studies* 38, no. 2 (Spring 1976): 145–58.

61. Menahem Ben-Sasson and Oded Zinger, "The Maghrib and Egypt," in Lieberman, *Jews in the Medieval Islamic World,* 129.

62. That nun was named Hroswitha and her definition of Córdoba gained global fame in Maria Rosa Menocal, *The Ornament of the World: How Muslims, Jews and Christians Created a Culture of Tolerance in Medieval Spain* (Boston: Back Bay Books, 2003), 12–13.

63. Abram Leon Sachar, *A History of the Jews* (New York: A. A. Knopf, 1940), 169.

64. Harris, *History of the Medieval Jews,* 60.

65. Richard Gottheil and Meyer Kayserling, "Granada," in Singer, *Jewish Encyclopedia,* 6:80.

66. Maria Angeles Gallego, "The Calamities That Followed the Death of Joseph Ibn Migash: Jewish Views on the Almohad Conquest," in *Judaeo-Arabic Culture in al-Andalus,* ed. Amir Ashur (Cordoba: Oriens Academics, 2013), 92.

67. Joel L. Kraemer, *Maimonides: The Life and World of One of Civilization's Greatest Minds* (New York: Crown, 2008), 215. Kraemer refers to the Arab physician Ibn Abi Usaybi'a, who wrote, "Moses ben Maimon served as physician to Saladin," adding that some historians question this report but that he sees no reason to doubt it.

68. The *Encyclopaedia Judaica* mentions this story as a "legend." "Maimonides, Moses," in Skolnik, *Encyclopaedia Judaica,* 13:382.

69. The quote, and the information about Richard the Lionheart, are in Henry S. Gehman, "Maimonides and Islam," *Muslim World* 25, no. 4 (October 1935): 386.

70. See Barnavi, *A Historical Atlas*, "A Golden Age in North Africa" (92–93), and "Berber North Africa and Mamluk Egypt" (116).

71. Joseph Telushkin, *Jewish Literacy: The Most Important Things to Know About the Jewish Religion, Its People, and Its History* (New York: William Morrow, 1991), 170. Telushkin adds: "During these three centuries, many Jews were invited to hold high government positions, and Jewish religious and cultural life flourished."

72. Barnavi, *A Historical Atlas of the Jewish People*, 116.

73. *Sunan ibn Majah*, 2842. The same commandment is also reported in other authoritative hadith collections, such as: *Sahih al-Bukhari*, 3014; *Sahih Muslim*, 1744b; and *Sunan Abi Dawud*, 2672.

74. The Biblical passage on Amalek is from I Samuel 15:3, whose own aggression against the Israelites provoked this ruthless response (see Deuteronomy 25:17–19). Pope Urban's labeling of Muslims as "Amalek" can be found in August C. Krey, *First Crusade* (Princeton: Princeton University Press, 1921), 36. Here we read that, "turning to bishops," the Pope said: "You, brothers and fellow bishops; you, fellow priests and sharers with us in Christ, make this same announcement through the churches committed to you, and with your whole soul vigorously preach the journey to Jerusalem. When they have confessed the disgrace of their sins, do you, secure in Christ, grant them speedy pardon. Moreover, you who are to go shall have us praying for you; we shall have you fighting for God's people. It is our duty to pray, yours to fight against the Amalekites. With Moses, we shall extend unwearied hands in prayer to Heaven, while you go forth and brandish the sword, like dauntless warriors, against Amalek."

75. This Crusader logic is paraphrased by Robert Chazan: "If war is waged against the Muslim nonbelievers, then the worst of the nonbelievers, the Jews, because of the sin of deicide attributed to them, should be the first target." Chazan, *European Jewry and the First Crusade* (Berkeley: University of California Press, 1987), 77.

76. Ibid., 53.

77. Simon R. Schwarzfuchs, "Crusades," in Skolnik, *Encyclopaedia Judaica*, 5:311.

78. Chazan, *European Jewry and the First Crusade*, 70.

79. Schwarzfuchs, "Crusades," 5:312.

80. Krey, *The First Crusade*, 261.

81. Amin Maalouf, *The Crusades Through Arab Eyes* (New York: Schocken, 1984), xiv.

82. Carole Hillenbrand, *The Crusades: Islamic Perspectives* (Chicago: Fitzroy Dearborn, 2018), 270.

83. Gil, *A History of Palestine, 634–1099*, 829.

84. Maalouf, *The Crusades Through Arab Eyes*, 137–38.

85. Jonathan Phillips, *The Life and Legend of the Sultan Saladin* (New Haven: Yale University Press, 2019), 23.

86. Shiite sources are often less sympathetic to Salah al-Din, which is an understandable reflection of the darker side of his legacy, which includes the destruction of the Shiite Fatimid Caliphate in Egypt, the execution of certain Shiite scholars, and other acts of sectarian persecution.

87. Ross Brann, "Jewish Perceptions of and Attitudes Toward Islam and Muslims, in Lieberman, *Jews in the Medieval Islamic World*, 81.

88. In "Saladin and the Jews," E. Ashtor-Strauss notes "some doubt has arisen as to the historical authenticity of his report," meaning that "in 1190 Saladin proclaimed that Jews could settle again in Jerusalem." Then he adds: "In order to examine the trustworthiness of al-Harizi's report, we should naturally ascertain whether such an act would have been in keeping with the policy of Saladin. The answer to this question must be in the affirmative." *Hebrew Union College Annual 1956*, no. 27 (Cincinnati, 1956): 324.

89. Brann, "Jewish Perceptions of and Attitudes Toward Islam and Muslims," 81. For a different translation, also see Judah al-Kharizi, *The Book of Tahkemoni: Jewish Tales from Medieval Spain*, trans. and ed. David Simha Segal (Portland, OR: Littman Library of Jewish Civilization, 2001), 556. "Ephraim" is the name of one of Ten Lost Tribes of Israel, but it can be used as a reference to all. Sources do not explain why al-Harizi may have used the term "all seed of Ephraim," but apparently it is some reference to Jews who were dispersed from their historical homeland.

90. Haïm Z'ew Hirschberg, "Saladin," in Skolnik, *Encyclopaedia Judaica*, 17:680.

91. Allan Harris Cutler and Helen Elmquist Cutler, *The Jew as Ally of the Muslim* (Notre Dame, IN: University of Notre Dame Press, 1987). Also see a mainly positive review of the book—as an "intriguing and even compelling argument"—by Daniel Pipes in *Commentary*, March 1987.

92. Jonathan Burton, "Christians, Turks, and Jews on the Early Modern Stage," in Burton, *Traffic and Turning: Islam and English Drama, 1579–1624* (Wilmington: University of Delaware Press, 2005), especially 196–210.

93. David M. Freidenreich, *Jewish Muslims: How Christians Imagined Islam as the Enemy* (Oakland: University of California Press, 2022), 1.

94. Krisztina Szilágyi, "Muhammad and the Monk: The Making of the Christian Bahira Legend," *Jerusalem Studies in Arabic and Islam* 34 (2008): 174, 177. Szilágyi adds that this Bahira legend is only one of the "stories about Jewish involvement in the foundation of Islam, which had been circulating among Christians already since the rise of Islam" (189).

95. Peter the Venerable, *Writings Against the Saracens*, trans. Irven M. Resnick (Washington, DC: Catholic University of America Press, 2016), 40.

96. Mehmet Karabela, *Islamic Thought Through Protestant Eyes* (New York: Routledge, 2021), 12.

CHAPTER 5: HALAL JUDAISM, KOSHER ISLAM

1. Jacob Neusner and Tamara Sonn, *Comparing Religions Through Law: Judaism and Islam* (London: Routledge, 1999), 246.
2. Elisha Russ-Fishbane, *Judaism, Sufism, and the Pietists of Medieval Egypt: A Study of Abraham Maimonides and His Times* (Oxford: Oxford University Press, 2015), 1–2.
3. Ibid.
4. Alan Brill, "Interview with Elisha Russ-Fishbane," Kavvanah.blog, January 23, 2016, https://kavvanah.blog/2016/01/23/interview-with-elisha-russ-fishbane -judaism-sufism-and-the-pietists-of-medieval-egypt-a-study-of-abraham -maimonides-and-his-circle/.
5. Ibid.
6. Obadiah Maimonides, *Treatise of the Pool*, trans. Paul Fenton (London: Octagon Press, 1981), 8.
7. S. D. Goitein, *Jews and Arabs* (New York: Dover Publications, 1955), 182.
8. Brill, "Interview with Elisha Russ-Fishbane."
9. Marc B. Shapiro, "Islam and the Halakhah," *Judaism: A Quarterly Journal of Jewish Life and Thought* 42, no. 3 (1993): 334–35.
10. Ibid.
11. "Halacha for Thursday 3 Tammuz 5783," Halacha Yomit, June 22, 2023, https://halachayomit.co.il/en/default.aspx?HalachaID=2367.
12. Rabbi Naftali Brawer, "Is It Forbidden for Jews to Enter a Church? An Orthodox and a Reform Rabbi Tackle Problems in Jewish Life," *Jewish Chronicle,* August 22, 2008, https://www.thejc.com/judaism/rabbi-i-have-a-problem /is-it-forbidden-for-jews-to-enter-a-church-1.4626.
13. "Can Muslims Eat Kosher?," Islam Question & Answer, March 25, 2012, https://islamqa.info/en/103701.
14. Yasir Qadhi, "Is Kosher Meat Halal? A Comparison of the Halakhic and Shar'ia Requirements for Animal Slaughter," *Muslim Matters,* June 22, 2012, https://muslimmatters.org/2012/06/22/is-kosher-meat-%E1%B8%A5alal-a -comparison-of-the-halakhic-and-shar%CA%BFi-requirements-for-animal -slaughter/.
15. The common proclamation, called *shahadatayn* (the two witnessings) includes also the prophecy of Muhammad. So it reads: "There is no god but God, and Muhammad is His messenger." But the earliest proclamations, found on coins and papyri, seem to include only the first part. See Fred Donner, *Muhammad and the Believers: At the Origins of Islam* (Cambridge, MA: Harvard University Press, 2010), 112.
16. See "Islam and Judaism: Some Related Religious Terminology," in Reuven Firestone, *An Introduction to Islam for Jews* (Philadelphia: Jewish Publication

Society, 2010), 253. Thanks to Rabbi Firestone for also, in a private correspondence, pointing out some nuances between these terms.

17. Bernard Lewis, *The Jews of Islam* (Princeton: Princeton University Press, 1987), 79.
18. Shelomo Dov Goitein, *Jews and Arabs: Their Contacts Through the Ages* (New York: Schocken Books, 1964), 10.
19. Ibn Khaldun, *The Muqaddimah,* trans. Franz Rosenthal (New York: Bollingen, 1958), 2:445.
20. Qur'an 3:3.
21. Qur'an 46:12.
22. Qur'an 3:93, 10:94, 17:101.
23. *Riyad as-Salihin,* 1380. A version of the hadith also appears in *Sahih al-Bukhari,* 3461.
24. S. B. (Sadreddin Berk) Metin, "De-Judaising Islam: Isrā'īliyyāt Discussions in Turkish New Media" (master's thesis, Leiden University Faculty of Humanities, 2020), 18.
25. Ibid.
26. Ibid. Among these modernists, Metin points to Muhammad Abduh, Rashid Rida, and Mahmud Abu Rayya, 18–27.
27. Ibid., 21.
28. See Muhammet Tarakci and Suleyman Sayar, "The Qur'anic View of the Corruption of the Torah and the Gospels," *Islamic Quarterly* 49, no. 3 (2005): 240.
29. Joseph Lumbard, "The Qur'anic View of Sacred History and Other Religions," *The Study Qur'an,* ed. Seyyed Hossein Nasr (San Francisco: Harper One, 2015), 1767.
30. The story of Job, Ayyub, is mentioned in the Qur'an in 21:83, 84, and 38:41–44.
31. Hava Lazarus-Yafeh, "Judeo-Arabic Culture," *The Encyclopaedia Judaica Yearbook 1977/1978* (Jerusalem: Keter, 1979), 101–2.
32. Qur'an 2:111–112.
33. Candice Liliane Levy, "Arbiters of the Afterlife: Olam Haba, Torah and Rabbinic Authority" (PhD dissertation, University of California, Los Angeles, 2013), 208.
34. Steven S. Schwarzschild, "Noachide Laws," in *Encyclopaedia Judaica,* 2nd edition, ed. Fred Skolnik (Detroit: Thomson Gale, 2007), 15:284.
35. These laws are mentioned in Babylonian Talmud, Sanhedrin 56a–59b. For an English translation, see I. Epstein, *The Babylonian Talmud* (London: Soncino Press, 1935), 381.
36. The modern liberal Jewish thinkers Moses Mendelssohn and Hermann Cohen stressed this "common ground." See Schwarzschild, "Noachide Laws," 285.
37. Ibid.

38. Ibid.

39. With thanks to Steven Grosby, who brought "Noahide Laws in the Qur'an" to my attention. The seventh law, "not to eat flesh torn from a living animal," is not found in this passage in chapter 17, but it can be detected in verses 2:173 and 5:3, both of which ban eating carrion. In hadith, the Prophet Muhammad also reportedly says: "Whatever is cut from an animal while it is alive, then it is dead flesh." *Jami' at-Tirmidhi,* 1480.

40. Jeffrey Spitzer, "The Noahide Laws," https://www.myjewishlearning.com /article/the-noahide-laws/.

41. Ibid.

42. Marc Lipshitz, "Are Muslims Going to Heaven According to Judaism?," https:// www.quora.com/Are-Muslims-going-to-heaven-according-to-Judaism.

43. Qur'an 2:62.

44. Qur'an 5:69.

45. Qur'an 3:85.

46. See my book *Reopening Muslim Minds: A Return to Reason, Freedom, and Tolerance* (New York: St. Martin's Press, 2021), 219–22.

47. Mohsen Kadivar, *Human Rights and Reformist Islam* (Edinburgh: Edinburgh University Press, 2021), 53.

48. Moses Mendelssohn, *Jerusalem: Or on Religious Power and Judaism,* trans. Allan Arkush (Waltham, MA: Brandeis University Press, 1983), 97.

49. Abdullah Saeed, "Inclusivism and Exclusivism Among Muslims Today Between Theological and Social Dimensions," *Interreligious Relations: Occasional Papers of the Studies in Inter-Religious Relations in Plural Societies Programme* (November/December 2020): 13.

50. Mohammad Hassan Khalil, *Islam and the Fate of Others: The Salvation Question* (Oxford: Oxford University Press, 2012), 13.

CHAPTER 6: HOW ISLAMIC RATIONALISM ENRICHED JUDAISM

1. Aaron W. Hughes, *Muslim and Jew: Origins, Growth, Resentment* (London: Routledge, 2018), 44.

2. Bernard Lewis, *The Jews of Islam* (Princeton: Princeton University Press, 1987), 80. Lewis writes: "The notion of a theology, of a formulation of religious belief in the form of philosophical principles, was alien to the Jews of Biblical and Talmudic times. The emergence of a Jewish theology took place almost entirely in Islamic lands. It was the work of theologians who used both the concepts and the vocabulary (either in Arabic or calqued into Hebrew) of Muslim kalam."

3. Aaron W. Hughes, "Theology: The Articulation of Orthodoxy," *The Routledge Handbook of Muslim–Jewish Relations,* ed. Josef Meri (New York: Routledge, 2016), 83.

4. For a study of the Karaites, which mentions the Muʿtazila influence on them, see Daniel J. Lasker, *Karaism: An Introduction to the Oldest Surviving Alternative Judaism* (London: Littman Library of Jewish Civilization, 2022).

5. Anan Ben David was declared by his followers as a rival exilarch, which led to his arrest. Then, "a fellow prisoner, identified in another Karaite work as the Muslim jurist-theologian Abū Ḥanīfa (d. 767), founder of the Hanafite school of Muslim jurisprudence, advised him to bribe the officials and to obtain a hearing before the caliph in order to claim that he represented a different faith distinct from that of his brother, and therefore was not guilty of the crime ascribed to him. According to this version, Anan stressed before the caliph that in matters pertaining to calculation of the calendar his method was akin to the Muslim system, namely it was based on observation and not on perpetual calculation. He was thus released." Leon Nemoy, "Anan Ben David," *Encyclopaedia Judaica*, 2nd edition, ed. Fred Skolnik (Detroit: Thomson Gale, 2007), 2:127.

6. Sarah Stroumsa, "Saadia and Jewish Kalām," in *The Cambridge Companion to Medieval Jewish Philosophy*, ed. Daniel H. Frank and Oliver Leaman (Cambridge: Cambridge University Press, 2003), 87.

7. The original source of the quote is Muhammad b. Futuh al-Humaydi, *Jadhwat al-Muqtabis*, ed., M. al-Tanji (Cairo, 1952), 101–2. The English translation here is from Alexander Altmann's introduction to his selected translation of *Saadya Gaon: The Book of Doctrines and Beliefs* (Oxford, 1946), 13–14. Emphasis added.

8. Hughes, "Theology: The Articulation of Orthodoxy," 84–85.

9. Ibid.

10. Mustafa Akyol, *Reopening Muslim Minds: A Return to Reason, Freedom, and Tolerance* (New York: St. Martin's Press, 2021), chapters 2–6.

11. Alexander Altmann, "Saadia's Conception of the Law," *Bulletin of the John Rylands Library* 28, no. 2 (1944): 320.

12. Also see David Sklare, "Muʿtazili Trends in Jewish Theology: A Brief Survey," *İslâmî İlimler Dergisi* 12, no. 2 (Fall 2017): 156.

13. Altmann, "Saadia's Conception of the Law."

14. Moses Maimonides, *The Guide for the Perplexed*, trans. Shlomo Pines (Chicago: University of Chicago Press, 1963), 166–67.

15. Sabine Schmidtke, "Rediscovering Theological Rationalism in the Medieval World of Islam," European Research Council Advanced Grant Research Proposal (2006), 15, https://albert.ias.edu/server/api/core/bitstreams/854de204 -a0a1-470b-8f45-903a028768f1/content. "By contrast," Schmidtke adds, confirming Maimonides, "Ashʾarite works and authors were received among Jewish scholars to a significantly lesser degree and in a predominantly critical way."

16. Sabine Schmidtke, "Intellectual History of the Islamicate World Beyond Denominational Borders," *Jewish History* 32, no 2/4 (December 2019): 206.

17. Mohammad Ali Amir-Moezzi and Sabine Schmidtke, "Rationalism and Theology in the Medieval Muslim World: A Brief Overview," *Revue de l'histoire des religions* 226, no. 4 (October 2009): xi, xxi. This Karaite genizah is different from the more famous Cairo Genizah mentioned before. For its story, see https://expositions.nlr.ru/eng/ex_manus/firkovich/sobr_second.php.

18. Schmidtke, "Intellectual History of the Islamicate World Beyond Denominational Borders," 208.

19. The attack on *istihsan* was launched by Imam Shafi, whose strict textualism had a long-lasting influence on Sunni jurisprudence. Therefore, in the words of Wael Hallaq, "with the emergence of a fully-fledged legal theory after the third/ninth century, no Sunni school could have afforded to hold a view in favor of a non-textually supported istihsan." See Hallaq, *A History of Islamic Legal Theories* (Cambridge: Cambridge University Press, 1999), 108. The term "underutilized tool" is from the PhD dissertation by Hassan Shahawy, "How Subjectivity Became Wrong: Early Hanafism and the Scandal of Istiḥsān in the Formative Period of Islamic Law (750–1000 CE)" (University of Oxford, 2019). As Shahawy demonstrates, "Much of the debate surrounding istiḥsān necessarily implicated theological debates. Most fundamental to this was whether humans can know the good absent of God's command (and relatedly, the Euthyphro dilemma: is something good because God commands it or does God command something because it is good)," 303.

20. See S. D. Goitein, "The Stern Religion: The Features of Judaism as Portrayed in Early Muslim Literature" (Hebrew) (Jerusalem, 1949), quoted in Gideon Libson, "A Few Remarks on Equity in Islamic, Jewish and English Law," in *Aequitas and Equity: Equity in Civil Law and Mixed Jurisdictions,* ed. Alfredo M. Rabello (Jerusalem, 1997), 157.

21. Ibid.

22. Al-Razi makes this argument in his *Grand Exegesis* in his commentary on verse 16:90, giving two examples: for murder, Jewish law commands retaliation, "the sharia of Jesus" commands forgiveness, while Islam takes the middle path by making retaliation optional. Similarly, Jewish law commands maximum distancing from a menstruating wife, "the sharia of Jesus" allows intercourse with her, while Islamic law bans intercourse but not distancing.

23. See Numbers 27:8–11. For an examination, also see Mary F. Radford, "The Inheritance Rights of Women Under Jewish and Islamic Law," *Boston College International and Comparative Law Review* 23, no. 2 (2000): 160–61. Radford adds: "In modern times, many Jews have mitigated this discriminatory effect through the use of testamentary bequests and devises."

24. Qur'an 4:7.

25. Qur'an 4:11. "God commands you that a son should have the equivalent share of two daughters."

26. Gideon Libson, "Jewish and Islamic Law: A Comparative Review," *Ency-*

clopaedia Judaica, 2nd edition, ed. Fred Skolnik (Detroit: Thomson Gale, 2007), 11:264–65.

27. Ibid., 11:262–70.

28. E. Wiesenberg, "Observations on Method in Talmudic Studies," *Journal of Semitic Studies* 11, no. 1 (Spring 1966): 28.

29. Eliezer Berkovits, *Essential Essays on Judaism* (Jerusalem: Shalem Press, 2002), 45. Berkovits further explains: "Principles from a sevara, sound common sense or logical reasoning, have the validity of a biblical statement. . . . A sevara may be so convincing that it may compel one's conscience to suppress the plain meaning of a biblical injunction and force upon a verse in the Bible a meaning that it can hardly bear textually. A sevara may show that in certain areas the consequences of a generally prevailing law would be unacceptable and, therefore, that those cases must be exempted from the authority of that law."

30. Shubert Spero, *Morality, Halakha, and the Jewish Tradition* (New York: Yeshiva University Press, 1983), 279.

31. Yehiel Kaplan, "Takkanah," in Skolnik, *Encyclopaedia Judaica,* 19:440.

32. Gideon Libson, "On the Development of Custom as a Source of Law in Islamic Law," *Islamic Law and Society* 4, no. 2 (1997): 132.

33. The comparison between the Jewish and Islamic conceptualizations of custom in their legal theory is covered in depth by Gideon Libson in his book *Jewish and Islamic Law: A Comparative Study of Custom During the Geonic Period* (Cambridge: Harvard University Press, 2003), especially 69–79. Gibson highlights the important fact that the early Hanafi jurist Abu Yusuf gave *urf,* or "custom," a higher status in legal theory, suggesting that it can even replace a sunnah, the practice of the Prophet, if this very practice was already based on a custom—yet later Hanafi jurists such as al-Sarakhsi rejected this theory, ruling that "custom cannot prevail over sunna" (73). For a shorter text by Libson, also see "On the Development of Custom as a Source of Law in Islamic Law," 131–55. Meanwhile, Hashim Kamali agrees that *urf* was "not given prominence in the legal theory" of Sunni Islam, for the very theological reason that I have stressed: "Islam's perspective on good and evil (*husn wa-qubh*) . . . are, in principle, determined by divine revelation. Hence when God ordered the promotion of *ma'ruf,* He could not have meant the good which reason or custom decrees to be such, but what He enjoins." See Mohammad Hashim Kamali, *Principles of Islamic Jurisprudence* (Cambridge: Islamic Texts Society, 2005), chapter 14: *'Urf* ("Custom").

34. Spero, *Morality, Halakha, and the Jewish Tradition,* 358.

35. Deuteronomy 6:18.

36. Aharon Lichtenstein, "Does Jewish Tradition Recognize an Ethic Independent of Halakha?," in *Modern Jewish Ethics,* ed. Marwin Fox (Columbus: Ohio State University Press, 1975), 69–71. Others agree that the Jewish legal

tradition "grants broad latitude to autonomous human judgment and acknowledges the independence of moral values"; see Avi Sagi and Daniel Statman, "Divine Command Morality and Jewish Tradition," *Journal of Religious Ethics* 23, no. 1 (Spring 1995): 63.

37. Qur'an 16:90.
38. George F. Hourani, *Reason and Tradition in Islamic Ethics* (Cambridge: Cambridge University Press, 2007), 32; Khaled Abou El Fadl, *Speaking in God's Name: Islamic Law, Authority and Women* (London: Oneworld, 2001), 160. Mariam Attar shows how this verse, 16:90, was referred by the Mu'tazila scholar Qadi abd al-Jabbar to argue for the value of justice (*adl*) and virtue (*ihsan*) independently of revelation: "The book [Qur'ān] testifies to the soundness of what we have mentioned, because the Exalted said: 'God commands justice and the doing of good.' As such He affirmed the two (*athbatahuma*) before the command. The Sublime said: 'He prohibited indecency, impropriety, and injustice.' As such he necessarily recognizes them as such before the prohibition." Mariam al-Attar, *Islamic Ethics: Divine Command Theory in Arabo-Islamic Thought* (London: Routledge, 2010), 120.
39. As *The Study Qur'an* notes, many classical exegetes "gloss justice as a reference to the fulfillment of obligatory duties and virtue as the performance of supererogatory or recommended deeds," 681. Al-Razi notes some of them in his *Grand Exegesis* while commenting on 16:90: justice means confirming the unity of God, where virtue is being sincere in this monotheism or performance of religious obligations. Conversely, *munkar,* or evil, is something that does not exist within any sharia or sunna.
40. Gideon Libson, "Jewish and Islamic Law: A Comparative Review," in Skolnik, *Encyclopaedia Judaica,* 11: 265.
41. Ibid.
42. See Benedikt Koehler, *Early Islam and the Birth of Capitalism* (Lanham, MD: Lexington Books, 2015).
43. Goyim simply means non-Jews, but the reference was clearly to Muslims, hence Goitein even translated the term as "mutual loan according to Muslim law." See S. D. Goitein, "The Interplay of Jewish and Islamic Laws," in *Jewish Law in Legal History and the Modern World,* ed. Bernard S. Jackson (Leiden: Brill, 1980), 68–69.
44. Rabbi Phil Lieberman, "Suftaja and the Laws of Interest in a Post-Biblical Economy," TheTorah.com, February 11, 2021, https://www.thetorah.com/article/suftaja-and-the-laws-of-interest-in-a-post-biblical-economy.
45. Libson, *Jewish and Islamic Law: A Comparative Study of Custom During the Geonic Period,* 84–85.
46. See Avraham Grossman, "Halakhic Decisions on Family Matters in Medieval Jewish Society," *Jewish Women's Archive,* https://jwa.org/encyclopedia/article/halakhic-decisions-on-family-matters-in-medieval-jewish-society.

47. Radford, "The Inheritance Rights of Women Under Jewish and Islamic Law," 135.
48. Ibid.
49. The term "basically static" is from Libson, "Jewish and Islamic Law: A Comparative Review," 267–68. From the Islamic point of view, Hashim Kamali seems to agree: "The sources of Sharia are . . . permanent in character and may not be overruled on grounds of either rationality or the requirements of social conditions. . . . [They are not] subjected to the limitations of time and circumstance"; Kamali, *Principles of Islamic Jurisprudence*, 7–8.
50. Libson, "Jewish and Islamic Law: A Comparative Review," 267–68. Elsewhere, Libson writes: "The difference between Islamic and Jewish law . . . stems from different perceptions as to the degree of authorship granted to the human factor, that is to say, legal scholars, in the development and renewal of law. The fact that Jewish law recognizes enactment, custom, and even *sevarah* (legal logic) as legitimate sources of the law derives from the basic conception that halakhic scholars are granted broad authority in relation to the development of Halakha. In Islamic law, theoretically at least, the human element is nonexistent. For Muslim legal scholars, everything comes from God, and human beings have no authority to legislate new laws on the basis of custom or through the use of enactment. Their function is limited to revealing the true law. In order to meet pressing needs of the times, they must seek other stratagems. Even consensus (*ijma*), which is recognized in Islamic law as a formal source, was intended solely to reveal the validity of a particular law and to maintain the unity of Islamic law, not, as is sometimes thought, to serve as a means in the creation of new laws." Libson, *Jewish and Islamic Law: A Comparative Study of Custom During the Geonic Period*, viii.
51. Deuteronomy 30:12.
52. One of the contemporary scholars who admits this unfair rejection of the Mu'tazila view on ethics is Ahmad al-Raysuni, a Maliki scholar from Morocco, who writes: "If the truth be told, the Ash'arites who have denied 'goodness' and 'badness' as rationally discernible properties which inhere in things and actions have been carried along by the force of the longstanding, contentious debate between them and their Mu'tazilite opponents. . . . As the days, years and indeed centuries passed, this struggle only grew fiercer and more intractable, while 'reaction' against the Mu'tazilite was such a dominant feature of Ash'arite thought that opposition to the Mu'tazilite became a kind of 'personal obligation' for every Ash'ari thinker! [. . .] Now, however, we need to apologize on behalf of those who denied self-evident truths and defended illusions and fantasies simply in order to vex and contradict the Mu'tazilite." Ahmad al-Raysuni, *Imam al-Shatibi's Theory of the Higher Objectives and Intents of Islamic Law*, (Herndon, VA: International Institute of Islamic Thought, 2005), 243.

53. The Maturidi school of theology takes its name from Abu Mansur al-Maturidi (d. 944), whose relatively more rationalist theology opened a second avenue within Sunni Islam, typically adopted by Hanafis, but still largely overshadowed by the dominance of Ash'arism. For some recent English-language works on Maturidi, who is rightly gaining more attention, see Lejla Demiri and Philip Dorroll, *Maturidi Theology: A Bilingual Reader* (Sapientia Islamica, 2022); Ramon Harvey, *Transcendent God, Rational World: A Maturidi Theology* (Edinburgh: Edinburgh University Press, 2023).

54. Ahmed Izzidien, "Shari'ah, Natural Law and the Original State," ed. Khalid Abou Fadl, et al., *Routledge Handbook of Islamic Law* (New York: Routledge, 2019), 52.

55. Kamali, *Principles of Islamic Jurisprudence,* 264.

56. Naomi Graetz, "Domestic Violence in Jewish Law," myjewishlearning.com, accessed January 25, 2024.

57. Naomi Graetz, *Silence Is Deadly: Judaism Confronts Wifebeating* (New York: Jason Aronson, 1998), 196.

58. Rami Koujah, "Divine Purposiveness and Its Implications in Legal Theory: The Interplay of Kalām and Uṣūl al-Fiqh," *Islamic Law and Society* 24, no. 3 (2017): 189. Koujah adds: "At its core, the Mu'tazilī position rests on assumptions regarding the understanding of God as a wise creator," and "All Mu'tazilīs affirm divine purposiveness. By contrast, it appears that the majority of Ash'arīs negated divine purposiveness" (188, 171). On the Mu'tazila origins of later *maqasid* theory, see Ahmed El Shamsy, "The Wisdom of God's Law: Two Theories," in *Islamic Law in Theory: Studies on Jurisprudence in Honor of Bernard Weiss,* ed. A. Kevin Reinhart and Robert Gleave (Brill: Leiden, 2014). Here El Shamsy notes: "[The] connection between human benefit and God's attribute of wisdom can be encountered among later Ash'aris, such as Fakhr al-Din al-Razi (d. 1210), but it appears to have originated among the Mu'tazilis of Baghdad, where it was closely linked to a broader debate regarding God's obligation to bring about the optimum, *al-aslah,* in creation as a whole" (24–25). Similarly, in the Islamic tradition the distinction between *aqliyyat* and *sam'iyyat* first appears clearly in the writings of the Mu'tazilite scholar al-Qadi Abd al-Jabbar (d. 1025), only to appear later in the writings of Ash'ari and Maturidi theologians. Yusuf Şevki Yavuz, "Akliyyât," *İslâm Ansiklopedisi* (İstanbul: TDV, 1989), 2:280.

59. Ahmad Raysuni, *Imam al-Shatibi's Theory of the Higher Objectives and Intents of Islamic Law* (Herndon, VA: International Institute of Islamic Thought, 2006), 188. Raysuni quotes this view from Shihab al-Din al-Zanjani, then discusses its truthfulness. His whole subsection, "Those Who Reject the Practice of Ta'lil," confirms that the issue has been controversial "in scholastic theology." He also quotes Taj al-Din al-Subki, an Ash'arite-Shafii scholar, who explained why he and other theologians denied *ta'lil*: "The scholastic

theologians do not support ta'lil—that is, the interpretation of legal rulings in light of their preservation of human interests—either as an obligation or even as a permissible practice. Indeed, this is the position which is most in keeping with their principles. They have stated that it is not permissible to interpret God's actions in light of some basis or purpose, since when some-one performs an action for a given purpose, the performance of the action, with respect to the actor, is most important, whether the purpose of the action had to do with the actor himself or with someone else. If so, this means that the actor is incomplete in himself and seeks completion through some other entity. But sublimely exalted is God, Glory be to Him, above any such thing" (193).

60. Ahmad Hasan, "The Legal Cause in Islamic Jurisprudence: An Analysis of 'Illat al-Hukm," *Islamic Studies* 19, no. 4 (Winter 1980): 250. Ahmad Raysuni also examines the different views on ta'lil, or identifying the illa ("cause") of divine commandments, and shows that the gap ultimately goes back to the split between the Mu'tazila and Ash'arites: "The question of whether inter-ests may be identified through human reason is, more or less, the equivalent of what has been known in the realms of scholastic theology and the funda-mentals of jurisprudence as the question of *al-tahsin wa al-taqbih,* that is, whether it is possible through human reason to determine whether a given act is good and praiseworthy, or evil and blameworthy, or whether this can only be determined based on explicit declarations of the Law. . . . According to the Ash'arites, nothing may be said to be either good or evil unless the Law declares it to be so." Raysuni, *Imam al-Shatibi's Theory of the Higher Objectives and Intents of Islamic Law,* 231.

61. For a study on the *maqasid* and its complexities, see Idris Nassery, Rumee Ahmed, and Muna Tatari, *The Objectives of Islamic Law: The Promises and Challenges of the Maqāṣid al-Sharī'a* (Lanham, MD: Lexington Books, 2018). Ahmed's chapter "Which Comes First, the Maqāsid or the Sharia?" is partic-ularly helpful in explaining the built-in limitations of the traditional *maqa-sid* perspective (239–62).

62. Gerald Y. Blidstein, "Commandments, Reasons For," in Skolnik, *Encyclo-paedia Judaica,* 5:86.

63. See Jonathan A. Jacobs, ed., *Reason, Religion, and Natural Law: From Plato to Spinoza* (Oxford: Oxford University Press, 2012), 91–92.

64. Hughes, "Theology: The Articulation of Orthodoxy," 86.

65. Blidstein, "Commandments, Reasons For." In a more detailed description, "Saadia distinguished between the rational commandments (*al-shara'i' al-'aqliyyah; mitzvoth sikhliyyot*), which in theory are discoverable by means of reason, and the traditional laws (*al-shara'i' al-sam'iyyah; mitzvoth shimm'iyot*), which comprise rituals and ceremonial laws (such as the dietary laws) that are not rooted in reason. Saadia is the first Jewish philosopher to

frame his discussion of ethical precepts in the context of rational apprehension. In the introduction to the work, Saadia distinguishes four sources of reliable knowledge (*'ilm*): sensation (*'ilm al-shahid; yedi'at hanir'eh*), reason or nous (*'ilm al-'aql; mada' ha-sekhel*), logical inference (*'ilm ma dafa'at al-darura 'ilayhi; yedi'at mah sheha-hekhreh mevi elav*), and reliable tradition (*al-khabr al-sadiq; ha-hagadah ha-ne'emenet or ha-masoret ha-amitit*)"; Tamar Rudavsky, "Natural Law in Judaism: A Reconsideration," in Jacobs, *Reason, Religion, and Natural Law: From Plato to Spinoza*, 91.

66. Howard Kreisel, *Judaism as Philosophy: Studies in Maimonides and the Medieval Jewish Philosophers of Provence* (Brookline, MA: Academic Studies Press, 2015), 365–66.

67. The point that Maimonides speaks of 'illa (Heb. *illah*) is noted in Blidstein, "Commandments, Reasons For," 86. It is worth reminding that in Islam, due to resistance to rationalist theology, the term *'illa* was controversial for centuries. In the words of Felicitas Opwis, "Understanding the ratio legis as reflective of the divine legislative intent of revealed rulings was not widely accepted prior to the late 5th/11th century. Rather, many influential legal theorists saw the ratio legis as a 'sign' for its ruling, disassociating it from any ethical purposive dimension." Opwis, "The Ethical Turn in Legal Analogy: Imbuing the *Ratio Legis* with *Maṣlaḥa*," in *Towards New Perspectives on Ethics in Islam* (whole issue): *Casuistry, Contingency, and Ambiguity*, ed. Feriel Bouhafa, *Journal of Arabic and Islamic Studies* 21, no. 2 (2021), 161.

68. Rudavsky, "Natural Law in Judaism: A Reconsideration," 105.

69. Today, among academics, there are different views on whether the *maqasid al-sharia* theory in classical Islam amounted to a theory of natural law. Anver Emon seems to think so, as he argued in *Islamic Natural Law Theories* (Oxford: Oxford University Press, 2010). Others disagree. See: Rami Koujah, "A Critical Review Essay of Anver M. Emon's Islamic Natural Law Theories," *Journal of Islamic and Near Eastern Law* 14, no. 1 (2015).

70. Maimonides writes: "There are persons who find it difficult to give a reason for any of the commandments, and consider it right to assume that the commandments and prohibitions have no rational basis whatever. . . . For they imagine that these precepts, if they were useful in any respect, and were commanded because of their usefulness, would seem to originate in the thought and reason of some intelligent being. But as things which are not objects of reason and serve no purpose, they would undoubtedly be attributed to God, because no thought of man could have produced them. According to the theory of those weak-minded persons, man is more perfect than his Creator. For what man says or does has a certain object, whilst the actions of God are different; He commands us to do what is of no use to us, and forbids us to do what is harmless. Far be this! On the contrary, the sole object of the Law is to benefit us." *Guide for the Perplexed*, 321.

71. Seeman, "Reasons for the Commandments as Contemplative Practice in Maimonides," *Jewish Quarterly Review* 103, no. 3 (2013): 298.

72. Deuteronomy 4–6.

73. Seeman, "Reasons for the Commandments as Contemplative Practice in Maimonides," 302.

74. Zalman Rothschild, "Sovereignty, Reason, and Will: Carl Schmitt and Hasidic Legal Thought," *Journal of Law and Religion* 37, no. 2 (2022).

75. Dimitri Gutas, *Greek Thought, Arabic Culture: The Graeco-Arabic Translation Movement in Baghdad and Early Abbasid Society* (New York: Routledge, 1998), 192.

76. Arthur Hym, "Philosophy, Jewish," *Jewish Encyclopedia,* ed. Isidore Singer (New York: Funk & Wagnalls, 1901), 16:76.

77. Ibid., 181. In Leaman's words, "Much of [Isaac Israeli's] work seems to be based on that of al-Kindī." Oliver Leaman, "Philosophy: The Intersection of Islamic and Jewish Thought," *The Routledge Handbook of Muslim-Jewish Relations,* ed. Josef Meri (New York: Routledge, 2020), 181.

78. Leaman, "Philosophy: The Intersection of Islamic and Jewish Thought," in Meri, *The Routledge Handbook of Muslim-Jewish Relations,* 183.

79. Shlomo Pines quotes this letter in his own introduction to his translation of the *Guide*: lix, lx. Pines adds: "He [Maimonides] advises against studying the commentaries on Aristotle of the Christian authors al-Tayyib, Yahya Ibn 'Adi, and Yahya al-Bitriq. To read them would be a sheer waste of time." Moses Maimonides, *The Guide for the Perplexed,* trans. Shlomo Pines (Chicago: University of Chicago Press, 1963), 1:lx.

80. A. Loewenthal and Kaufmann Kohler, "Averroes, or Abul Walid Muhammed Ibn Ahmad Ibn Roshd," in Singer, *Jewish Encyclopedia,* 2:346.

81. Shlomo Pines, Bernard Suler, Suessmann Muntner, and Steven Harvey, "Averroes," in Skolnik, *Encyclopaedia Judaica,* 2:723.

82. Leaman, "Philosophy: The Intersection of Islamic and Jewish Thought," 185–88.

83. See my book *Reopening Muslim Minds,* 1–10.

84. Loewenthal and Kohler, "Averroes, or Abul Walid Muhammed Ibn Ahmad Ibn Roshd," 347.

85. For a list of the forty-nine known works of Ibn Rushd, fourteen of which are extant not in Arabic but in Latin and mostly Hebrew translations, see Fouad Ben Ahmed and Robert Pasnau, "Ibn Rushd [Averroes]," *The Stanford Encyclopedia of Philosophy* (Fall 2021), ed. Edward N. Zalta, https://plato.stanford.edu/archives/fall2021/entries/ibn-rushd/.

86. The unfairness of al-Ghazali's accusation of apostasy, and the political motives behind it, are discussed by the contemporary scholar of Islamic studies Ebrahim Moosa: "Commenting on Ghazālī's attitude towards the philosophers, the legendary Indian Muslim scholar Muḥammad Shiblī

Nuʿmānī (d. 1914) was courageous enough to raise questions about Ghazālī's strictures to sustain a healthy conversation within Muslim theology. Nuʿmānī argued that Ghazālī often found sympathetic interpretative solutions to rescue several Sufis from being accused of doctrinal waywardness for their semi-heretical utterances. Why, he asked rhetorically, did Ghazālī not show the same generosity or hermeneutic charity to the Muslim philosophers as he did the Sufis? While this is a rhetorical question any conclusive reply is difficult unless we can pose the question to Ghazālī himself! One speculative reply would be that Ghazālī was invested in the experiences of the Sufis and shared their metaphors more empathetically. He possibly found philosophy useful as an epistemic framework but was less invested in its experiential reality. Politically also the stakes were too high for Ghazālī to give an inch to the Muslim philosophers, given that the philosophy-loving Ismāʿīlīs posed a political threat from Egypt, challenging his Seljuk-Abbasid patrons." "Ghazālian Insights on Scholarly Critique and Freedom," in *Free Speech, Scholarly Critique and the Limits of Expression in Islam,* ed. Liyakat Takim (Proceedings of the 9th AMI Contemporary Fiqhī Issues Workshop, July 1–2, 2021) (Birmingham, UK: AMI Press, 2022), 164.

87. In the words of Oliver Leaman and Sajjad Rizvi, al-Ghazali's "deep internalisation of logic, the core rationalist technique, within the fundamental disciplines of the religion, ensured that later kalam texts were well equipped to present a systematic theology which progressed on strictly ratiocinative lines to prove the truths of religion, as well as deploying reason to interpret the content of revealed doctrine." "The Developed Kalam Tradition," *The Cambridge Companion to Classical Islamic Theology,* ed. Tim Winter (Cambridge University Press, 2008), 78.

88. As F. E. Peters observed, after the eleventh century, "*Kalam* was progressively more *falsafah*-ridden both in form and in substance, but *falsafah* itself no longer had an independent existence in the Islamic East." F. E. Peters, *Aristotle and The Arabs: The Aristotelian Tradition in Islam* (New York: New York University Press, 1968), 230. Carl Sharif El-Tobgui also puts this nuance, conversely, as follows: "While al-Ghazālī's attack on the Muslim Peripatetic tradition was long understood in Western scholarship to have spelled the death of philosophy in the Muslim world, this is only true in one limited sense, namely, that there was no continuation of an independent philosophical tradition pursued along the largely Aristotelian lines of classical falsafa." El-Tobgui, *Ibn Taymiyya on Reason and Revelation: A Study of Darʾ taʿāruḍ al-ʿaql wa-l-naql* (Leiden: Brill, 2022), 72.

89. Dimitri Gutas, "Avicenna and After," in *Islamic Philosophy from the 12th to the 14th Century,* ed. Abdelkader Al Ghouz (Gottingen: Bonn University Press, 2019), 52.

90. Frank Griffel, "Toleration and Exclusion: Al-Shāfi'ī and al-Ghazālī on the Treatment of Apostates," *Bulletin of the School of Oriental and African Studies* 64, no. 3 (2001): 339–54. According to Griffel, with the al-Ghazali effect, "While before the fifth/eleventh century apostasy was the outward profession of a break-away from Islam, it was now a supposedly heretical conviction or a heretical religious tenet" (352).

91. Hamza Yusuf, "Medina and Athena: Restoring a Lost Legacy," *Renovatio*, June 10, 2019, https://renovatio.zaytuna.edu/article/medina-and-athena-restoring-a-lost-legacy.

92. Ibid.

93. In his popular book, *The Balance of Truth*, Katip Çelebi criticized some of the Islamic attitudes of his time, from sectarianism to rejection of philosophy. In his view, Islam was initially open to all learning, but it was later dominated by dogmatists who repudiated any source of knowledge other than explicitly religious ones. "They passed for learned men," Çelebi wrote, "while all the time they were ignoramuses, fond of disparaging what they called 'the philosophical sciences,' and knowing nothing of earth or sky." Katip Çelebi, *The Balance of Truth*, trans. G. L. Lewis (London: George Allen and Unwin, 1957), 25.

94. Makdisi, *The Rise of Colleges: Institutions of Learning in Islam and The West* (Edinburgh, UK: Edinburgh University Press, 1981), 233, 290–91. Hamza Yusuf also agrees with these views in his *Renovatio* article.

95. See Ahmet T. Kuru, *Islam, Authoritarianism, and Underdevelopment: A Global and Historical Comparison* (Cambridge: Cambridge University Press, 2019).

96. Alfred North Whitehead, "An Appeal to Sanity," *The Atlantic*, March 1939. Reprinted in Alfred North Whitehead, *Science and Philosophy* (New York: Philosophical Library, 1948), 79.

97. Haim Hillel Ben-Sasson, Raphael Jospe, and Dov Schwartz, "Maimonidean Controversy," in Skolnik, *Encyclopaedia Judaica*, 13:375.

98. See Barry S. Kogan, "Al-Ghazali and Halevi on Philosophy and the Philosophers," *Medieval Philosophy and the Classical Tradition: In Islam, Judaism and Christianity*, ed. John Inglis (London: Curzon Press, 2002), 54–80. Kogan argues that each thinker "recovered from that crisis by selectively appropriating a part of his philosophical inheritance to reestablish a basis for religious belief and action" (55). Also see Steven Harvey, "The Changing Image of al-Ghazālī in Medieval Jewish Thought," in *Islam and Rationality: The Impact of al-Ghazālī*, ed. Georges Tamer (Leiden: Brill, 2015). Harvey says, "Ha-Levi indeed seems to have been influenced by al-Ghazālī's critique of the philosophers" (290).

99. Heinrich Graetz, *History of the Jews* (Philadelphia: Jewish Publication Society of America, 1894), 3:542.

100. Ibid.
101. Leaman, "Philosophy: The Intersection of Islamic and Jewish Thought," 192.
102. Daniel Jeremy Silver, "Heresy," in Skolnick, *Encyclopaedia Judaica* (2008), 9:21.
103. For discussions on Islamic laws and attitudes on apostasy, blasphemy, and heresy, and their roots in medieval Muslim politics, see my book *Reopening Muslim Minds*, chapters 9, 11, 12, 13.

CHAPTER 7: THE JEWISH HASKALAH AND THE ISLAMIC ENLIGHTENMENT

1. H. C. Hillier, "The Rationalism of Jewish Law in Moses Mendelssohn," *Canadian Theological Review* 1, no. 2 (2013): 106.
2. Maurice Harris, *History of the Medieval Jews* (New York: Bloch Publishing, 1916), vi.
3. David Sorkin, *The Religious Enlightenment: Protestants, Jews, and Catholics from London to Vienna* (Princeton: Princeton University Press, 2008), 167.
4. Perez Zagorin, *How the Idea of Religious Toleration Came to the West* (Princeton: Princeton University Press, 2003), 2.
5. Notably, these seventeenth-century thinkers were preceded by the French jurist Jean Bodin (1530–1596), whose pioneering defense of religious tolerance included a positive reference to Islamic states of his time: "Is it not better to admit publicly all religions of all peoples in the state, as in the kingdom of the Turks and Persians, rather than to exclude one?" Jean Bodin, *Colloquium of the Seven About Secrets of the Sublime*, trans. Marion Leathers Daniels Kuntz (Princeton: Princeton University Press, 1975), 152.
6. Toland's suggestion that "the Jews should all be naturalized ran directly counter to the prevailing logic which had simply been to grant them privileges but never to recognise them as equals. . . . [It] was striking for its audacity." Pierre Lurbe, "John Toland and the Naturalization of the Jews," *Eighteenth-Century Ireland / Iris an Dá Chultúr* 14 (1999): 46.
7. Michael A. Meyer, *The Origins of the Modern Jew* (Detroit: Wayne State University Press, 1967), 15.
8. Michah Gottlieb, *Faith and Freedom: Moses Mendelssohn's Theological-Political Thought* (Oxford: Oxford University Press, 2011), 46.
9. "Immanuel Kant," *Encyclopaedia Judaica*, 2nd edition, ed. Fred Skolnik (Detroit: Thomson Gale, 2008), 11:769.
10. Ibid.
11. Wojciech Kozyra, "Kant on the Jews and Their Religion," *Diametros* 17, 65 (2020): 42.
12. Ibid.

13. Michael Schulson, "Why Do So Many Americans Believe That Islam Is a Political Ideology, Not a Religion?," *Washington Post,* February 3, 2017. Also see Asma T. Uddin, *When Islam Is Not a Religion: Inside America's Fight for Religious Freedom* (New York: Pegasus Books, 2019).

14. Allan Arkush, "Theocracy, Liberalism, and Modern Judaism," *Review of Politics* 71, no. 4 (Fall 2009): 640.

15. Numbers 15:35.

16. Leviticus 24:16.

17. Deuteronomy 13:7, 10.

18. John Locke, *The Works of John Locke, etc. (The Remains of John Locke . . . Published from His Original Manuscripts),* 3rd edition (London: A. Bettesworth, 1727), 2:247.

19. Arkush, "Theocracy," 638.

20. Haim Hermann Cohn, "Herem," in Skolnik, *Encyclopaedia Judaica,* 9:15.

21. Ibid.

22. Yirmiyahu Yovel, *Dark Riddle: Hegel, Nietzsche, and the Jews* (University Park: Pennsylvania State University Press, 1998), 198.

23. "Search for Light and Right: An epistle to Moses Mendelssohn," in Moses Mendelssohn, *Jerusalem: A Treatise on Ecclesiastical Authority and Judaism,* trans. Moses Samuel (London: Longman, Orme Brown and Longmans, 1838), 124.

24. Ibid., 129.

25. Ibid., 126–29.

26. Genevieve Lloyd, ed., *Spinoza: Critical Assessments* (London: Routledge, 2001), 1:59.

27. Moses Mendelssohn, *Jerusalem: Or on Religious Power and Judaism,* trans. Allan Arkush (Waltham, MA: Brandeis University Press, 1983), 128.

28. Ibid., 132.

29. 1 Samuel 8:19–20.

30. Mendelssohn, *Jerusalem* (1983), 130.

31. Ibid., 131.

32. Alexander Altmann, *Moses Mendelssohn: A Biographical Study* (Liverpool: Liverpool University Press, 1984), 549.

33. Alexander Altmann, "Reasons for the Commandments," *Jewish Values,* ed. Geoffrey Wigoder (Jerusalem: Keter Books, 1974), 243.

34. Mendelssohn quotes Jesus in *Jerusalem,* 132. Mendelssohn, anticipating the modern scholarship on Jesus as a pious, law-abiding Jew, also wrote: "Jesus of Nazareth was never heard to say that he had come to release the House of Jacob from the law. Indeed, he said, in express words, rather the opposite; and, what is still more, he himself did the opposite. Jesus of Nazareth himself observed not only the law of Moses but also the ordinances of the rabbis; and whatever seems to contradict this in the speeches and acts ascribed to him appears to do so only at first glance" (*Jerusalem,* 134).

35. Ibid. (1983), 133.
36. Arkush, "Theocracy," 71:645.
37. Gottlieb, *Faith and Freedom,* 10.
38. Mendelssohn, *Jerusalem* (1983), 45.
39. Ibid. (1983), 45, 56.
40. Ibid. (1983), 88.
41. Ibid. (1983), 93.
42. Ibid. (1983), 23. Altmann's paraphrasing.
43. Ibid. (1983), 94.
44. Michah Gottlieb puts it this way: "Taking as my starting point Mendels-sohn's invoking of the medieval adage that 'truth cannot conflict with truth,' I argue that Mendelssohn is so firmly convinced of the truth of both Judaism and of the German Enlightenment that he simply cannot imagine a contradiction between them." Gottlieb, *Faith and Freedom,* 9.
45. Mendelssohn, *Jerusalem* (1983), 52.
46. Ibid. (1983), 45.
47. Ibid. (1983), 44.
48. Ibid. (1983), 44–45.
49. Gottlieb, *Faith and Freedom,* 51.
50. Kenneth Hart Green, "Moses Mendelssohn's Opposition to the *Herem*: The First Step Toward Denominationalism?," *Modern Judaism* 12, 1 (February 1992): 41.
51. Mendelssohn, *Jerusalem* (1983), 87.
52. Ibid. (1983), 139.
53. Sorkin, *The Religious Enlightenment,* 21.
54. Ibid.
55. Judith R. Baskin, "Haskalah," in Skolnik, *Encyclopaedia Judaica,* 8:435.
56. Chaim N. Saiman, *Halakhah: The Rabbinic Idea of Law* (Princeton: Princeton University Press, 2018), 243.
57. Gottlieb, *Faith and Freedom,* 11.
58. As Altmann says, "Saadia's theory which, as we have seen, springs mainly from Islamic sources, helped to introduce the doctrine of natural Law into medieval thought." Alexander Altmann, "Saadia's Conception of the Law," *Bulletin of the John Rylands Library* 28, no. 2 (1944): 333. Sorkin also believes that "Mendelssohn's commentary provided a bridge between medieval and eighteenth-century philosophy" Sorkin, *The Religious Enlightenment,* 178. He also writes: "A watershed in creating the Haskalah library was the re-publication by the Wolffian press of two of Maimonides's major works. His *Mishneh Torah,* the first systematic presentation of Jewish law, appeared in 1739 (it had last been reprinted in Amsterdam in 1702–3). Three years later came the first reissue in almost two centuries of his *Guide for the Perplexed,* a central text of medieval Jewish philosophy notable for its systematic effort to reconcile Judaism with Aristotle. David Fränkel (1707–1762), the rabbi of

Dessau and Moses Mendelssohn's teacher, tacitly approved these publications." (Sorkin, *The Religious Enlightenment*, 171.

59. For an overview of the "Islamic Enlightenment" and the "counter-Enlightenment," see Christopher de Bellaigue, *The Islamic Enlightenment: The Modern Struggle Between Faith and Reason* (New York: Random House, 2017).

60. Oliver Leaman, "Philosophy: The Intersection of Islamic and Jewish Thought," in *The Routledge Handbook of Muslim-Jewish Relations*, ed. Josef Meri (New York: Routledge, 2016), 197.

61. See Michelangelo Guida, "Seyyid Bey and the Abolition of the Caliphate," *Middle Eastern Studies* 44, no. 2 (March 2008).

62. Abdel Raziq's argument is summarized in Souad T. Ali, *A Religion, Not a State: Ali 'Abd al-Raziq's Islamic Justification of Political Secularism* (Salt Lake City: University of Utah Press, 2009), 86.

63. Qur'an 24:54.

64. Ali, *A Religion, Not a State*, 96.

65. Ibid., 61, 70.

66. Ali Abdel Razek, *Islam and the Foundations of Political Power* (Edinburgh: Edinburgh University Press, 2013), viii.

67. See Abdullahi Ahmed An-Na'im, *Islam and the Secular State: Negotiating the Future of Shari'a* (Cambridge, MA: Harvard University Press, 2010).

68. Claudia Mende, "The Reinvention of Islam: Interview with the Islamic Scholar Ebrahim Moosa," Qantara.de, March 22, 2016, https://en.qantara .de/content/interview-with-the-islamic-scholar-ebrahim-moosa-the -reinvention-of-islam.

69. Zohaib Ahmad, "Marginalization and Reform of Religion: A Comparative Study of Moses Mendelssohn and Syed Ahmad Khan," *Journal of Islamic Thought and Civilization* 9, no. 2 (Fall 2019): 190.

70. Oliver Leaman, *Islamic Philosophy* (Cambridge: Polity Press, 2009), 201.

71. Christopher de Bellaigue makes this argument forcefully in *The Islamic Enlightenment*.

72. See Orlando Crowcroft, "Sharia Law UK: Britain's Jewish Beth Din Court 'an Example' for Muslim Legal System," *International Business Times*, January 28, 2016; Michael J. Broyde, "Jewish Law Courts in America: Lessons Offered to Sharia Courts by the Beth Din of America Precedent," *New York Law School Review* 57, no. 2 (January 2013).

73. Mendelssohn "provided the philosophical underpinning for a redefinition of the mitzvot that was a necessary precursor to the development of the Reform movement." Arden Eby, "Mendelssohn and Reform: Redefining the Mitzvot," Academia.edu, 1.

74. Ibid.

75. Dana Evan Kaplan, *American Reform Judaism: An Introduction* (New Brunswick, NJ: Rutgers University Press, 2003), 8.

76. Michael Berenbaum, "Pittsburgh Platform," in Skolnik, *Encyclopaedia Judaica,* 16:90.

77. Kaplan, *American Reform Judaism,* 15.

78. Berenbaum, "Pittsburgh Platform."

79. See Amel Brahmi, "A Quiet Revolution: The Female Imams Taking Over an LA Mosque," *The Guardian,* November 24, 2021.

80. For a comparison between the prominent "lady imam" Amina Wadud and Abraham Geiger, see Judith Frishman and Umar Ryad, "Islamic and Jewish Legal Traditions," in Meri, *The Routledge Handbook of Muslim-Jewish Relations,* 168.

81. Timur Kuran, a Turkish American academic, ponders "the absence of liberal Islamic schisms" in his book *Freedoms Delayed: Political Legacies of Islamic Law in the Middle East* (Cambridge: Cambridge University Press, 2023), 190–211.

CHAPTER 8: THE GOOD ORIENTALISTS

1. Susannah Heschel, "German Jewish Scholarship on Islam as a Tool for De-Orientalizing Judaism," *New German Critique,* no. 117 (Fall 2012): 93.

2. Andreas Alm, "Egyptology in the Periphery: Valdemar Schmidt and the Making of Egyptology in Denmark 1872–1925" (master's thesis, Lund University, 2019), 2.

3. Edward Said, *Orientalism* (New York: Vintage Books, 1979), 17.

4. Suzanne L. Marchand, *German Orientalism in the Age of Empire: Religion, Race, and Scholarship* Reprint Edition (Cambridge: Cambridge University Press, 2009), xviii.

5. Ibid.

6. Pedro A. Piedras Monroy, "Edward Said and German Orientalism," *Storia della Storiografia* 44 (2003): 96–103.

7. Said, *Orientalism,* 18. Later in the discussion, Said also says: "Yet what German Orientalism had in common with Anglo-French and later American Orientalism was a kind of intellectual authority over the Orient within Western culture" (19). However, that vague argument does not seem to take account of the German Jewish identification with the Orient—a theme one cannot find in Said's book.

8. Ibid.

9. Susannah Heschel, "German Jews, Orientalism, and Islam," conference paper presented at the 129th Annual Meeting of American Historical Association, 2015; Bernard Lewis, "The Pro-Islamic Jews," *Judaism: A Quarterly Journal of Jewish Life and Thought* 17, no. 4 (1968): 395.

10. As Susannah Heschel explains: "Jews were called 'German speaking Orientals' by the historian Heinrich von Treitschke, 'orientalische Fremdlinge'

by the publicist Wilhelm Marr, and 'Wüstenvolk und Wandervolk' by the economist Werner Sombart. Furthermore, Jews functioned as 'Orientals' in the scholarship of European Christians, who viewed the Orient as a shelter from the vicissitudes of progress, or better put, presented Islam as timeless and Judaism as regressing. Both the philologists Friedrich Max Müller and Ernest Renan spoke of 'Semitic monotheism' as the product of desert nomad foreign to European Aryans." Susannah Heschel, "Orientalist Triangulations: Jewish Scholarship on Islam as a Response to Christian Europe," in *The Muslim Reception of European Orientalism: Reversing the Gaze*, ed. Susannah Heschel and Umar Ryad (London: Routledge, 2018), 147.

11. Ibid.
12. Ibid.
13. Michael L. Miller, "European Judaism and Islam: The Contribution of Jewish Orientalists," in *A History of Jewish-Muslim Relations: From the Origins to the Present Day*, ed. Abdelwahab Medde and Benjamin Stora (Princeton: Princeton University Press, 2013), 828.
14. Mark R. Cohen, "Islamic Attitudes and Policies," in *Cambridge History of Judaism*, vol. 5, *Jews in the Medieval Islamic World*, ed. Phillip I. Lieberman (Cambridge: Cambridge University Press, 2021), 92.
15. Aaron Hughes, *Shared Identities: Medieval and Modern Imaginings of Judeo-Islam* (Oxford: Oxford University Press, 2017), 123.
16. John M. Efron, "From Mitteleuropa to the Middle East: Orientalism Through a Jewish Lens," *Jewish Quarterly Review* 94, no. 3 (Summer 2004): 493. The historian Jane S. Gerber also observes: "The Jewish historical experience in al-Andalus became a subject of much interest and delight in the nineteenth century. Its larger-than-life personalities who functioned in the public arena and mastered secular knowledge provided a perfect foil for a European Jewish scholarly class seeking human models in their battle to obtain civic rights in Europe. . . . Jewish historians tended to ascribe exaggerated qualities of tolerance and enlightenment to Andalusian Islamic rule, juxtaposing the 'tolerance' and interfaith amity of Muslim Spain to a largely persecutory medieval Christendom. Their apologetic analyses formed one voice in a broader movement of romanticization of medieval Spain associated with the publication of such works as Washington Irving's *Tales of the Alhambra* in the United States." Jane S. Gerber, "The Jews of Muslim Spain," Lieberman, *Jews in the Medieval Islamic World*, 167–68.
17. Efron, "From Mitteleuropa to the Middle East," 495.
18. Ibid., 497.
19. Miller, "European Judaism and Islam," in Medde and Stora, *A History of Jewish-Muslim Relations*, 829.
20. Bernard Lewis, *Islam in History: Ideas, People, and Events in the Middle East* (Chicago: Open Court, 1993), 142.

21. Gustav Weil, *A History of the Islamic Peoples,* trans. Khuda Bakhsh (Calcutta: University of Calcutta, 1914), 27–28. Before these quoted words, Weil also criticized "his weakness for the fair sex," as he had other critical remarks as well. But his largely positive tone offers a refreshing contrast to the grimmer view about Muhammad that then dominated Western literature.

22. Ottfried Fraisse, ed., *Modern Jewish Scholarship on Islam in Context: Rationality, European Borders, and the Search for Belonging* (Berlin: Walter de Gruyter, 2018), 101.

23. Efron, "From Mitteleuropa to the Middle East," 502.

24. Heinrich Graetz, *History of the Jews* (Philadelphia: Jewish Publication Society of America, 1894, 1974 reprint), 3:85.

25. Martin Kramer, ed., *The Jewish Discovery of Islam: Studies in Honor of Bernard Lewis* (Tel Aviv: Moshe Dayan Center for Middle Eastern and African Studies, 1999), 5–6.

26. Ibid., 6.

27. Ibid., 5.

28. Anouar Majid, *We Are All Moors: Ending Centuries of Crusades Against Muslims and Other Minorities* (Minneapolis: University of Minnesota Press, 2009), 107.

29. Susannah Heschel, "Judaism's Embrace of Islam: An Historical Inquiry into the Role of Islam in Modern Jewish Thought," Lecture at the Center for Middle Eastern Studies at Harvard University, 2013, https://cmes.fas.harvard.edu/event/judaisms-embrace-islam-historical-inquiry-role-islam-modern-jewish-thought. The point that German Jewish scholars had begun to study the Jewish Mu'tazila is from Sabine Schmidtke, "Intellectual History of the Islamicate World Beyond Denominational Borders," *Jewish History* 32, no. 2 (December 2019): 209.

30. Heschel, "Judaism's Embrace of Islam."

31. Lewis, *Islam in History,* 144.

32. Raphael Patai, *Ignaz Goldziher and His Oriental Diary: A Translation and Psychological Portrait* (Detroit: Wayne State University Press, 1987), 28.

33. Ibid., 20.

34. Tamás Turán, "Academic Religion: Goldziher as a Scholar and a Jew," in *Modern Jewish Scholarship in Hungary: The Science of Judaism Between East and West,* ed. Tamás Turán and Carsten Wilke (Berlin: Walter de Gruyter, 2016), 263.

35. In the words of Susannah Heschel, Goldziher was "an advocate of liberalizing Judaism and his arguments about the Hadith bear clear implications for liberalizing rabbinic law." Heschel, "Orientalist Triangulations," 148.

36. Joshua Little, "A Summary of Early Sunni Hadith Criticism," *Islamic Origins,* November 15, 2022, https://islamicorigins.com.

37. Ignaz Goldziher, *Introduction to Islamic Theology and Law* (Princeton: Princeton University Press, 1981), 68.

38. See Kevin A. Reinhart, "Juynbolliana, Gradualism, the Big Bang, and Ḥadīth Study in the Twenty-First Century," *Journal of the American Oriental Society* 130, no. 3 (July–September 2010): 413–44.

39. The early hadith critics in Islam, the "theologians" most of whom were Mu'tazilites, "accepted no reports about the accuracy of which there is the smallest doubt and they believed that hadith, being of uncertain veracity, should never be allowed to rule on the Qur'an. They were, in fact, reluctant to accept any extra-Qur'anic evidence for legal problems dealt with in the Qur'an and tended to regard questions not referred to in the Qur'an as having been left deliberately unregulated by God." Daniel Brown, *Rethinking Tradition in Modern Islamic Thought* (Cambridge: Cambridge University Press, 1999), 14.

40. Ibid., 116.

41. This was an observation by the late Josef Van Ess, another "good Orientalist." Josef Van Ess, "Goldziher as a Contemporary of Islamic Reform," Goldziher Memorial Conference (Budapest: Hungarian Academy of Sciences, 2005), 37.

42. Kramer, *The Jewish Discovery of Islam*, 16.

43. Susannah Heschel, in Heschel and Ryad, *The Muslim Reception of European Orientalism*, 95.

44. Guy G. Stroumsa, *The Idea of Semitic Monotheism: The Rise and Fall of a Scholarly Myth* (Oxford: Oxford University Press, 2021), 176.

45. Hüseyin Akgün, *Goldziher ve Hadis* (Ankara: Araştırma Yayınları, 2019), 303, 305–6.

46. Mehmet Hayri Kırbaşoğlu, "Understanding Goldziher, Goldziher'i Anlamak," September 19, 2021, http://www.hayrikirbasoglu.net.

47. Alan Barnard and Jonathan Spencer, eds., *The Routledge Encyclopedia of Social and Cultural Anthropology* (London: Routledge, 2009), 514.

48. See Avishai Margalit and Ian Buruma, *Occidentalism: The West in the Eyes of Its Enemies* (New York: Penguin, 2005).

49. Franz Rosenthal's foreword in Bruce Lawrence, *Shahrastani on the Indian Religions* (Berlin: De Gruyter, 1976), 5.

50. In an assessment, the Muslim academic Amjad Mahmud Hussain points to "a pressing need for Muslims to study not only the various religions, but also the various modern philosophies of life." However, he adds: "Perhaps an even more pressing issue is the question as to how to carry out this task. The methodology of suspension of judgment (epoche) seems to be highly irreconcilable with the Muslim mindset since it is unreasonable to ask a Muslim to successfully 'detach' from one's identity that is multifaceted as a Muslim whilst studying the 'other.'" Amjad Mahmud Hussain, "The Muslim Approach to the

6666666666

Study of Religions," *International Journal of Advanced Science and Technology* 29, no. 7 (2020): 3468.

51. Lenn E. Goodman, *Religious Pluralism and Values in the Public Sphere* (New York: Cambridge University Press, 2014), 173.

52. Ibid., 173–74.

53. Ibid.

CHAPTER 9: THE OTTOMAN HAVEN

1. Samuel Usque, *The Consolation for the Tribulations of Israel,* trans. Martin A. Cohen (Philadelphia: Jewish Publication Society of America, 1965), 231.

2. Salih Keramet Nigar, *Halife İkinci Abdülmecid* (İstanbul: Derin Tarih, 2013), 10–11, with my translation from Turkish. (The first edition of the book was published in 1964 by İnkılap ve Aka Kitabevi.)

3. Ibid., 10.

4. Ibid., 10–11.

5. Isaiah Friedman, "Ottoman Empire," *Encyclopaedia Judaica,* 2nd edition ed. Fred Skolnik (Detroit: Thomson Gale, 2007), 15:520.

6. Lucien Gubbay, "The Rise, Decline and Attempted Regeneration of the Jews of the Ottoman Empire," *European Judaism: A Journal for the New Europe* 33, no. 1 (Spring 2000): 60.

7. Alan Mikhail, *God's Shadow: Sultan Selim, His Ottoman Empire, and the Making of the Modern World* (New York: Liveright, 2020), chapter 11.

8. Isaiah Friedman, "Ottoman Empire," in Skolnik, *Encyclopaedia Judaica,* 15:521.

9. Mikhail, *God's Shadow.*

10. Bernard Lewis, *The Jews of Islam* (Princeton: Princeton University Press, 1987), 135–36.

11. Ibid.

12. Rabbi Joseph Telushkin, *Jewish Literacy* (New York: William Morrow, 1991), 193.

13. Matthew Carr, *Blood and Faith: The Purging of Muslim Spain, 1492–1614* (Oxford: Oxford University Press, 2017).

14. Telushkin, *Jewish Literacy,* 194.

15. Mikhail, *God's Shadow.*

16. Eli Barnavi, *A Historical Atlas of the Jewish People,* revised edition (New York: Schocken Books, 2002), 130.

17. F. M. Loewenberg, "Outlawed Visitors on al-Haram al-Sharif: Jews on the Temple Mount During the Ottoman and British Rule of Jerusalem, 1517–1967," *Hakirah* 28 (2020): 287.

18. "Women at the Western Wall, 1910," National Library of Israel, https://web.nli.org, accessed June 16, 2023. Also see Gudrun Krämer, *A History of Pal-*

estine: From the Ottoman Conquest to the Founding of the State of Israel (Princeton: Princeton University Press, 2011), 25.

19. Loewenberg, "Outlawed Visitors on al-Haram al-Sharif," 291.

20. Ibid., 292.

21. Telushkin, *Jewish Literacy,* 194.

22. Yasin Meral, *Yüzyıl İstanbul Yahudi Cemaatinde İlmî Hayat* (Ankara: Ankara Üniversitesi, 2016), 593.

23. Yasin Meral, *İstanbul'da Yahudi Matbuatı: İbrahim Müteferrika Öncesi (1493–1729)* (Ankara: Divan Kitap, 2016), 239.

24. The Turkish historian Ekmeleddin İhsanoğlu makes this point, with a quote from the Italian man of letters Comte de Marsigli, who visited Istanbul in the 1670s: "Turks do not always get their works printed; but this is not, as commonly believed, because printing is forbidden or because their works are not worth printing. *They do not want to prevent all the copyists whose number reached ninety thousand when I was in Constantinople, from earning their living*; and this is what Turks themselves told the Christians and Jews who wanted to introduce printing techniques to the empire in order to make profits." Ekmeleddin Ihsanoglu, *Science, Technology and Learning in the Ottoman Empire* (Farnham, UK: Ashgate Publishing, 2004), 47.

25. Meral, *Yüzyıl İstanbul,* 594.

26. Ibid., 595.

27. Ekmeleddin İhsanoğlu, *Studies on Ottoman Science and Culture* (New York: Routledge, 2021), 65.

28. Meral, *Yüzyıl İstanbul,* 597–98.

29. Gubbay, "The Rise, Decline and Attempted Regeneration of the Jews of the Ottoman Empire," 61.

30. Ibid.

31. For a story on the Sarajevo Haggadah, see Geraldine Brooks, "The Book of Exodus: A Double Rescue in Wartime Sarajevo," *New Yorker,* November 25, 2007.

32. See Barnavi, *A Historical Atlas of the Jewish People,* 156. For the story of Zevi and his followers, see Gershom Scholem, *Sabbatai Sevi: The Mystical Messiah* (Princeton: Princeton University Press, 1973).

33. In the words of Marc David Baer, "The *Dönme* character—a secret Jew hiding in the guise of the nation's leader who surreptitiously aims to destroy the Turkish culture, nation, and people on behalf of world Jewry—has been the stock figure in antigovernment conspiracy theories promoted by Islamists dispossessed of their authority, extreme rightists, and most recently leftists and secularists divested of their power." Marc David Baer, "An Enemy Old and New: The Dönme, Antisemitism, and Conspiracy Theories in the Ottoman Empire and Turkish Republic," *Jewish Quarterly Review* 103, no. 4 (Fall 2013): 528.

34. Lewis, *The Jews of Islam*, 158.

35. Ibid., 158–59.

36. Given at Constantinople, 12th Ramazan, 1256 (November 6, 1840). The translation is from Moses Montefiore's original words in: *Diaries of Sir Moses and Lady Montefiore, Comprising Their Life and Work as Recorded in Their Diaries, from 1812 to 1883, Volume 1* (Chicago: Belford-Clarke, 1890), 279–80.

37. Jonathan Frankel, *The Damascus Affair: "Ritual Murder," Politics, and the Jews in 1840*, (Cambridge: Cambridge University Press, 1997), 378; Jonathan Frankel, "'Ritual Murder' in the Modern Era: The Damascus Affair of 1840," *Jewish Social Studies* 3, no. 2 (1997): 378.

38. Frankel, *The Damascus Affair*, 378.

39. The full name of the museum is the Quincentennial Foundation Museum of Turkish Jews, which stands next to Istanbul's historic Neve Şalom synagogue. It can be virtually visited at https://www.muze500.com. The Quincentennial Foundation was founded in 1989 to celebrate the five hundredth anniversary of the welcoming of the Jewish people to the Ottoman Empire after their expulsion from Spain in 1492. It is worth noting that the four hundredth anniversary of the same event was also celebrated, in 1892, by Ottoman Jews. Yaacov Geller, Haïm Z'ew Hirschberg, and Leah Bornstein-Makovetsky, "Ottoman Empire," in Skolnik, *Encyclopaedia Judaica*, 15:543.

40. A notable case was the remarks of the late King Faysal of Saudi Arabia, in a 1972 interview with Fu'ad al-Sayyid, an Egyptian journalist, where he asserted the Jews keep murdering children in their rituals, which proves that "Israel has had malicious intentions since ancient times." See Norman A. Stillman, "New Attitudes Toward the Jew in the Arab World," *Jewish Social Studies*, 37, no. 3/4 (Summer–Autumn 1975): 197. Stillman also observes that "as with much of the antisemitic imagery now current in Middle Eastern literature, the 'Blood Libel' is of fairly recent vintage and is a European import." Ibid.

41. İlber Ortaylı, *İmparatorluğun En Uzun Yüzyılı* (İstanbul: Kronik Kitap, 2018).

42. Niyazi Berkes, *The Development of Secularism in Turkey* (London: C. Hurst & Co., 1998), 145.

43. "Rescript of Reform, Islahat Fermanı," Boğaziçi University, Atatürk Institute of Modern Turkish History, https://www.anayasa.gen.tr/reform.htm.

44. "The Ottoman Constitution," December 23, 1876, Boğaziçi University, Atatürk Institute of Modern Turkish History, http://www.ata.boun.edu.tr.

45. This is the observation Ottoman statesman and scholar Ahmed Cevdet Paşa shares in his *Tezakir*, or chronicles. The English translation is available at: Norman A. Stillman, *Jews of Arab Lands: A History and Source Book* (Philadelphia: Jewish Publication Society, 1998), 361.

46. Ibid. Meanwhile, it is worth noting that this communal ranking, which

placed Jews at the bottom, was a late invention: "The chief rabbis of İstanbul ... preceded the Greek Orthodox patriarchs in the Ottoman protocol until 1697, when an intervention by the English and French ambassadors changed the established order." İlker Aytürk, "Anti-Judaism and Judaism in Medieval Islam," in *Encyclopedia of Jews in the Islamic World,* ed. Norman Stillman (Leiden: Brill, 2010), 1:225.

47. Due to concerns with political Zionism, from 1882 onward, Ottoman authorities banned foreign Jews from settling in Palestine and purchasing land, while also stating "Jews could settle in any part of the Ottoman state except for Palestine, on the condition that the newcomers adopt Ottoman nationality and obey Ottoman law." Büşra Barın, "The Ottoman Policy Towards Jewish Immigration and Settlement in Palestine: 1882–1920," Thesis at Middle East Technical University, 2014, 35–36. Yet still, Jewish immigration to Palestine continued, in waves called the First Aliyah (from 1882 to 1903), which brought in some nearly 35,000 Jews mainly escaping from Russian pogroms, and then the Second Aliyah (from 1904 to 1914), which brought in some additional 40,000 Jews, most of them socialists also fleeing Czarist Russia (Jewish Virtual Library, www.jewishvirtuallibrary.org).

48. In the words of Bernard Lewis: "The ideas of the French Revolution, and the whole intellectual ferment that followed in the early decades of the nineteenth century and caused such a tremendous stir among the Greeks and Armenians, seem to have had no impact among the Ottoman Jews, who continued undisturbed in their old ways." Lewis, *Jews of Islam,* 175.

49. İlber Ortaylı, "Ottomanism and Zionism During the Second Constitutional Period, 1908–1915," *Studies on Ottoman Transformation* (Istanbul: Isis Press, 2010), 86.

50. This was a comment by Nâzım Bey, a prominent member of the Party of Union and Progress. Isaiah Friedman, "The Young Turks and Zionism: International Implications," *Cemoti,* no. 28 (1999): 32.

51. Ebüziyya Tevfik's writings, including his 1888 book *Millet-i İsrâiliye (The People of Israel),* "parroted many of the anti-Semitic discourses rampant in Europe at the time, copying those almost verbatim from the anti-Semitic literature in French." Aytürk, "Anti-Judaism and Judaism in Medieval Islam," in Stillman, *Encyclopedia of Jews in the Islamic World,* 1:225. Also see Osman Özkul, Nadir Çomak, and Hilal Uzun, "Osmanlı Devleti'nde Yahudilik: Ebüzziya Tevfik'in *Millet-i İsrâiliye* Kitabı," *Filistin Araştırmaları Dergisi,* no. 5 (2019): 79.

52. "Among Ottoman bureaucrats and intellectuals there were some who had been affected directly or indirectly by European antisemitism. In general, however, it would appear that educated Ottomans did not have a prejudiced attitude vis-à-vis Judaism or Zionism." Ortaylı, "Ottomanism and Zionism During the Second Constitutional Period, 1908–1915," 89.

53. Stanford J. Shaw, *The Jews of the Ottoman Empire and the Turkish Republic* (Houndmills, UK: Macmillan, 1991), 188–91.

54. "Black-and-white offset print reproduction of the interior of the Ahrida Synagogue in Istanbul, during prayers offered for the victory of Turkish armies in the Russo-Turkish War of 1877–1878, in the presence of Ibrahim Edhem Pasha." Published in the June 9, 1877, edition of *The Illustrated London News,* https://lcdl.library.cofc.edu/lcdl/catalog/lcdl:51039.

55. "In Fear of Greeks, Jews Plead for Aid," *New York Times,* April 3, 1913.

56. Lewis, *Islam in History,* 137.

57. Ibid.

58. Thomas Power O'Connor, *Lord Beaconsfield, A Biography.* People's ed. (Bennett Brothers, 1880), 236–37. Bernard Lewis also quotes this passage, with his comments, in Lewis, *Islam in History,* 138.

59. O'Connor, *Lord Beaconsfield, A Biography,* 237.

60. Ibid.

61. "Past Prime Ministers: Benjamin Disraeli, The Earl of Beaconsfield," UK Government, https://www.gov.uk/government/history/past-prime-ministers /benjamin-disraeli-the-earl-of-beaconsfield.

62. O'Connor, *Lord Beaconsfield, A Biography,* 237.

63. Edward Augustus Freeman, *The Ottoman Power in Europe: Its Nature, Its Growth, and Its Decline* (Macmillan and Company, 1877), xviii, xix.

64. Ibid., xix.

65. Ibid.

66. Lewis, *Islam in History,* 141.

67. O'Connor, *Lord Beaconsfield, A Biography,* 610–11.

68. Gülsen Sevinç and Ayse Fazlioğlu, "Turkish Participation to 1893 Chicago Exposition," *The Turkish Yearbook,* vol. 31, 27.

69. Isidor Lewi, "Yom Kippur on the Midway," *Report of the Committee on Awards of the World's Columbian Exposition* (Washington, DC: Government Printing Office, 1901), 2:1691–2.

70. Ibid.

71. Ibid.

72. This narrative is common in Islamist sources across the contemporary Muslim world. In Turkey in the late 2010s, it was even promoted on state TV in a drama titled *Payitaht Abdülhamid,* which purportedly presented the life and times of the Ottoman sultan Abdülhamid II, but with many historical fictions that unmistakably reflected the ideological narratives of the post-Ottoman Islamist movement.

73. "Zionism," in Skolnik, *Encyclopaedia Judaica,* 21:566.

74. "There were Jewish political activists who supported the constitutional movement and who had been in contact with the Unionists since the days of Abdülhamid. This group overlapped to some extent with the previous

one and included Nissim Masliah, Albert Ferid Asseo, Albert Fua and the *Mesveret* newspaper group in Paris, the famous Emmanuel Carasso, Nissim Russo and Avram Galante. These Ottomanized Jewish intellectuals were genuinely staunch supporters of the ideals of the Second Constitutional Period. Their support was not 'tactical' and should not be regarded as a national 'compromise.' . . . It was rather a direct result of their Ottoman Patriotism." Ortaylı, "Ottomanism and Zionism During the Second Constitutional Period, 1908–1915," 87.

75. This was a statement by Reuben Qattan, a Jewish poet from İzmir. Michelle U. Campos, "Between 'Beloved Ottomania' and 'The Land of Israel': The Struggle over Ottomanism and Zionism Among Palestine's Sephardi Jews, 1908–13," *International Journal of Middle East Studies* 37, no. 4 (November 2005): 471. The Ottoman Chief Rabbi Haim Nahoum also stated in 1909 that most Ottoman Jews were "absolutely indifferent to the [Zionist] movement." *New York Times*, July 26, 1909.

76. Louis Fishman, "Understanding the 1911 Ottoman Parliament Debate on Zionism in Light of the Emergence of a 'Jewish Question,'" in *Late Ottoman Palestine: The Period of Young Turk Rule*, ed. Yuval Ben-Bassat and Eyal Ginio (London: I. B. Tauris, 2011), 105. Ortaylı agrees: "Ottoman Zionists generally supported the principle of the state's territorial integrity and focused primarily on activities aimed at Jewish cultural revival." Ortaylı, "Ottomanism and Zionism During the Second Constitutional Period, 1908–1915," 88.

77. "Jews served actively in the Ottoman army during the Balkan Wars and during World War I, and they also strove to demonstrate their loyalty to the government by getting young non-Ottoman Jewish volunteers to enlist in the military. . . . Jewish bankers in and out of the empire and Jewish charitable organizations provided money for wartime expenditure." Geller, Hischberg, and Bornstein-Makovetsky, "Ottoman Empire," in Skolnik, *Encyclopaedia Judaica*, 15:543. Also see Stanford Shaw, *Jews of the Ottoman Empire and the Turkish Republic* (New York: New York University Press, 1991), 230–32.

78. As a Turkish academic notes: "The perception of the Young Turks with regard to the Jews and Palestine was not different than that of Abdülhamid. . . . Young Turk leaders were not against Jewish immigration into the Ottoman Empire at large; however, they were concerned about the fact that Zionism as a national movement might have separatist ambitions." Barın, "The Ottoman Policy Towards Jewish Immigration and Settlement in Palestine: 1882–1920," 103.

79. "Young Turks Oppose a Zionist State," *New York Times*, July 26, 1909. The story also reported: "The leaders of the Young Turks, [Bernstein] found, are unalterably opposed to the autonomy of any of the individual races in the Ottoman Empire. The Zionist movement, accordingly, with which thousands

of Jews are affiliated, and to which vast sums of money have been donated, seems almost futile in its aspirations as long as the Young Turks are in power."

80. Isaiah Friedman, "German Intervention on Behalf of the Yishuv, 1917," *Jewish Social Studies* 33, no. 1 (January 1971): 37.

81. Lewis, *The Jews of Islam,* 178.

82. Baer, "An Enemy Old and New," 531.

83. Burhanettin Duran and Cemil Aydın, "Competing Occidentalisms of Modern Islamist Thought: Necip Fazıl Kısakürek and Nurettin Topçu on Christianity, the West and Modernity," *Muslim World* 103, no. 4 (October 2013): 491.

84. Daniel Pipes, *The Hidden Hand: Middle East Fears of Conspiracy* (New York: St. Martin's Griffin, 1998), 297.

85. Bernard Lewis, "Muslim Antisemitism," *Middle East Quarterly* 5, no. 2 (June 1998): 43–49.

86. Ibid.

87. John Connelly, *From Enemy to Brother: The Revolution in Catholic Teaching on the Jews, 1933–1965* (Cambridge, MA: Harvard University Press, 2012).

88. Yona Malachy, "Protestants," in Skolnik, *Encyclopaedia Judaica,* 16:631.

EPILOGUE

1. Post on X by @AkyolinEnglish on October 7, 2023. https://x.com/AkyolinEnglish/status/1710636268562874662?s=20.

2. In traditional Islamic ethics of war, noncombatants are not legitimate targets. However, in the past few decades, some supporters of Hamas and similar factions bypassed this ethical concern, with arguments such as that most Israelis serve in the army, settlers are default aggressors, imbalance of power requires terrorism, or they are acting on the basis of "eye for an eye." See Beverley Milton-Edwards, *Hamas: the Islamic Resistance Movement* (New York: John Wiley & Sons, 2013); Peter Mandaville, *Islam and Politics* (New York: Routledge, 2014), 291. Meanwhile, justifications of unrestrained "anticolonial" violence have long been advocated by radical left-wing groups.

3. These are quotes from some of the posts that appeared on my X timeline in the days after October 7, 2023.

4. "Biden takes a tougher stance on Israel's 'indiscriminate bombing' of Gaza," *Associated Press,* December 12, 2023.

5. "Death Toll in Gaza Passes 30,000," *New York Times,* February 29, 2024. The story added, "experts say it is likely an undercount."

6. "Israel Intensifies Raids Against Palestinians in West Bank," *Wall Street Journal,* January 19, 2024.

7. "Israeli President Suggests That Civilians in Gaza Are Legitimate Targets," *Huffington Post,* October 16, 2023.

8. For Herzog's correction, see: "Israeli President Blasts ICJ's Portrayal of His Remarks, Says There Are Innocent Palestinians in Gaza," *Haaretz*, January 28, 2024. For examples of the "no innocent civilians" line, see: Daniel Greenfield, "The myth of Gaza's innocent civilians," *Jewish News Syndicate*, November 23, 2023; Mark Levin, "There Are No 'Innocent Palestinians'" *Townhall*, December 7, 2023; "French-Israeli lawyer: There are no innocent civilians in Gaza," *Middle East Monitor*, November 1, 2023; "The people of Gaza are NOT innocent civilians," The Dershow With Alan Dershowitz, December 11, 2023, https://www.youtube.com/watch?v=wg7P8VjSiPU.

9. Noah Lanard, "The Dangerous History Behind Netanyahu's Amalek Rhetoric," *Mother Jones*, November 3, 2023. The Biblical command on Amalek is from 1 Samuel 15:3. One should add that modern Jewish thought has tended to interpret the Biblical command to destroy Amalek as a metaphorical call to fight evil in all its expressions, and not a call to eradicate an ethnic or national group. Yet Netanyahu's reference to "Amalek" in the beginning of a catastrophic war could easily be taken literally, as some Israeli soldiers seem to have done. See: "Israeli Soldiers Deployed in Gaza Post Their Abuses on Social Media," *Le Monde*, February 28, 2024.

10. Alan Dowty, *Arabs and Jews in Ottoman Palestine: Two Worlds Collide* (Bloomington: Indiana University Press, 2019), 303.

11. Yitzhak Y. Melamed, "Hasidic-Muslim Relations in Ottoman Palestine," TheTorah.com (2018). https://thetorah.com/article/hasidic-muslim-relations-in-ottoman-palestine.

12. Scholar Noah Feldman also stresses the political nature of the conflict: "Even the prevalence of antisemitism among Islamist groups like Hamas isn't primarily driven by religion. Rather, it is part of their politically motivated effort to turn a struggle between two national groups for the same piece of land into a holy war." Noah Feldman, "The New Antisemitism," *Time*, February 27, 2024.

13. Bernard Lewis, *The Jews of Islam* (Princeton: Princeton University Press, 1987), 191.

14. Some 850,000 Jews who used to live in Muslim-majority countries of the Middle East were displaced in the mid-twentieth century. Many of them migrated to Israel. Jewish Virtual Library, "Jewish Refugees from Arab Countries," https://www.jewishvirtuallibrary.org/jewish-refugees-from-arab-countries.

15. Massoud Hayoun, *When We Were Arabs: A Jewish Family's Forgotten History* (New York: New Press, 2019).

16. Esther Webman, "Rethinking the Role of Religion in Arab Antisemitic Discourses," *Religions* 10, no. 7 (2019): 5.

17. United States Holocaust Memorial Museum. "Protocols of the Elders of Zion," *Holocaust Encyclopedia*, accessed January 23, 2024, https://encyclopedia.ushmm.org/content/en/article/protocols-of-the-elders-of-zion.

18. Seyyid Kutub, *Yahudi ile Savaşımız,* trans. Abdülhamid Dağdeviren (Istanbul: Hikmet Yayınları, 2007).

19. Israeli scholar Meir Bar-Asher observes this modern-day tendency in his book *Jews and the Qur'an,* for which I had the chance to write a foreword. He writes: "While Jews and Judaism do occupy a major place in the Qur'an, they do not appear solely as antagonists, and the Jewish question is far from being central to the preoccupations of classical Muslim discourse. As we have also seen, traditional exegesis tended to focus more on specifying the circumstances in which a given verse should apply, whereas the modern tendency is to absolutize its meaning and transform it into an ideological weapon. It is the vicissitudes of history that have pushed this theme to the foreground of contemporary discourse, and it would be a mistake to conclude from what one hears today that Islam is somehow 'irrevocably' anti-Jewish." Meir M. Bar-Asher, *Jews and the Qur'an* (Princeton: Princeton University Press, 2022), 140.

20. Farid Esack, "The Portrayal of Jews and the Possibilities for Their Salvation in the Qur'an," in *Between Heaven and Hell: Islam, Salvation, and the Fate of Others,* ed. Mohammad Hassan Khalil (Oxford University Press, 2013), 19–20. As Esack shows here, almost all classical exegetes understood this "apes and pigs" story as a physical transformation that happened to a particular group among ancient Jews. Ibn Kathir, for example, "specifically notes as well that the transformed creatures died after three days, thus leaving no offspring amongst today's Jewish population."

21. This prophecy comes from a hadith reported in a few classical sources including the most authoritative *Sahih al-Bukhari*: "The last hour would not come unless the Muslims will fight against the Jews and the Muslims would kill them until the Jews would hide themselves behind a stone or a tree and a stone or a tree would say: Muslim, or the servant of Allah, there is a Jew behind me; come and kill him; but the tree Gharqad would not say, for it is the tree of the Jews" (Book 54, Hadith 103).

22. See Qur'anic verses 6:50, 6:59, 10:20, 11:31, 16:77, 72:25. Hence, in Turkey's encyclopedia of Islam, theologian İlyas Çelebi argues, "all reports attributed to the Prophet which give detailed information about events that will take place after him must be considered with caution." "Fiten ve Melâhim," *İslam Ansiklopedisi* (İstanbul: TDV, 1996), 13:151. Moreover, even if the "Gharqad tree" hadith is to be accepted as authentic, it seems to foretell not an attack on all Jews, but "combatants in the Antichrist's army . . . who are themselves involved in killing innocent people." Justin Parrott, "The Myth of An Antisemitic Genocide in Muslim Scripture," *Yaqeen Institute,* March 28, 2017, https://yaqeeninstitute.org/read/paper/the-myth-of-an-antisemitic-genocide -in-muslim-scripture.

23. *Muwatta Malik,* 971. This hadith, which has similar versions in other sources, is widely quoted in both classical and modern text on Islamic rules of war. For a broader discussion on the theme, see Asma Afsaruddin, *Jihad: What Everyone Needs to Know* (New York: Oxford University Press, 2022).

24. For a summary and critique of "jihadist" views that justified attacks on non-combatants see Muhammad Munir, "Suicide Attacks and Islamic law," *International Review of the Red Cross* 90, no. 869 (March 2008).

25. Susannah Heschel, "German Jewish Scholarship on Islam as a Tool for De-Orientalizing Judaism," in *New German Critique,* no. 117 (Fall 2012): 93.

26. Anne Cohen, "Honoring the Moroccan King Who Saved the Jews," *Forward,* December 22, 2015.

27. For example, see: Isaac Chotiner, "The Extreme Ambitions of West Bank Settlers," *The New Yorker,* November 11, 2023.

28. Avraham Burg, "The end of Zionism?: A failed Israeli society is collapsing," *International Herald Tribune,* September 6, 2003.

29. Post on X by @AmiDar on December 23, 2023. https://twitter.com/AmiDar/status/1737839793109962888?s=20.

30. For this argument see Rashid Khalidi, *The Hundred Years' War on Palestine: A History of Settler Colonialism and Resistance, 1917–2017* (New York: Metropolitan Books, 2020).

31. See: https://www.alandforall.org/english/.

32. Exodus, 22:20.

33. Qur'an, 5:8.

INDEX

Aaron, 18, 27–29, 34
Abbasid Caliphate, 87, 93, 100, 125, 127, 142
Abd al-Malik ibn Marwan, 86, 87
Abdel-Haleem, Muhammad, 1
Abduh, Muhammad, 168, 169
Abdülhamid II, 218, 220, 221
Abdullah ibn Salam, 44
Abdul Majid Daryabadi, 28–29
Abdülmecid I, 208–10
Abdülmecid II, 197–99
Aben Tofail, 143, 145
Abrahamic religions, 5, 7, 13, 14, 23, 34, 44, 63, 92, 93, 107, 115, 124, 142, 173
Abu Bakr, 35, 169
Abu Hanifa, 47, 126–27
Abu Sufyan, 52
Abyssinia, 13, 63, 64, 79
Ahmad, Barakat, 56
Ahmed Cevdet Paşa, 211
Akgün, Hüseyin, 193
Akiba, Rabbi, 111
al-Afghani, Jamal al-Din, 192, 193
Al-Andalus, 97, 108, 202
al-Aqsa Mosque, 82, 203
al-Baladhuri, 90–91
Albert of Aix, 102–4

al-Biruni, 194
Albo, Joseph, 163
al-Fadil, 99
al-Farabi, Abu Nasr, 143, 144
al-Ghazali, 123, 138, 146–49
al-Hakim, 101
Alhambra Decree, 202
al-Harizi, Judah, 105–6
al-Humaydi, 127
Al-Husayni, Hajj Amin, 232
Ali, 35
Ali, Souad T., 171
al-Juwayni, 138
al-Kamil, al-Malik, 109
al-Kindi, 143
Ally, Shabir, 56
Al-Madinah, 53
Almansor (Heine), 188
al-Maqdisi, 58–59, 85
al-Maqrizi, 118
al-Masudi, 103
Almohads, 98–100, 108
al-Mutawakkil, 87–88
al-Samiri, 28–29
al-Shahrastani, 194
al-Shatibi, 138–39
al-Tabari, Ali, 6, 82–83
Altmann, Alexander, 129, 160–61

al-Wahidi, 49, 66
Amalek, 101, 227, 235
Amr ibn Hisham, 26
Anan Ben David, 126–27
Anatolia, 100–101, 199
An-Na'im, Abdullahi Ahmed, 172
Aqaba, 32, 33
aqliyyat, 140
Arabian Peninsula, 61, 63, 65, 80
Arabs and Jews in Ottoman Palestine
      (Dowty), 228
Arafat, Walid N., 55–56
Aristotle, 108, 143, 144, 148, 277n58
Ark of the Covenant, 35
Arkush, Allan, 156, 161
Armenians, 212
Asad, Muhammad, 189
Ash'arites, 129, 138
Ashura, 43
aslah, 138
astronomy, 204–5
Atatürk, Mustafa Kemal, 170, 197
Augustine, Saint, 101
Avempace (Ibn Bajja), 143, 144
Averroes (Ibn Rushd), 143–47
Averroës and Averroism (Renan), 145
Avicenna (Ibn Sina), 143, 144
Aws, 32, 33, 38, 39, 54
Aydın, Cemil, 222

Babylonia, 16, 105
Bacon, Roger, 148
Badr, Battle of, 51–52
Baghdad, 93
Baha'i, 46
Bahira, 106–7
Balfour Declaration, 229
Balkans, 214, 234
Banu Nadir, 38, 39, 41, 51–54, 73
Banu Qaynuqa, 38, 39, 41, 52, 73
Banu Qurayza, 38, 39, 41, 54–58, 73
Banu Tha'laba, 42
Bar Kokhba revolt, 84

Barnavi, Eli, 89–90, 99–100
Barton, John, 23
Bayezid II, 202–4
Bayle, Pierre, 152
Berber dynasty, 98
Berkovits, Eliezer, 133
Bernstein, Herman, 221
Bey, Javid, 220
Bible, 69, 111, 119, 206, 227
   Abraham in, 23
   distortions of, 118
   Esther, 16
   Exodus, 15, 19
   golden calf in, 27–30
   Haman in, 16
   Hebrew, 7, 14, 101; *see also* Torah
   Job in, 119
   laws in, 133–34, 136–37, 141, 155,
      178
   Moses in, 18–30
   parting of the sea in, 24–26
   plagues in, 24
   prophets in, 45
   Qur'anic Uzair and, 73–74
blasphemy, 52, 159, 169, 192
blood libel, 207–10, 223, 231
Book of Beliefs and Opinions, The
      (Saadia Gaon), 128
Book of Raids, The (al-Waqidi), 39
books
   burning of, 149, 188
   printing of, 204
Bosnia, 206
Bowersock, G. W., 67
Britain, *see* Great Britain
Bu'ath, Battle of, 32, 39
Burg, Avraham, 233
Byzantine Empire, 61–63, 65–67, 71,
      78–81, 89–92, 101, 199, 200

Caesarea, 90–91
Cairo Genizah, 83, 99
Canaan, 55

Carasso, Emmanuel, 220
Çelebi, Katip, 25, 147
Chosroes Parwiz, King, 62, 78–79
Christianity, 5, 115, 122, 125, 126,
        178
    Bible in, see Bible
    in Byzantine Empire, 61, 62
    Catholicism, 94, 114, 152, 188, 202,
        223–24
    clergy in, 114
    conspiracy stories about origin of,
        107
    departures from Judaism, 5
    Enlightenment and, 153, 179
    Gospel in, 5, 64, 116, 118
    Islam and, 48, 65–68, 81
    Jewish, 68
    Judeo-Christian tradition, 7, 63,
        223–24
    just war theory in, 101
    Protestant, 152, 224
    religious laws and, 5, 6
    salvation in, 120, 122
    in triangle with Judaism and
        Islam, 7
    Trinity in, 5, 68, 113, 122
Christians, 57, 80, 116, 143, 149
    Crusades of, 100–105, 117, 216,
        227
    in Jerusalem, 81–85
    Jewish-Arabic cabal and, 90–96
    Jews persecuted by, 62–63, 70, 151,
        200, 202, 207–11, 223–24,
        231
    in Muslim states, 87–90, 97, 99,
        210–14
    in Ottoman Empire, 210–14
    in Qur'an, 63, 65–69, 73
    reconquest campaigns by, 97, 188,
        202
churches, 113
circumcision, 113, 174, 203, 228
Cole, Juan, 67

colonialism, 174, 180–82, 192, 193,
        226, 233–34
Comprehensive Guide for the Servants
        of God (Maimonides), 110
conscience, 155, 164, 173
conspiracy theories, 9, 73, 91, 107,
        192, 206, 216, 217, 219–23,
        231
Constantinople, 61, 63
Córdoba, 96, 97
Cranz, August Friedrich, 157–60
Crimean War, 203
Crone, Patricia, 4
Crusades, 100–105, 117, 216, 227
Crusades Through Arab Eyes
        (Maalouf), 102–3
Cutler, Allan Harris, 106
Cutler, Helen Elmquist, 106
Cyrus, King, 105

Damascus, 105
Damascus Affair, 207–9
Dar, Ami, 233
David, King, 45
Dawud al-Muqammis, 128
Deuteronomy, 55
dhimmi (protected) status, 42, 59, 71,
        88–90, 99, 201, 210–12
Dhu Nuwas, 63, 65
Disraeli, Benjamin, 216–18
Donner, Fred, 56
Dowty, Alan, 228
Duran, Burhanettin, 222
Dürrüşehvar Sultan, 199

Eby, Arden, 175
Egypt, 46, 80, 99, 100, 108, 110, 143,
        172, 230
    disasters and plagues in, 24
    Israelites' Exodus from, 3, 22–23,
        28–29
    Pharaoh of, 3, 15, 17–22, 24–26,
        28, 30, 43, 44, 64, 242n16

Enlightenment, 143, 145, 152–54,
    166–67, 174, 179, 185
  Islamic, 167–68, 173–74
  Jewish, 145, 150, 166–67, 173–74,
    179, 233
Enoch, 34, 74
Europe, 151–52, 166–67, 182–84,
    188, 201–2, 207, 210, 214,
    217–18, 228, 231, 233
Ezra, 73

Faith and Freedom (Gottlieb), 165
fasting, 43
Faysal of Saudi Arabia, 285n40
Ferdinand, King, 202, 204
financial tools, 134–35
Finhas, 49, 74
Firestone, Reuven, 14, 46–47
France, 181, 183, 200, 203, 220, 221,
    234
Franks, 103–5
Freeman, Edward Augustus,
    216–17
Freidenreich, David M., 106
Freytag, Georg, 184

Gabriel, Angel, 2, 49
Gaza, 225–29, 234
Geiger, Abraham, 175, 178, 184–86,
    190
German Orientalism in the Age of
    Empire (Marchand), 181
Germany, 174, 175, 182, 187, 201
  Nazi, 188–89, 206, 231, 232
  Orientalists in, 181–83, 189
Gershom, Rabbi, 135
Gershon, Abraham, 228
Ghassanids, 67, 79
Gibbon, Edward, 95
Gibraltar, 95
Gil, Moshe, 83, 87, 90, 93, 103–4
Godfrey of Bouillon, 101, 102
God in the Qur'an (Miles), 20–21

Goitein, Shelomo Dov, 111, 115, 119,
    189
golden calf, 27–30
Goldziher, Ignaz, 189–93
Goodman, Lenn, 195
Gospel, 5, 64, 116, 118
Gottlieb, Michah, 165
Graetz, Heinrich, 187
Graetz, Naomi, 137
Granada, 98, 202
gratitude, 129
Great Britain, 181, 203, 214–18, 220,
    221, 229, 234
Greece, 213–14
Greek philosophy, 108, 126, 139,
    142–43, 146–48, 205
Guadalete, Battle of, 95
Guide for the Perplexed, The
    (Maimonides), 108, 130, 141,
    144, 149, 162, 271n70, 277n58
Gürkan, Saime Leyla, 72
Gutas, Dimitri, 143

Ha-Amen, 16
ha-Cohen, Shelomo, 99
Hadrian, 84
Hagar, Hagarenes, 92
Haggai, 45
Haifa, 103–4
Halakha, see Jewish law
halal food, 113, 174
Halevi, Judah, 148
Haman, 16–17
Hamas, 73, 226, 230n, 234
Hamidullah, Muhammad, 40
Hamza ibn Abdul-Muttalib, 36
Hanbalism, 88, 129
Harris, Maurice, 93, 98, 151
Haskalah, 166–67, 179, 233
Hattin, Battle of, 105
Hayy ibn Yaqzan (Ibn Tufayl), 145
Hebron, 90
Heine, Heinrich, 188

Heraclius, 62, 67, 78–79, 83, 92
herem, 157, 158
heretics, 129, 149, 150, 152, 158–59, 253n21
Herzl, Theodor, 220
Herzog, Isaac, 227
Heschel, Susannah, 182–83, 188, 232
Hijaz, 59, 60
Himyarite Kingdom, 63, 65
Hind bint 'Utbah, 42
Hindus, 80
hisba, 169
History of the Jews, A (Sachar), 97–98
History of the Jews, The (Graetz), 187
History of the Medieval Jews (Harris), 93
Holland, Tom, 57
Holocaust, 189, 206, 224, 231, 232
Hud, 14
Hughes, Aaron W., 126, 128

Iberia, 94–98
Ibn al-Arabi, 25
Ibn Asakir, 88
Ibn Bajja (Avempace), 143, 144
Ibn Gabirol, 143
Ibn Hisham, 32
Ibn Ishaq, 32–33, 37, 39, 45–48, 54–56
Ibn Kathir, 53, 117
Ibn Khaldun, 116, 118
Ibn Rushd (Averroes), 143–47
Ibn Sa'd, 38
Ibn Sina (Avicenna), 143, 144
Ibn Tufayl (Aben Tofail), 143, 145
Ibn Tumart, 98
Ibn Wahshiyya, 140
Ibrahim, Ayman, 57
idolatry, 26–27, 33, 63, 66, 72, 74, 109, 110, 112–13, 122, 155
    golden calf, 27–30
İhsanoğlu, Ekmeleddin, 205
Ikhwan al-Safa, 143

'illa, 138, 140
Incoherence of the Incoherence (Ibn Rushd), 146
Incoherence of the Philosophers (al-Ghazali), 146, 148
India, 75, 194, 199
inheritance rights, 136
Inquisition, 188, 206
Iran, 46, 234
Iraq, 93, 125, 230
Isaac, 23, 93, 244n43
Isabella, Queen, 202
Ishmael, 3, 8, 12, 23, 77, 81, 85, 86, 92, 93, 109
Islahat, 211
Islam, 5–6
    Christianity and, 48, 65–68, 81
    conspiracy stories about origin of, 106–7
    Jewish converts to, 44
    Jewish distrust of, 67–70
    Judaism and, see Judeo-Islamic tradition
    kalam in, 125–28
    liberalism and, 158, 172, 219
    martyrs of, 13, 36–38, 42
    Medinan Arabs' embrace of, 32–34
    military doctrine of, 101, 232
    modernism in, 168
    as monotheism, 123–24
    Orientalism and, 145–46, 180–96
    philosophy in, 143–48, 162
    pillar of faith in, 113–14
    political nexus and, 67
    prayer direction in, 51
    rationalism in, 125–50
    reform in, 172–73, 177–79, 191–92
    as religion versus state, 168–72
    religious freedom in, 53–54, 56, 169, 172
    religious terminology of, 113–14
    salvation in, 120–24
    Shiite, 123, 141, 147

Islam (*continued*)
  studied by non-Muslims, 182–89,
    194–95
  Sufism in, 25, 109–11, 272n86
  Sunni, 47, 73, 105, 115, 123, 127,
    137, 138, 141, 146, 147, 149,
    264n19, 266n33
  as theocratic, 170–71
  in triangle with Judaism and
    Christianity, 7
  truth and, 30
  ulema in, 114–15
  Western critics of, 154, 173
  see also Muslims
*Islam and the Foundations of
  Governance* (Raziq), 169–70
Islamic empire, *see* Muslim states and
  dynasties
Islamic Enlightenment, 167–68,
  173–74
Islamic law (Sharia), 6, 113, 121–22,
  125, 131–37, 147–48, 150, 169,
  172, 174, 183, 268n50
  hadith in, 191
  intentions of, 138–42, 175, 177–78
Islamophobia, 113, 174, 184, 230n
Israel, 118, 220–21, 228–29, 232
  October 7 attack on, 225–29, 234
  Palestinian conflict with, 225–36
Israeli, Isaac, 143
Israelites, 3, 5, 12, 19–20, 23, 24–28,
  44–45, 55, 68, 72, 109, 117, 118,
  155, 156, 231
  Exodus from Egypt, 3, 22–23,
    28–29
  God's mercy for, 29–30
Isra'iliyyat, 115–20
Istanbul, 197–98, 200–205, 208, 209,
  214, 220
istihsan, 131, 133, 137

Jabal al-Nour and Hira cave, 3, 12
Jabal al-Tariq, 95

Jacob ben Asher, 141
Jacobson, Israel, 175
Jebara, Mohamad, 56
Jemal Pasha, 221
Jerusalem, 34, 82, 84, 105, 109, 203,
  230
  Christians in, 81–85
  Church of the Holy Sepulchre in,
    82, 101
  Crusaders' invasion of, 101–3, 105
  Dome of the Rock in, 34, 86, 87
  Jews in, 81–87, 105–6, 203
  Muslim conquest of, 80, 81–87
  Muslim reconquest of, 104–6
  prayer toward, 51
  Sassanid invasion of, 62, 83
  Temple Mount in, 84–87, 109, 203
Jerusalem (Mendelssohn), 15, 161,
  162, 165–66, 168
Jesus, 4, 5, 14, 34, 68, 107, 132, 156,
  161, 244n43
  birth of, 4, 11, 64, 68
  Crucifixion of, 4, 62, 63, 69
  divinity of, 5, 6, 68–70, 73, 74
  as Messiah, 68, 69
  Muhammad and, 11, 48, 69–70
  in Qur'an, 4, 64, 68, 69
  Romans and, 4, 5, 107
Jethro, 18
Jew as Ally of the Muslim, The (Cutler
  and Cutler), 106
Jewish Christianity, 68
Jewish Enlightenment, 145, 150,
  166–67, 173–74, 179, 233
Jewish law (Halakha), 5, 6, 113, 125,
  131–37, 149, 153, 165, 167, 172,
  174, 183, 268n50
  reasons for commandments in,
    138–42, 165, 175
  Talmud in, *see* Talmud
Jewish Muslims (Freidenreich), 106
Jewish Orientalists, 182–88, 192, 193,
  232

Jews
    antisemitism and, 7, 63, 66, 113,
        151, 167, 174, 182, 207–11, 213,
        221–23, 228, 231, 232, 234
    Ashkenazi, 151–52, 200
    blood libel against, 207–10, 231
    in Byzantine Empire, 62–63, 66,
        67, 89
    Christian intolerance of, 62–63, 70,
        151, 200, 202, 207–11, 223–24,
        231
    churches and, 113
    Covenant of Medina and, 39–43,
        51, 58, 70, 71
    Crusades and, 100–105, 216
    in Europe, 151–52, 166–67,
        182–84, 188, 201–2, 217–18
    in Germany, 182, 187, 188
    Hasidic, 141, 228
    in Holocaust, 189, 206, 224, 231,
        232
    in Iberia, 94–98
    Islam distrusted by, 67–70
    Islamic architecture as influence
        on, 187–88
    Islam studied by, 182–89
    in Jerusalem, 81–87, 105–6, 203
    Jesus and, 68
    in Medina, 32–35, 36–60, 64, 65,
        67–75, 78, 231
    Messiah expected by, 45, 78, 81
    Muhammad and, 39, 44–47, 49–50,
        54–57, 59–60, 64, 72
    Muslim conquests welcomed by,
        90–97
    in Muslim countries, 42, 59, 71,
        75, 87–90, 97–100, 115, 151,
        183–85, 187, 198–224, 230,
        232
    Muslim persecution of, 98–99
    in Ottoman Empire, 198–224
    in Qur'an, 30–31, 44, 63–64,
        66–68, 71–75, 118, 231
    in Roman Empire, 38, 76–78, 81,
        84–85, 156, 159
    Sassanids and, 62, 66, 81, 83
    Sephardic, 151, 158, 203–5
    in Spain, 95–100, 183, 185, 198,
        202, 205, 206, 216, 218
    Visigoth persecution of, 94–95, 218
    in Yemen, 59, 63, 230
Jews of Yemen, The (Tobi), 59
jizya (poll tax), 42, 80, 88–89, 97
Job, 119
John Chrysostom, 63
John the Baptist, 123
Joseph, 14, 34
Joseph ibn Naghrella, 98
Josephus, 156
Judaism, 5, 109–11
    Conservative, 177
    European concerns about, 153–54
    Islam and, *see* Judeo-Islamic
        tradition
    Judeo-Christian tradition, 7, 63,
        223–24
    Kabbalah, 111
    Kant on, 153
    laws in, *see* Jewish law
    liberalism and, 155, 156, 161–62,
        165, 167, 174, 233
    Muhammad and, 184–85
    Orthodox, 167, 175, 177, 190
    philosophy in, 143, 148–50, 154,
        162
    pillar of faith in, 114
    rabbis in, 114–15, 157, 160, 161,
        177, 178
    Reform, 175–78, 186, 190
    religious terminology of, 113–14
    salvation in, 120–24
    Talmud in, *see* Talmud
    as theocratic, 4, 155–62
    Torah in, *see* Torah
    in triangle with Christianity and
        Islam, 7

*Judaism, Sufism, and the Pietists of
    Medieval Egypt* (Russ-Fishbane),
    109
Judeo-Islamic tradition, 7, 10, 34,
    35, 75, 81, 107, 113, 181, 188,
    215–17, 224
    Arab-Israeli conflict and, 225–36
    Covenant of Medina and, 42–43,
        58
    Islamic rationalism's influence on
        Judaism in, 125–50
    Isra'iliyyat in, 115–20
    Jewish distrust of early Islam in,
        67–70
    Mu'tazilites and, 88, 128–31, 134,
        137–42, 165, 188, 281n39
    Ottoman dynasty and, 198–224
    Reform Judaism and, 177
    salvation in, 120–24
    similarities between Judaism
        and Islam, 6–8, 51, 81, 106–7,
        108–24, 174
    Sufism in, 109–11
justice, 134, 162

Kaaba, 13, 112
Ka'b al-Ahbar, 85
Kabbalah, 111
Ka'b ibn al-Ashraf, 51–52
Kadivar, Mohsen, 124
kalam, 125–28
Kamali, Hashim, 137
Kant, Immanuel, 153
Karaites, 126–27
Kemal, Namık, 193
Khadija, 12
Khan, Syed Ahmad, 173
khawarij, 99
Khaybar, 53, 58
Khazraj, 32, 33, 38, 39, 42
Kırbasoğlu, Hayri, 193
Kısakürek, Necip Fazıl, 222
kizyat, 89

Korkut, Derviš, 206
kosher food, 113, 174, 176
Kramer, Martin, 187–88
Kuran, Timur, 178
Kuru, Ahmet, 148

Last Caliph Abdülmecid, The (Nigâr),
    198–99
laws, 5, 6, 113
    in Islam, *see* Islamic law
    in Judaism, *see* Jewish law
    Mosaic, 5, 121, 132, 155–56, 158,
        161, 176
    natural, 121, 140–41, 152, 153,
        162, 163
    Noahide, 121–22
    women and, 113, 132, 134–37,
        169
Lazarus-Yafeh, Hava, 119
Leaman, Oliver, 149, 168, 173
Lecker, Michael, 33, 67
Leder, Stefan, 91
Leibniz, Gottfried Wilhelm, 154
Letter Concerning Toleration, A
    (Locke), 155–56
Levi ben Yefet, 130
Levites, 30
Lewi, Isidor, 218–19
Lewis, Bernard, 114–15, 126, 207,
    217–18, 230
Liberal Constitutionalist Party, 172
liberalism, 166
    Islam and, 158, 172, 219
    Judaism and, 155, 156, 161–62,
        165, 167, 174, 233
Libson, Gideon, 132, 133, 136
Life of the Messenger of God (Ibn
    Ishaq), 32–33
lifnim mishurat hadin, 133–34
loans, 135
Locke, John, 152, 154–56, 165, 178
Lot, 14
Lumbard, Joseph, 118

Maalouf, Amin, 102–3
Maghreb, 96
Mahdi, 98
Maimonides, Abraham, 74, 108–12
Maimonides, Moses, 6, 74, 99, 108,
    112, 121, 124, 130, 140–41,
    144, 148–49, 156, 162–63, 189,
    271n70, 277n58
Makdisi, George, 147
Malachi, 45
Maller, Allen S., 70
Mamluks, 100, 203
Mandeans, 123
Manzikert, Battle of, 101
maqasid al-sharia, 138–42, 175,
    177–78
Marchand, Suzanne L., 181
marriage, 132, 134–36, 167, 192
Martel, Charles, 95
Mary, mother of Jesus, 4, 64, 68–70
Masihiyyat, 116
Maturidi school, 137
al-Mawdudi, Abul, 31
Mecca, 3, 12, 13, 15, 24, 26, 30–32,
    34–35, 40, 72, 112, 236
    Muhammad's hijra to Medina
        from, 3, 13, 31–35, 36, 38, 39,
        42, 43, 48, 60, 64, 67
    polytheists of, 33–35, 36–38, 41,
        42, 51–54, 58, 59, 235
    prayer toward, 51
Medina, 15, 31, 38–39, 72, 75, 79
    Banu Qurayza affair in, 54–58
    Covenant of, 39–43, 51, 55, 58, 67,
        70, 71
    Islam embraced in, 32–34
    Jews in, 32–35, 36–60, 64, 65,
        67–75, 78, 231
    Muhammad's hijra to, 3, 13, 31–35,
        36, 38, 39, 42, 43, 48, 60, 64, 67
Mehmed II, 200–202
Mendelssohn, Moses, 124, 154–55,
    157–73, 175, 178, 233

Mesopotamia, 123, 221
Messiah, 45, 78, 81, 98
    Jesus as, 68, 69
    Muhammad as, 33, 45, 78, 85
Metatron, 77
Metin, Sadreddin Berk, 117
Meyer, Michael A., 153
Midian, 17–18
Midrash, 47, 87, 184
Mikhail, Alan, 201
Miles, Jack, 20–21, 30
Miller, Michael L., 183
millet system, 201, 211
minhag, 133
Mishneh Torah (Maimonides), 108,
    156, 277n58
Moghul, Haroon, 67
Mohammed V, 232
Mongols, 100
monotheism, 4–6, 33, 43, 44, 46–48,
    63, 66, 72, 74, 109, 112–13, 115,
    122, 176, 183, 184
    Islam defined as, 123–24
    Muhammad and, 13
    salvation and, 122–23
    two visions of, 23
Montefiore, Moses, 208–9
Moosa, Ebrahim, 172
morality police, 169
moral values, 129
Moses, 34, 46, 116, 124, 136–37,
    235–36
    al-Samiri and, 28–29
    in Bible, 18–20
    burning bush encounter of, 3, 11,
        18
    constitution of, 159–60
    Exodus from Egypt led by, 3, 22–23
    golden calf and, 27–30, 45
    as *kalimullah*, 27
    laws of, 5, 121, 132, 155–56, 158,
        161, 176
    mother of, 17, 18

Moses (*continued*)
  Muhammad and, 3–4, 11, 12, 44,
    92, 130
  in parting of the sea, 24–26
  Pharaoh and, 15, 17–22, 24–26, 28,
    43, 64, 242n16
  in Qur'an, 2, 3, 14–15, 17–30, 64,
    72
  tablets given to, 27, 29
Moses of Narbonne, 145
Mosque of Umar, 82
Mount Hira, 3, 12
Mount Horeb, 3, 11
Muawiya, 91
Muhammad, Prophet, 91–93, 115,
    124, 130, 132, 134, 185, 266n33
  Amr ibn Hisham and, 26
  authenticity of stories about,
    55–57, 191, 193, 250n75
  Baha'i and, 46
  Bahira and, 106–7
  Banu Qurayza affair and, 54–57
  caliphate following, 76, 169–71,
    197
  death of, 48, 70, 76, 77
  early life of, 11
  hadith of, 43, 49, 54, 58, 117,
    190–93, 117, 190–93, 291n21
  hijra from Mecca to Medina, 3, 13,
    31–35, 36, 38, 39, 42, 43, 48, 60,
    64, 67
  Jesus and, 11, 48, 69–70
  Jews and, 39, 44–47, 49–50, 54–57,
    59–60, 64, 72
  Judaism and, 184–85
  letters to kings sent by, 78–79
  Medina community established by,
    13, 169–71
  as messenger, 170, 171, 185
  as Messiah, 33, 45, 78, 85
  military doctrine of, 101, 232
  Moses and, 3–4, 11, 12, 44, 92, 130
  Mukhayriq and, 37

  Night Journey of, 34
  prophecies attributed to, 231–32
  prostrations and, 111
  in Qur'an, 2–3, 57, 58, 170
  Qur'an transmitted to, 2, 12
  revelations of, 3, 12, 185
  Tabuk expedition of, 79
  Weil on, 186
Muhammad, the World-Changer
    (Jebara), 56
Muhammad Ali of Egypt, 208
Muhammad and the Jews (Ahmad),
    56
Muhammad at Medina (Watt), 71
Muhammad's Military Expedition
    (Ibrahim), 57
Mukhayriq, Rabbi, 36–38, 42, 44
Muqaddimah, The (Ibn Khaldun),
    116
Muqatil ibn Sulayman, 46, 55, 73
Murad III, 204–5
Muslims
  antisemitism among, 231, 232, 234
  Baha'i and, 46
  Covenant of Medina and, 39–43,
    51, 58, 70, 71
  Crusades against, 100–105, 216,
    227
  endowment tradition in, 37
  Jewish persecution by, 98–99
  meaning of term, 23, 25, 40
  Meccan polytheists and, 33–35,
    36–38, 41, 42, 51–54, 58
  Medina community established by,
    13, 169–71
  in Medina, conflicts between Jews
    and, 42–55, 59–60
  mosques of, 187–88, 219
  Occidentalism and, 194–96
  oppression of, 14, 15, 17, 22, 26
  Orientalism and, 145–46, 180–96
  political power achieved by, 15
  prayer direction and, 51

study of other religions by, 194–95
in Uhud battle, 36–38, 42, 52, 53,
73
umma and, 40
see also Islam
Muslim states and dynasties, 75, 76,
77, 81, 110
Abbasid Caliphate, 87, 93, 100,
125, 127, 142
Christian reconquests and, 97, 188,
202
Christians in, 87–90, 97, 99,
210–14
conquests by, 76, 80–81, 90–96,
100–101, 169
dhimmi status in, 42, 59, 71, 88–90,
99, 201, 210–12
Jews in, 42, 59, 71, 75, 87–90,
97–100, 115, 151, 183–85, 187,
198–224, 230, 232
laws on non-Muslims in, 87–90
Ottoman Empire, *see* Ottoman
Empire
Spain, 75, 95–100, 143, 183, 185,
198, 202, 205, 206, 216, 218
Umayyad Caliphate, 76, 86, 87,
91, 95
mustad'afin, 26
Mut'a, Battle of, 79
Mu'tazilites, 88, 128–31, 134, 137–42,
165, 188, 281n39

Nabatean Agriculture (Ibn
Wahshiyya), 140
Nachmanides, 133
Nahda, 168
Najashi, King, 64, 79
Najran, 63, 65
namus, 12
Nasser, Gamal Abdel, 172
nationalism, 212–14, 220–22, 228,
234–35
Nazism, 188–89, 206, 231, 232

Netanyahu, Benjamin, 227
Nethanel ben al-Fayyumi, 47
New York Times, 214, 221
New York Tribune, 218
Nigâr, Salih Keramet, 198–99
Nineveh, Battle of, 62
Noah, 14, 121–22, 124
Nur ad-Din, 104–5

Obadiah the Proselyte, 112
Occidentalism, 194–96
O'Connor, Thomas P., 215–18
Orhan, Sultan, 200
Orientalism, 145–46, 180–96, 232
Orientalism (Said), 180–82, 193, 194
Origins of the Modern Jew, The
(Meyer), 153
Ortaylı, İlber, 212
orthopraxy and orthodoxy, 125
Osman I, 199, 200
Ottoman Empire, 197–224, 228, 229,
234
Constitution of, 211
decline of, 221, 222
Russia's war with, 214, 215
violent conflict in, 211–12
Ottoman Power in Europe, The
(Freeman), 216–17
Öztürk, Mustafa, 26

pagans, 63, 66, 67, 70, 84, 87, 139,
140, 165, 184
see also polytheists
Palestine, 80, 176, 212, 220–21,
228–30
Israeli conflict with, 225–36
Palmerston, Lord, 214
Paul, Saint, 5, 6, 107
People of the Book, 48, 63–64, 66–68,
72, 74, 80, 87, 98, 101, 116, 118
Persia, 61, 66, 79, 90
Peters, F. E., 86–87
Peter the Venerable, 107

Pharaoh, 3, 15, 17–22, 24–26, 28, 30, 43, 44, 64, 242n16
Philo of Alexandria, 126
philosophy, 142
　Greek, 108, 126, 139, 142–43, 146–48, 205
　Islamic, 143–48, 162
　Jewish, 143, 148–50, 154, 162
Pico della Mirandola, Giovanni, 145
poll tax (*jizya*), 42, 80, 88–89, 97
polygamy, 135, 136
polytheists, 5, 32, 44, 48, 66, 70, 80
　Muhammad and, 13, 21
　of Mecca, 33–35, 36–38, 41, 42, 51–54, 58, 59, 235
prayer, 51, 110, 111
Priesand, Sally Jane, 177
printing press, 204
Protocols of the Elders of Zion, The, 213, 223, 231

Qadhi, Yasir, 113
Qayrawan, 96
qibla, 51
qirad, 134–35
Qur'an, 1–5, 13–14, 40, 44, 48, 50, 85, 88, 115, 134, 170, 171, 178, 184, 186–92, 231, 235
　Abraham in, 23
　Banu Qurayza affair and, 55
　chapters of, 15, 17, 19–20, 24, 26, 28–31, 34, 44, 65, 68, 71–72, 79–80, 120, 121
　Christians in, 63, 65–69, 73
　on covenants, 58
　disasters in, 24
　divine mercy in, 29–30
　fasting in, 43
　first words of, 12
　golden calf in, 27–30, 45
　Haman in, 16–17
　historical stories in, 14
　Jesus in, 4, 64, 68, 69

Jewish religious knowledge in, 116–17
　Jews in, 30–31, 44, 63–64, 66–68, 71–75, 118, 231
　laws in, 121–22
　Job in, 119
　Mary in, 64, 68–69
　misinterpretation of, 118
　Moses in, 2, 3, 14–15, 17–30, 64, 72
　Muhammad in, 2–3, 57, 58, 170
　parting of the sea in, 24–26
　People of the Book in, 48, 63–64, 66–68, 72, 74, 80
　political matrix defined by, 81
　preexisting traditions and, 185
　prophecies and, 231–32
　religious tensions and, 44–45, 48–49
　salvation in, 120, 122–24
　transmission to Muhammad, 2, 12
　Verse of the Sword and Verse of the Jizya in, 80
Qur'an, The: A New Translation (Abdel-Haleem), 1
Quraysh, 13, 32, 33, 40, 41, 52
Qutb, Sayyid, 231

Ramadan, 43
Rashidun Caliphate, 76, 80–81
rationalism, 125–50, 153, 162–63, 165, 166, 168, 171–72, 175
al-Razi, Fakhr al-Din, 33, 34, 73, 132, 254n37
Raziq, Ali Abdel, 169–72
Receswind, King, 94
Refik, Ahmet, 189
Reis, Kemal, 202
religion
　freedom of, 53–54, 56, 152–62, 164, 169, 171, 172, 174, 178–79, 183–84, 199
　separation of state from, 155, 164
Renaissance, 143, 145, 147

Renan, Ernest, 145, 146, 192–93
Reşid Paşa, Mustafa, 210
Richard the Lionheart, 99
Roman Empire, 62, 65, 79, 86
    Eastern, see Byzantine Empire
    Jesus and, 4, 5, 107
    Jews in, 38, 76–78, 81, 84–85, 156, 159
Rosenthal, Franz, 189, 194
Rudavsky, Tamar, 140
Russ-Fishbane, Elisha, 109, 111
Russia, 203, 207, 210, 213–16, 228

Saadia Gaon, 128–30, 139–41, 165
Sabbath, 5, 37, 38, 42, 155, 177, 225
Sabians, 123, 124
Sachar, Leon, 97–98
Said, Edward, 180–82, 193, 194
sakina, 35
Salafis, 141
Salah ad-Din, 99, 105–6
Salih, 14
Salmon ben Yeruham, 84–85
salvation, 120–24
Samaritans, 28
sam'iyyat, 140
Samuel, Prophet, 159
Samuel ibn Tibbon, 144
Sarajevo Haggadah, 205–6
Sassanid Empire, 61–62, 65–67, 71, 78, 80–81, 83, 89
Schmidtke, Sabine, 130, 131
Sebeos, Bishop, 92–93
Secrets of Rabbi Shimon bar Yohai, The, 76–78, 81, 85, 87
Selim I, 203
Seljuk Turks, 100–101
Sergius, 107
sevarah, 133
Seyyid Bey, Mehmed, 170
Shapur I, 62
Sharia, see Islamic law
Shaw, R. Dykes, 94

Shaw, Stanford J., 213
al-Shaybani, Muhammad, 47
shekhina, 35
Shimon bar Yohai, 76–78, 81, 85, 87
Shneur Zalman of Liadi, 141
Shoemaker, Stephen J., 78, 92–93
Sisebut, King, 94
Sklare, David, 131
slavery, 13, 54, 55, 89, 122
Solomon ben Abraham, 149
Sophronius, Saint, 82–84
sorcery, 21–22, 34
Sorkin, David, 166
Spain, 75, 95–100, 143, 147, 183, 185, 188, 198, 201, 202, 205, 206, 216, 218
Spinoza, Baruch, 158, 160
suftaja, 135
Suleyman the Magnificent, 203
Sumayyah bint Khabbat, 13
Sykes-Picot Agreement, 220
Syria, 58, 79, 80, 93, 109, 230

ta'amei ha-mitzvot, 138–42, 165, 175
al-Tabari, 58, 73–74
Tabuk, 79
takkanah, 133–35
Talmud, 45, 69, 107, 110, 113, 128, 135, 149, 152, 158, 167, 178, 184, 204, 223
Tancred, 103–4
Tanzimat, 210–11
Taqi ad-Din, 204
Tarik b. Ziyad, 95
Tariq ibn Ziyad, 95, 96
Tayma, 59
Taymiyya, 117
Teaching of Jacob, 91–92
Telushkin, Joseph, 100
terrorism, 232, 234
Tevfik, Ebüziyya, 213
theocracy, 4, 155–62

Theological-Political Treatise
    (Spinoza), 158
Thomas Aquinas, 148
Tishri, 43
Tobi, Yosef, 59
Toland, John, 152–53
Toledo, 96
Torah, 3, 5, 6, 18, 31, 33, 53, 55, 85,
    108, 116, 118, 126, 132, 133, 166,
    178, 204, 235
Tours, Battle of, 95
trade, 134
Trench, Battle of the, 54, 73
Tripoli, 91
truth, 162–63, 176, 185
Ṭuʻmah ibn Ubayriq, 50
Turkey, 197–99, 202, 206, 214, 222,
    223

Uhud, Battle of, 36–38, 42, 52, 53, 73
Umar ibn ʻAbd al-Aziz, 87
Umar ibn al-Khattab, 49, 58, 80,
    82–86, 105
    Pact of, 87–90, 169
Umayyad Caliphate, 76, 86, 87, 91,
    95
umma, 40
Understanding Goldziher
    (Kırbasoğlu), 193
United Nations, 229
Uqba ibn Nafi, 96
Urban II, Pope, 100, 101, 227
urf, 133
Uthman ibn Affan, 190
Uzair, 73–74

Vahdeti, Derviş, 221
Visigoths, 94–96, 218

Wadi al-Qura, 59
al-Waqidi, 39, 48–49, 51–52
Waraqa, 12, 13
Watt, Montgomery, 58, 69, 71
Webbman, Esther, 231
Weil, Gustav, 185–87
Weiss, Leopold, 189
*What Did Mohammed Take from
    Judaism?* (Geiger), 184–85
Whitehead, Alfred North, 148
Wise, Isaac Mayer, 176
Wolff, Christian, 154
women, 89, 113, 132, 134–37,
    167–69, 176–78, 192
World's Fair of 1893, 218–19
World War I, 174, 212, 219–21
World War II, 206

Xerxes the Great, 16

Yarmuk, Battle of the, 80
Yasir ibn Amir, 13
Yemen, 59, 63, 99, 109, 230
Yeruham, Salmon ben, 86
Yom Kippur, 43, 219
Yosef, Ovadia, 112
Young Turks, 220–21
Yovel, Yirmiyahu, 157
Yusuf, Hamza, 56, 147

Zangi, Imad al-Din, 104
Zarfati, Isaac, 201–2
Zayd ibn Samin, 50
Zechariah, 45
Zevi, Sabbatai, 206
Zionism, 219–23, 228–29, 230n, 232,
    234
Zoroastrianism, 61, 62, 80, 126